PRESTON
TUCKER

and His Battle to Build the Car of Tomorrow

PRESTON TUCKER

and His Battle to Build the Car of Tomorrow

STEVE LEHTO

◆

FOREWORD BY
JAY LENO

CHICAGO
REVIEW
PRESS

Library of Congress Cataloging-in-Publication Data
Names: Lehto, Steve, author.
Title: Preston Tucker and his battle to build the car of tomorrow / Steve
    Lehto; foreword by Jay Leno.
Description: Chicago, Illinois: Chicago Review Press, [2016] | Includes
    bibliographical references and index.
Identifiers: LCCN 2016009223 | ISBN 9781613749531 (hardback) | ISBN
    9781613749562 (epub edition) | ISBN 9781613749555 (kindle edition)
Subjects: LCSH: Tucker, Preston, 1903–1956. | Tucker automobile—History. |
    Experimental automobiles—United States—History—20th century. |
    Automobile industry and trade—United States—History—20th century. |
    BISAC: BIOGRAPHY & AUTOBIOGRAPHY / Business. | HISTORY / United States /
    20th Century. | BUSINESS & ECONOMICS / Industries / Automobile Industry.
Classification: LCC HD9710.U54 T854 2016 | DDC 338.7/629222092—dc23
LC record available at https://lccn.loc.gov/2016009223

Typesetting: Nord Compo

Printed in the United States of America
5 4 3 2 1

*In honor of Preston Tucker
and every other person who has dared
to launch a business in America*

A man with a dream can't stop trying to realize that dream any more than an artist can stop painting, or a composer composing. Other men failed before me. Henry Ford failed twice. Willys failed twice. Today their names are known in every corner of the globe. It's no disgrace to fail against tough odds if you don't admit you're beaten. And if you don't give up.

—Preston Tucker, 1952

Contents

Foreword BY JAY LENO

Many cars are known by their creators: Ford, Porsche, Ferrari. But no other carmaker has overshadowed his own creation like Preston Tucker. And that is probably what led to his downfall, and that of his company.

Tucker was a big deal in 1947, and the fact that people today know his name is a testament to that. They even did a movie about him, starring Jeff Bridges. Tucker made headlines by announcing that he was going to launch a new car at a time when America really needed one. In the years after World War II, there was a car shortage, and the big American car companies planned to fill the market with warmed-over designs from before the war.

And along came Tucker. He promised to build not just any car, but a car that would be revolutionary and futuristic. It would be aerodynamic, rear-engine, and rear-wheel drive. It would have a lot of revolutionary new safety features, like a pop-out windshield and a safety cell a passenger could dive into in the event of a crash. It would have a headlight on each front fender and a cyclops light in the middle that moved with the steering wheel. It would also have something Tucker called a hydraulic drive that would power the rear wheels using fluid instead of gears—but that never got past the experimental stage. And it would be affordable. It was exactly what

America wanted to hear, and soon letters were flooding in from across the country from people wanting to know where they could buy one of these cars. The problem was that the car didn't exist yet.

Tucker knew a lot about cars. He'd been a car salesman his whole life, and he loved cars. What's interesting is that his idea wasn't *completely* revolutionary—the car he envisioned was a lot like the Czechoslovakian Tatra T87. That car had an engine in the rear and a trunk in the front and was quite groundbreaking before the war. In fact, when the Germans invaded Czechoslovakia, many high-ranking German officials commandeered them as staff cars because of how fast they were. The trouble was they were deceptively fast. The combination of the cars' sleek aerodynamics, engine in the rear, and swing axle made them tricky to drive, especially in turns. As a result the Germans, who were not familiar with the cars' handling characteristics, crashed many of the cars.

A story went around during the war that within the first week following the Nazi invasion, seven German officers had died driving Tatras. A popular joke told of how the Tatra had killed more Germans than the Czechoslovakian army. Afterward, Hitler was said to have banned the use of the Tatra by his officers or Nazi officials. This could explain why so few of them ended up in Germany after the war.

So, many of Tucker's ideas were workable. But the trouble with Tucker was that he was a better car salesman than he was an engineer. Although he had some great ideas, he didn't have the business acumen to put them in place. He ended up being chased by the federal government, who said he committed fraud. He used customer deposit money in such a way that it looked like he was building a car today with money from a buyer who was promised a car tomorrow, and so on. To some, it looked like a Ponzi scheme. If that was what he was doing, technically it would have been fraud. Some even tried arguing that Tucker never intended to build any cars, but later facts would show that to be untrue. Tucker wound up being acquitted after a lengthy trial. But by then the damage was done and his company was gone.

Tucker did get the last laugh. He built fifty-one cars. And most of those are still around and are highly valued. They routinely sell at auction in the millions. A few years ago, rumors that someone had found a previously unknown Tucker convertible caused a frenzy in the car collecting community until it was disproven. That shows the intensity of the interest in these cars.

Preston Tucker's legacy is that of the ultimate underdog, the everyman whose optimism would allow him to triumph against great odds. He almost made it, but in the end . . . well, Tucker's company did not survive. But so many of the Tucker cars did. And that certainly stands for something.

1

An Early Morning Car Crash

September 24, 1948.

Eddie Offutt had been driving all night at 90 mph. It felt slow to him as the stands flashed by his car. Here, on the Indianapolis Motor Speedway, he normally drove much faster.[1] Even so, the rough brick surface of the two-and-a-half-mile oval chewed the car's tires. Offutt sailed around the oval with the pedal almost to the floor, watching the miles add up on the odometer of his "waltz blue" Tucker.

Offutt was in charge of a team testing the revolutionary Tucker '48 sedan, then the hottest thing in the automotive world. More than 150,000 people had written letters to the car's manufacturer asking how they could buy one. So many people paid admission to see one displayed in New York City that the venue outgrossed some Broadway plays running nearby.

The car's namesake, Preston Tucker, had unveiled the car to the world on June 19, 1947. Tucker, a brilliant salesman and showman, was promising a newer, safer, and more reliable car than those the auto giants in Detroit churned out. His rear-engine, rear-wheel-drive automobile featured better traction and more passenger space than its competitors, along with disc brakes and an automatic transmission, long before those became standard in

1

the industry. Its padded dash and sturdy frame would better protect passengers in a collision, and the car would drive more smoothly and cost less than other vehicles on the market. The established car companies had stopped assembling new automobiles in 1942, spending the last few years building tanks and airplanes for America's forces in World War II. Now, as peacetime production resumed, these companies were struggling to bring fresh new models to the market. Tucker's bold alternative was raising a stir.

Eddie Offutt lapped the track at 90 mph, worrying little about business problems as he noted how smoothly Tucker #1027 ran. Offutt, Preston Tucker's lead mechanic, had met his employer at Indianapolis years before, when Tucker had worked with famed race car builder Harry Miller. Now Tucker had sent his team to Indy with a fleet of seven Tucker '48s to test the cars' endurance and resolve last-minute bugs. The cars weren't in mass production yet, but Tucker had assembled enough to display them around the country and build consumer interest.

As daylight began to break at Indianapolis, Offutt's drive took a dramatic turn. Just as he entered a curve at high speed, the sedan's engine stalled. In a fraction of a second, the rear of the car swung out from behind him. As he fought to regain control, the right rear tire blew out. The vehicle's tires, with a new tubeless design by Goodrich, had seen nothing but heavy driving in the previous days as the team had clocked a thousand miles at high speed, virtually nonstop around the speedway, often without even slowing for corners.

Offutt lost control. He skidded onto the grass of the infield and the car turned sideways. Then it flipped. The driver held on as it tumbled over and over again, three times in all. The windshield popped out. Finally, the car landed on its wheels.[2]

Offutt climbed out and surveyed the damage. He had bruised an elbow but suffered no other injuries.[3] Other than the missing windshield, some minor body damage, and the tire that had blown out as he lost control, Offutt saw nothing wrong with the car.

Later, Offutt and the others would realize the accident was the result of a simple mistake made in the early morning darkness. At 4:15 AM, Offutt had stopped to refuel the car. A mechanic had reached for the wrong container in the dark and placed aviation fuel in the vehicle, which the Tucker engine was not tuned to run on.[4] For now, Offutt replaced the tire and drove the vehicle off the track.

The Tucker team was conducting the Indianapolis tests in strict secrecy. The Tucker '48 had been subjected to oddball rumors and gossip, like a persistent story that the car could not drive in reverse. No matter how many times they demonstrated the cars backing up, the story dogged Tucker's men. Tucker could not afford leaked test results, especially if something went wrong.

Fortunately, the tests were a spectacular success. The team logged thousands of miles in the Tucker '48s and found only a few minor problems, all easily resolved. And Offutt's crash was not caused by the failure of a Tucker part. If anything, the crash underscored Tucker's assertions about his car's safety: it had rolled three times after crashing at 90 mph, and the driver had walked away with nothing but scrapes and bruises. The team drove the caravan of Tucker '48s back to Chicago, satisfied with their results. Only the damaged Offutt car had to be trailered home—because it was missing its windshield.

But not all was well at the Tucker Corporation in Chicago. Even though the American public clamored to buy the cars, and Tucker had raised $20 million from enthusiastic investors, powerful forces in Washington were gunning for him. The Securities and Exchange Commission had announced that it was investigating Tucker, suspecting him of bilking investors with a massive fraud scheme. The latest headlines about Tucker accused him of perpetrating a hoax, suggesting that his cars weren't real and his factory was a sham.

But everyone who saw the Tucker '48 sedan believed Tucker had built an amazing car. The vehicle was revolutionary, and Tucker had built it despite vocal critics who said it was impossible. Tucker had not resolved one problem though: the cars were taking too long to get to market. Could Tucker save his business?

Offutt would witness just how serious the disconnect was between the reality and the government's suspicions in early 1949, when he was summoned to appear before a grand jury and grilled about the Tucker '48s. The

US attorney not only believed the cars were fake but thought Offutt knew it too. Offutt told the attorney about the successful tests at Indianapolis. The attorney then asked him, "How were the cars taken to Indianapolis—trucked down or driven down?"

Offutt said the cars had been driven to Indianapolis from Chicago.

"Are you sure you drove them down?" the attorney pressed, giving Offutt the chance to change his story in case he was lying.

Offutt stuck to his answer, which was the truth. The cars had not been "trucked" down; they had all been driven to Indianapolis under their own power. Offutt offered to let the attorney and the jurors visit the Tucker plant and see the cars. The offer had been made before, many times.

Again they declined the offer.

And so the stage was set for a trial that would ruin an innocent man, Preston Tucker, and doom the corporation building the spectacular Tucker '48 automobile.

2

Preston Thomas Tucker

People who met Preston Tucker described him as an extraordinary sales-man. Six feet tall, he exuded a confidence that could make you believe what-ever he was pitching at the moment. He was always well dressed in public, usually in a suit with a fancy necktie. But his most striking characteristic was his ability to speak easily with anyone, to put his listener at ease. His powers of persuasion worked on journalists too: several interviewed Tucker and wrote about him in such glowing terms it was apparent they had fallen under his spell.

He did not come across as slick. He spoke in a folksy style, sometimes misusing words, much to the dismay of his close friends and family mem-bers. Speaking of a car with its gas pedal depressed, he might say that the car "exhilarated," or when talking finance to board members, he would refer-ence the recent "physical year." His daughter tried more than once to help him with his vocabulary; he told her not to bother. "They know what I'm talking about."[1]

Those who knew him best said there was much more to the salesman than an unpretentious charm. To Cliff Knoble, an advertising man who worked closely with Tucker, "he possessed a warmth and humanness that made men eager to help him." He was loyal to those he knew and deter-mined to follow through on the ideas he believed in. This, perhaps, was his biggest flaw. People who worked with Tucker in his most important years said that he sometimes discarded advice from experts and deferred instead to friends. Knoble referred to it as a "naiveté" that left him "susceptible to the blandishments of an occasional highly skilled parasite."[2]

Family members saw Preston not as a salesman, of course. To them he was trusting, taking people at face value. His granddaughter says he was not suspicious of anyone. Loving and warm to those around him, he was often even goofy, especially with children. His home was overrun with his own and those of other family members. And he would speak to anyone, always as an equal.[3]

As many have attested, Preston Tucker had a magnetic personality. People were drawn to him.

———

Preston Thomas Tucker was born in Capac, Michigan, a small farming community about thirty miles west of Port Huron, roughly sixty miles north of Detroit, on September 21, 1903. His father, Shirley Harvey Tucker, was a railroad engineer, and his mother's maiden name was Lucille Caroline Preston. Shortly after Preston's birth, the young family moved in with Lucille's parents, Milford A. Preston and Harriet L. Preston, in Evart, Michigan. Lucille gave birth to another boy, William, in 1905. Preston's father died of appendicitis on February 3, 1907, when Preston was three.[4] To make ends meet, Lucille taught at the local one-room schoolhouse in a community known as Cat Creek, just west of Evart.

When he was in the fourth grade, Preston befriended a boy a year older, Fay Leach. In later years, Leach would watch Tucker's name appear in the news and remember the time the two had spent in the nearby farm fields. While Leach and the others were doing their chores, Tucker would be talk-ing and asking questions of the older kids. Often, the conversation turned to what fascinated Tucker the most: "these new machines—the automobile."[5]

In 1914 Lucille decided to move to Detroit to look for work. She briefly worked in an office and then returned to teaching. Money was tight; by 1920 the family had six lodgers living with them.[6]

Cars continued to fascinate Preston, and as a teenager he spent much of his time frequenting local service stations and used car lots, talking to the workers and examining the cars. He even landed a job in the auto industry as an "office boy" at Cadillac in 1916.[7] His stint there was short but legendary. He worked for D. McCall White, an executive at the company, who had Tucker running around quite a bit. The teenager decided he could do his job more efficiently if he were on roller skates, so he began skating around the offices at Cadillac. One day Tucker rounded a corner at the office with an armful of papers and slammed into his boss. Tucker's time as an office boy came to an end shortly thereafter, but there must not have been any hard feelings; White would end up working for Tucker a few decades later.[8]

When Preston was sixteen, he convinced his mother to let him use his savings to buy a car. He found an Overland touring car for sale and negotiated the seller down to $300. He drove it for a year and a half and then sold it for the same amount he'd paid, using the money to buy a Ford Model T. There was something mechanically wrong with the Ford, so his mother told him to sell it rather than endure the headaches of maintenance and repair costs. Tucker found a buyer at $350. The profit inspired him. He sought another car deal and located someone selling a Chandler for $750. Tucker offered the $350 he had made from the Model T sale and struck a deal.

The Chandler had a defective transmission, and Tucker was reluctant to pay someone else to fix it. He tore the transmission apart himself and laid the parts out on the floor of the family's garage. To remember where the parts went, he numbered them as he took them out, writing the numbers on the floor by each part with chalk. Despite his system, Tucker could not get the transmission to run properly. He relented and paid a mechanic to rebuild it. Sixty-four dollars later, he sold the Chandler for $610, a tidy profit. After all, Tucker was still in high school, attending classes at Detroit's Cass Technical and working odd jobs in the evenings and on weekends.

After Tucker left high school, his family moved to the Detroit suburb of Lincoln Park. Preston found a job riding motorcycles for a living with the

Lincoln Park Police Department. Only nineteen, he lied about his age and became a police officer, patrolling a stretch of town near the Detroit River, trying to enforce Prohibition. Canada, where bootleggers acquired alcohol to smuggle into the United States, was just across the river. It was 1922, and the outlaws had discovered the lucrative nature of the import business, which meant Tucker would not be able to spend as much of his working time as he hoped simply cruising around on a motorcycle. His mother did not like the danger of his work, and she told his supervisor that he was underage. As a result, the police force ousted him for the time being.[9]

Tucker had met Vera Fuqua when he was eighteen, and the two had begun dating. They married in 1923. By this time, while Vera worked for the phone company in Detroit, Tucker had returned to the auto industry and was now working on Ford's assembly line. He didn't enjoy standing at a machine all day and asked for a different job, but he didn't like his new job either. He left Ford and ran a gas station for a short time.[10] When he turned twenty-one in 1924, he rejoined the police department; now that he was old enough, his mother couldn't stop him.

Tucker enjoyed police work and collared a bank robber and an auto thief along with some alcohol smugglers. But his creativity and knowledge of cars soon got him in trouble with the department. His squad car had no heater, and Tucker thought he could remedy that easily enough. He drove to the public works department and borrowed an acetylene torch, which he used to cut a hole through the car's firewall, which separates passengers from the engine compartment. This would allow engine compartment heat to keep him warm while on patrol. It was a crude alteration, and word soon got around that Tucker had butchered a city-owned police car without permission. He was moved to foot patrol and saw the handwriting on the wall.[11]

In 1924 Preston and Vera welcomed their first child, Shirley—named after Tucker's father—followed by Preston Jr. in 1925. The couple would go on to have three more children over the next five years—Marilyn, Noble, and John.

Around 1925 Tucker became good friends with Mitchell Dulian, the owner of a Studebaker dealership in Hamtramck, a Detroit suburb with a booming immigrant population.[12] Dulian hired Tucker as a salesman, and

Tucker took to selling cars in ways that Dulian, a veteran, had never seen. Tucker would take a "parade" of cars through town and set up near a street corner, where he would pitch the cars to people on the streets as if he were an "old time medicine man."[13] He paid commissions to local shopkeepers and businessmen for sending him prospects. Dulian's was soon the top-selling Studebaker outlet in the Detroit area.

Tucker quickly became disillusioned with working in Hamtramck, though, because the commute from Lincoln Park took away too much of his family time. In 1926 he returned to the police force one last time.[14]

Dulian, meanwhile, moved to Memphis, where he owned two dealer-ships. He asked Tucker to come down and manage one of them. This Tucker could not resist. As soon as he got the telegram offering the job, he sent back a telegram accepting it. According to one biographer, he left in such a hurry that he didn't have time to resign from the Lincoln Park PD. Instead, they termed it a leave of absence. Arguably, Tucker was a member of the Lincoln Park PD until the day he died,[15] but he actually left on March 18, 1927.

After a few years in Memphis selling Studebakers and Chryslers, Tucker and his family moved back to Lincoln Park. Tucker repeated this pattern several times—spending time outside Michigan for a year or two and then returning to the Detroit area.

In 1931 Pierce-Arrow Motor Car Company offered Tucker a job as a zone manager. He and his family moved to Buffalo, New York.[16] Shortly there-after, Preston got a job at a Packard dealership in Indianapolis, and the family moved to the home of the Indy 500.[17] He attended races there, as well as the several weeks of practice and qualifying that preceded them. In the garages at the track, Tucker talked to car owners and builders, including Harry Miller, whom he had first met on a visit to the city in 1925. The two remained in contact even after Tucker moved back to the Detroit area.[18]

After returning to Michigan in 1933, Tucker tried one of the few ventures in his life that was not car-related: he ran for mayor of Lincoln Park.[19] He announced his candidacy in January, running against two well-known can-didates, Mark Goodell and Arthur Zirkalosa. He distributed flyers outlining his populist stance. In them, after describing how politicians had not been doing enough to solve recent financial problems, he stated:

> I have no paid-for campaign workers, nor paid-for propagandists, and made no promises, nor do I intend to, and if you people see fit to place me in office, you may feel sure that your future Mayor will deal fairly with all of you.
>
> My qualifications are these: Beginning as an automobile mechanic, I continued in this field until I reached the position of general sales manager of a nationally known manufacturer, my work including the actual budgeting and financial lay-outs of various sizes of businesses. My earlier record as a policeman in Lincoln Park is one of action and loyalty.[20]

Despite his impressive record and the campaign's homespun appeal, he came in third in the primary that March. The winner, Zirkalosa, had 1,729 votes, Goodell 516, and Tucker 275.[21]

But most of Tucker's endeavors stayed closer to his area of expertise. At one point, he helped the Mundus Brewing Company of Detroit with their fleet of beer delivery trucks, designing the truck bodies as well as an automated loading and unloading system for the kegs.[22] And he continued his association with engineer Harry Miller—a partnership that would pave the way for his automotive odyssey to follow.

3

Harry Miller

Preston Tucker could not have risen so high in the auto industry had he not made a name for himself by working with engineering genius Harry Arminius Miller.

Miller was born in Wisconsin and dropped out of school at thirteen to work in a machine shop.[1] In 1895, at the age of twenty, he moved to Los Angeles, where he made racing parts for bicycles. After marrying in California, he returned home to Wisconsin to work in a foundry, where he tinkered with car engines, motorcycles, and even boat motors.[2] There he designed and built a four-cylinder engine that impressed his coworker Ole Evinrude, the man whose name would become synonymous with outboard boat motors. But Miller quickly moved on, relocating to San Francisco to work on motorcycles and developing and patenting a spark plug, which he sold to fund more of his projects. One writer has called this a demonstration of Miller's "characteristic inability to concentrate on any one project at a time."[3] Indeed, restlessness defined Miller's career. He spent half his time working for others and half tinkering and inventing.

By 1906 he was in Michigan working for the Olds Motor Works in Lansing as a mechanic. The following year he invented a carburetor with two-stage jets. At idle and low speeds, one set fed fuel to the engine. At higher speeds, the second set opened so both sets fed the engine. The carburetor worked well and seemed ideal for a race engine. In 1911 he went to the Indianapolis speedway and pitched his carburetor to race teams there, who after seeing how well it worked, jumped at buying them. The Miller Master carburetor dominated the race for the next decade.[4]

After World War I, increasing speeds at the races concerned the Indianapolis 500 organizers. Crashes often resulted in serious injury or death. Could the cars be slowed down and still present an entertaining race? Organizers introduced new rules limiting engine size to a displacement of 3 liters—or roughly 183 cubic inches. To Miller it was an engineering challenge: he set out to build the most powerful 183-cubic-inch engine possible. Two drivers funded Miller as he built an eight-cylinder racing engine that would meet the new threshold.[5] By 1922 Miller's refined engine dominated the race. That year, the Miller 183 won at Indianapolis and nine other major races.

The new engine-size rule did not slow the cars. They still managed speeds that worried race organizers. The 1922 race winner averaged a speed of 94.5 mph. The organizers tried to slow the cars more, reducing engine displacement by another third. The following year engines could be no larger than 2 liters, or 122 cubic inches.

Miller designed a high-performance 122-inch engine, and because of his reputation with the Miller 183, racers placed orders with him for the 1923 season. Again Miller's engine outperformed many of its larger predecessors. A Miller 122–powered car won the 1923 Indy 500, along with eight other races. And, contrary to race organizers' plans, average speeds had again increased despite the engine downsizing. Winning race speeds that year exceeded 100 mph.[6] Drivers started asking Miller if he would also build cars to go with his engines, and Miller obliged.

Again in 1926, race officials sought to slow the cars down and mandated that engines in the race cars on that circuit could displace no more than 1.5 liters, or 91.5 cubic inches. And again, Miller designed a smaller, more powerful engine. His engines were so dominant that most drivers used them. Besides Indy-style racing, the engines powered other record-setting events.

One driver ran a lap in Atlantic City at over 147 mph. Another set a straight-line record at Daytona Beach, covering a mile at over 180 mph.[7] Between 1922 and 1929, Miller engines won 79 percent of major US races, and in the 1929 Indy 500, Miller engines powered twenty-seven of the thirty-three starting positions.[8]

Unfortunately, Miller's reputation as a genius engine and car builder was offset by his inability to make money from his work. While his engines dominated the tracks and made drivers famous, Miller toiled away, often flirting with bankruptcy.

———

Meanwhile, Preston Tucker was spending more and more time at Indianapolis each year, particularly in the pits and garages, where he studied the cars and got to know the car builders. He met Harry Miller in 1925[9] and told him he could help him turn his business profitable. Tucker had no shortage of the salesmanship skills Miller lacked. Miller agreed to work with Tucker.

By 1931 news reports were referring to Miller and "his manager, Preston Tucker." But it was Miller's latest innovation for making race cars run faster that garnered the headlines: MILLER BUILDS FOR SPEEDWAY: PLANS FOUR-WHEEL DRIVE RACER TO APPEAR AT INDIANAPOLIS. Most race cars had always been two-wheel drive, but Miller had made front-wheel-drive racers previously, and he believed he could gain an advantage by putting power to all four wheels at Indianapolis. The story noted that Miller, along with "manager" Tucker, had designed the racer in Detroit, and that their car would be "the first of its kind Indianapolis has ever seen." One senses that Tucker influenced the reporter: without quoting Tucker or Miller, the story said their car would have a sixteen-cylinder engine.[10] In reality, the car hit the track with a four-cylinder engine.

In the following years Miller and Tucker were involved in a partnership off the track as well. Marmon, a car company located in Indianapolis, had been building cars since 1902 but had fallen on hard times. In 1933, at the height of the Depression, the company entered receivership. A variety of plans were floated to save the company, including an effort in 1934 to bring aboard Harry Miller and Preston Tucker. The announcement touted Miller's expertise in engine design and building and Tucker's salesmanship. The new company would resume making Marmon autos and also aviation and marine engines. It might even build race cars designed by Miller.[11] But despite organizers' high hopes, the deal fell apart and Marmon stopped making automobiles. Its founder, Walter Marmon, focused his attention on building four-wheel-drive vehicles under the name Marmon-Herrington—without the help of Miller or Tucker.

By 1935, the two men had formed their own company, Miller-Tucker. Inspired by the fact that Studebaker had sponsored five cars in the previous two Indianapolis 500s, Tucker wondered whether he could convince a car company to underwrite race cars built by Miller-Tucker.[12] Tucker pitched the idea to Henry Ford, and he agreed to try it. Ford would sponsor a contingent of ten Miller-Tucker cars that they would build using engines and parts furnished by Ford. Ford would invest $25,000 in the project. Tucker and Miller would keep any prize money won, and their company would retain the cars' ownership afterward. All Ford would gain from the relationship would be bragging rights.[13]

And if the project failed, Ford recognized, all he would earn was *bad* publicity. To manage that potential downside, he decided not to negotiate a contract directly with Miller-Tucker. Instead, Ford engaged N. W. Ayer & Son, one of America's most prestigious advertising agencies, to draft a two-page contract. Ayer would control how the cars were presented, from what advertising they might carry to what the press would be told about them.[14] Presumably, they would act on behalf of Ford and do their utmost to protect the Ford image.

Tucker oversold Ford on how soon the cars could be built. The contract was sent to Miller and Tucker on January 28, 1935. The race was scheduled for May 30, 1935.[15] The team would need to work nonstop, especially because Miller wanted to make something special: front-wheel-drive, all-independent-suspension racers. They would be the first of their kind at Indy. And he needed to build ten of them in time to test and qualify them for the race.[16]

As agreed, Ford provided the money and parts to Miller-Tucker, which frantically worked to get the cars built in time. It quickly became clear that the budget of $25,000 was insufficient. Among other things, Ford had not given Miller-Tucker enough parts to assemble complete cars—Ford only donated engines, differential gear assemblies, gauges, and brakes.[17] Tucker asked Ford for more money, and Ford tripled his investment to $75,000.[18]

While Miller built the cars, Tucker recruited drivers, getting commitments from some of the biggest names in racing. And the initial publicity proved a bonanza for Ford. Newspapers covering the practice and qualifying runs at the speedway featured photos and headlines about the Ford entries. HENRY FORD HAS ENTERED TEN OF THESE IN BIG RACE, read an Associated Press photo caption beneath a photo of the Miller-Tucker car. The description claimed they were "85 per cent stock cars,"[19] presumably so Ford could get car buyers to equate the success of the racers with the quality of Ford's consumer cars.

Unfortunately, the task of building ten cars on such short notice, even for Harry Miller, proved too difficult. Peter DePaolo had won the race in 1925 and agreed to drive one of the cars. He took it for a test run and the steering didn't seem right to him. He asked Miller about it. "You just drive it," Miller is said to have snapped back, impatiently trying to solve too many problems at once.[20] DePaolo quit the team instead.[21]

At first, Miller's problems readying the cars for the race were kept quiet. Reporters continued pushing the story about Miller and Ford returning race cars to the time when they were more stock and less exotic. One columnist said Miller had done an "about face" with the project, but also denied that Henry Ford was behind it. He wrote, "The project was financed by a group of dealers whose identity has not been revealed. Miller is the front man for them."[22] Perhaps Henry Ford was going to wait for the results of the race before actively promoting his connection to the venture. The columnist also noted that only five of the cars had drivers but did not doubt that all ten would race. The cars impressed all who saw them, even those unaware of the cutting-edge setups inside the cars. One authority said the Miller-Tucker creations were "the best looking, best streamlined cars ever seen at the speedway."[23]

Ultimately, only five cars were ready for qualifying and only four of them qualified. On the plus side, the cars were more than fast enough; they hit speeds of 130 mph in practice, and the fastest qualifiers entered the field at 120 mph.[24]

Ford still hoped for a publicity bonanza. The pace car for the race that year was even a Ford convertible.[25] But on race day the Miller-Tucker cars did not fare well. One dropped out early, leaking fluid. The rest all suffered identical steering gear failures.[26] Miller later diagnosed the problem: a portion of the steering mechanism was mounted too near the exhaust manifold and overheated, causing the gear to fail.[27] The longest-lasting of the cars made it to lap 144 out of 200, good for only sixteenth place. Miller must have had mixed feelings watching his latest creations fail, since all of the top twelve finishers of the race that day used Miller engines.[28]

Henry Ford was upset by the embarrassing show. Worse, Miller-Tucker sent a bill to Ford for the $117,000 that it had expended developing the cars, even though Ford had only agreed to pay $75,000 toward the project. The parties squabbled, and eventually Ford settled with Miller and Tucker by agreeing to pay them if he could keep the cars. He wanted to make sure the cars did not tarnish his company's name any further.[29] Rumor had it that Henry Ford ordered the cars destroyed, but for some reason they survived. A few even returned to the track in later years, no longer affiliated with Ford, proving that they were competitive once the bugs had been worked out of them. At least two of the cars made the field for the 500-mile race as late as 1947.[30]

As for Henry Ford, the experience scared him away from auto racing. He died in 1947, and Ford Motor Company would not return to auto racing until 1952.[31] Miller and Tucker, on the other hand, were convinced their cars were spectacular and would have done much better if only they'd had a little more time. Their partnership dissolved, and Miller returned to working on cars by himself.

Miller eventually sold his company, and ran into financial difficulty again. Meanwhile, his cars continued showing up at Indy. In 1941 the field of the 500 contained three cars of his design, with the engine in the rear powering all four wheels.[32] However, when the United States entered World War II, the Indianapolis Motor Speedway shut down for four years.[33] Many racers and car builders returned to more mundane professions. Miller established a shop in Detroit and hoped to work with the auto industry, but his ventures away from the race tracks never did well.

4

The Tucker Combat Car

Back in Michigan, Tucker and his family moved to Ypsilanti, thirty-five miles west of Detroit. It was there that he started a company called Ypsilanti Machine and Tool in 1939. Some of it occupied a wooden barn that stood behind the family home on Park Street; a larger two-story metal building a little farther back was where production took place. The business did well, and soon the small facilities were crowded with workers. Joe Butcko, a tool and die maker, worked for Tucker at the facility starting in 1943, after apprenticing in nearby Plymouth, Michigan, when he was sixteen. He remembers the barn as unbelievably busy and crowded. Two shifts of workers kept it running around the clock, seven days a week. "That barn was so damn crowded, even the mice were hunchbacked."[1] Whenever Tucker came through, he was always wearing a suit and a tie, even if he was spending time working in the shop.

Tucker's universe was geographically quite small. He would walk from his house to his shop out back, meaning he was never very far from his family. The house they lived in was huge and left in the able hands of wife Vera to run. Whenever Tucker went into town he came home with fresh-cut flowers for Vera. And when Preston traveled, he would bring back even bigger gifts for her. One time he returned with fifty rosebushes, which he planted all around the yard and down both sides of the driveway.[2]

The Tuckers frequently invited others over, and the large house was often packed, with plenty of food for anyone who stopped by.[3] Tucker also loved classical music and listened to it whenever he could, furthering the welcoming feel of the Tucker home.

At work, Tucker began exploring the possibility of furnishing goods to the military. He envisioned an armored vehicle driven by a powerful engine, racing around a battlefield faster than the lumbering army tanks of the day. Working with Harry Miller, he developed a prototype, which he called the Tucker Tiger Tank. The vehicle was wheeled, not tracked, so it would more properly be considered not a tank but an armored car. It was also fast, powered by a Packard V-12 engine Miller had modified for this application.[4]

Tucker got good publicity for his project. He showed it to *Mechanix Illustrated*, which ran an article titled "Armored Tank Attains Speed of 114 M.P.H." According to the piece, published in February 1939, the vehicle's body was welded together and weighed ten thousand pounds. Heavy by automobile standards, it still weighed a ton less than similar armored vehicles and was faster than other vehicles in its class. Tucker claimed that it attained speeds of 78 mph over rough ground and 114 mph on "level road." The accompanying photograph showed the camouflaged car, bristling with machine guns, while Tucker, whom the magazine called "an armament manufacturer," stood inside it, pointing at the gun turret on the roof. The vehicle's main punch was delivered by a 37 mm cannon mounted in it.[5]

Although World War II had not started by this point, many people thought a European conflict was likely coming. But the US Army had already decided against buying armored vehicles like Tucker's, opting instead for lighter reconnaissance cars.[6] However, the main gun turret Tucker had designed for his armored car was of interest.

During World War I, the air forces of the world had experimented with airplane-mounted machine guns to shoot at other planes. Shooting accurately from a moving target proved difficult. Airplane designers developed turrets to allow gunners to swivel, but as the planes moved faster and the guns got larger and heavier, accuracy became a problem. Tucker's gun turret used electric motors to rotate the gun, allowing the gunner to aim more swiftly and track a target in flight.

Tucker applied for a patent on his "Gun Control Mechanism" on July 18 1939, and demonstrated it to US Army Air Corps representatives who visited his Ypsilanti shop.[7] They were impressed. The chief of the air corps called the turret "ingenious" and invited Tucker to a conference at Wright Field to discuss the needs of gun turrets with the military.[8]

A postwar report noted that Tucker's turret had shown promise by solving one particular problem other turret designers had encountered: when his electric motors were suddenly reversed during tests, they did not arc as those of other manufacturers had. His turret's motor was better insulated and less prone to burning out from excessive use. Air corps officials thought Tucker's turret moved too slowly but were curious to know if it could be improved. They gave Tucker a $10,000 development contract to work on it.

But in the end the military did not care for the results. Part of the problem had been caused by delays in getting parts from the government, so Tucker earned some sympathy from the decision-makers, but nevertheless they passed on his design.[9]

Tucker was undeterred. In 1940 he started a new company he called Tucker Aviation Corporation, hoping to build airplanes for the military. He envisioned a small plane—built around a powerful Miller engine, of course—cheaply made and mass-produced. His plane, the XP-57, would be rear-engine with a driveshaft running through the single-seat cockpit to the propeller at the front of the plane. Although unusual, this configuration was not unheard of. Bell manufactured the P-39 Airacobra with an engine behind the pilot and a driveshaft to the propeller. The P-39 first flew in 1939 and was in mass production by 1941.[10]

Tucker's XP-57, nicknamed the Peashooter, had some novel features that could have made it attractive for mass production. The airframe was to be made of metal tubing and its fuselage from aluminum. Plywood wings meant it would not use much aluminum, in short supply during the war. Officials liked the idea enough on paper to ask Tucker to build one, but the contract expired without a prototype being built. A US Air Force fact sheet on the XP-57 claimed that the project failed because of "financial problems" at Tucker Aviation.[11]

Another part of the problem may have been that the rear-engine design was not optimal for an airplane. Pilots noted that the Bell P-39 had strange "spin characteristics" because of the plane's odd balance. The design never caught on, and most P-39s built during the war were given to other countries; the United States continued to use airplanes with front-mounted engines.[12] But the root of the issue may have been something simpler: Tucker was not an aeronautical engineer, and airplanes were beyond his realm of expertise.

So he returned his focus to his terrestrial designs. He heard that the government was having a hard time getting turrets made for B-17 bombers. He met with air corps representatives and left believing they would buy turrets from him, even though no contract had been signed. The turret he proposed was capable of handling the .50 caliber machine guns on the B-17. Tucker built a prototype, but it was deemed "unsatisfactory."[13]

Perhaps the biggest problem facing Tucker was the size of his company, or lack thereof. He had allies—several companies had agreed to manufacture the turrets for him if he got the contract—but none of them were the size of Bendix, Westinghouse, General Electric, and Sperry, the giants who were bidding on this project.[14]

Tucker continued working on the prototype and in 1941 filed for another patent on a "Gun Mounting and Control Mechanism," which looked much like the ball turrets eventually used in American airplanes during the war. The primary claims Tucker made about his electrically driven ball turret were that the gunner could swing the guns quickly and the turret would prevent the gunner from accidentally shooting his own plane.[15]

Then Tucker decided to revive his armored car concept to create a platform for his gun turret. In 1942 *Mechanix Illustrated* once again ran a piece on the vehicle, now described as a "mobile anti-aircraft fortress." The magazine said it was being manufactured "for the U.S. Army by a Michigan firm." It did not mention Tucker by name but said the car would chase after airplanes flying overhead and, because of its amazing speed, would be able to fire thousands of rounds at them before they got away.[16] Again, it came to nothing. Tucker's combat car was never purchased by the US military.

Nor did he land any big contracts with the government to make his gun turrets—though stories persist that he did. Some of the claims began quite early, but it is unclear who started them. One 1946 newspaper article detailing Tucker's life story noted that he held a variety of patents, which was true, but then it added, "His wartime royalties on the gun turret alone would probably have run more than $100 million—if the government hadn't confiscated the patents. Tucker got around $200,000."[17]

The story may have been encouraged by the public relations department of Tucker's company. According to its 1948 film *Tucker: The Man and the Car*,[18] Tucker "turned the patents over to the United States during the war." No mention was made of the value of the patents or whether Tucker was compensated for them, however, and it sounded more like he had given them up willingly as an act of patriotism than had them confiscated.[19]

Even more pervasive is the myth that the Tucker turret was widely used by US forces during World War II.[20] There is little evidence to support the story, and authoritative sources debunk it. In 1947 the US Army Air Forces commissioned a report on gun turret procurement before and during the war. Titled *Development of Aircraft Gun Turrets in the AAF*, the report was declassified in 1959, almost three years after Preston Tucker passed away. It described the methodical approach military planners had used in acquiring turrets for warplanes:

> In the hectic early days of the war in Europe, the Materiel Division sought to accelerate experimental work on fire control equipment by breaking the whole problem into separate components, each to be a project within itself. Tentatively, and as a point of departure, the major industrial concerns interested in turret development were assigned specific airplanes to arm. In this way it came about that Sperry designed equipment for the B-17, Bendix for the B-25, Martin for the B-26, and General Electric for the A-20.[21]

When Tucker received the $10,000 in development money, other planes' turrets were already assigned to Sperry, Bendix, Martin, and GE. A plane no one was designing a turret for was the B-18, and it was assigned as Tucker's project. The B-18 Bolo airplane would see little use during the war and was "already obsolescent" when Tucker received the assignment. As such, his turret project was "doomed to failure."[22] The government did not order any Tucker turrets for its airplanes. In addition, the report noted that Tucker's turret was too slow and never had much hope of success.

5

Andrew Higgins

In March 1942 a man named Andrew Higgins announced that he had bought Tucker Aviation Corporation. Higgins's claim to fame was supplying boats to the US military. He had built boats in New Orleans before the war, and when the war started, he focused on boats for the navy and the marines. He became known for patrol torpedo boats, commonly called PT boats, and smaller boats designed to bring soldiers ashore and let them disembark quickly on a beach. These "Higgins boats" would be instrumental in many Allied wartime operations. News reports at the time said Tucker's company held contracts with the government worth $250 million,[1] but it is unclear where that story originated and it most likely was not true. It is possible that reporters confused Tucker's contract with one Higgins had received around the same time for "200 freighters, said to be the largest single order for shipbuilding ever made in the United States."[2]

Preston Tucker told the press that his negotiations with Andrew Higgins had taken only ten minutes. The men had known each other for a couple years and had simply written an agreement on a piece of paper and signed it. Though Higgins became the owner of Tucker Aviation, the arrangement constituted a joint venture between the two men, focusing on "airplane and boat armament production."[3] Tucker would become vice president of Higgins Industries, "overseeing the new Higgins-Tucker division."[4] He would move his operation down to New Orleans, into a new plant Higgins promised to build for it.

The following year, Tucker did indeed move his entire enterprise to New Orleans, with perhaps a hundred workers in tow. Joe Butcko was one of the Michigan workers transplanted. Though it was Tucker's then eighteen-year-old son, Preston Jr., who had hired Butcko as a tool and die maker for his father's company in January 1943,[5] the employee got to know Preston Sr. well, something quite common for the workers there. "He was easy to get to know. Very few people called him Mr. Tucker. He was referred to as Pres."[6]

When the Tucker contingent first arrived in Louisiana, they began work on engines for landing craft.[7] Though the Tucker turret had not been purchased and the XP-57 project had evaporated, perhaps Higgins believed Tucker could make a military contract materialize now that a large manufacturer had acquired his operation.

"When we went to New Orleans, [Preston] really treated the people swell," Butcko remembers. He would stop and talk to the workers on the plant floor, always dressed impeccably in business attire. Still, Butcko never saw Tucker lingering on the plant floor. "He always walked like he was going someplace in a hurry."

Tucker was also a heavy smoker, although few people thought much of it in that era. Seemingly everyone smoked cigarettes. Tucker often kept a pack inside his suit jacket and would reach in and retrieve a cigarette without removing the pack from his pocket. It was a helpful maneuver during the years of wartime scarcity, when people might be inclined to ask for a cigarette from someone brandishing a pack, but Tucker would continue to employ it even after the war was over.[8] As a result, many people noticed he had a lit cigarette in his hand as he spoke, often waving his hands to make a point, but no one could tell where the cigarette had come from.

For an eighteen-year-old like Joe Butcko, working for Higgins-Tucker was an adventure. He kept his toolbox next to that of Arthur Chevrolet, brother of one of the founders of the car company of that name. Arthur seemed a natural fit for Tucker's business, since he had spent time in Indianapolis building race engines. Now he was in charge of testing the engines being built on a dynamometer, which measures their mechanical force.[9]

The Higgins-Tucker collaboration started well. "They used to throw parties for us, Higgins and Preston," Butcko recalls. "It was pretty damn classy." Dinner parties at the nicest restaurants in town could not save the partnership once trouble started, however. Higgins had an ego. Butcko once heard Higgins say, "I am Andrew Jackson Higgins, the Henry Ford of the South."[10] A little over a year after they started working together, Higgins and Tucker had a falling out. Higgins said nothing publicly and Tucker returned to Ypsilanti. Higgins-Tucker quietly became Higgins Engines. Neither partner ever commented officially on the breakup, but Higgins's daughter later said her father came to believe that Tucker was "all fluff and no substance."[11] It might just have been that the two men's personalities clashed.

Around this same time, Harry Miller was running a machine shop in Detroit. He was working on a monstrous aircraft engine that he said would generate more than 3,000 horsepower—an obvious frontier for the engineer to conquer, since he had done so much with marine and automotive engines. But in 1943, after six weeks of hospitalization, he died of a heart attack. He was sixty-five.[12]

6

Tucker's Automobile Plans

Harry Miller was gone and the partnership with Andrew Higgins had crumbled, but Preston Tucker remained determined to make his mark. He returned to the realm of automobile manufacturing, studying the recent advances in hydraulics. Hydraulic systems, using fluid to drive accessories on an automobile, had been gaining more widespread use before the war. Power steering was already in development, and people wondered to what other uses hydraulics might be put.

Tucker saw the advantages hydraulics offered over typical mechanically driven systems. For example, the fluid in a hydraulic system cushioned the movement of mechanical parts so there was no jerky start at the beginning or harsh stop at the end of an action. Tucker theorized that the same drive technology might be used to actually propel cars, by replacing the automotive drivetrain with a fluid drive system.[1] He studied other advances made recently in automobiles as well, particularly the high-performance components and aerodynamic styling used on race cars. He imagined that an all-new line of cars, packed with the latest improvements, would be the easiest thing he'd ever had the chance to sell. And he'd build them himself.

He would have the opportunity due in large part to the changes in American industry brought about by World War II, which was now in its final years. As the United States was drawn into the conflict, the bulk of American manufacturing had been commandeered for the war effort.[2] By far the most important sector to be harnessed was the automobile industry. Spread over most of the country, in practically every city, were more than a thousand industry contractors and at least ten times as many subcontractors. Half a million Americans were producing vehicles before the United States started sending forces overseas, and the industry employed more than seven million.[3] The US government switched that production capacity over to manufacturing weapons of war, particularly tanks and airplanes for the army.

One government department, the Supply Priorities and Allocations Board, simply ordered the auto industry to stop making cars. The industry resisted at first, asking if it could continue producing autos while also producing armaments. The government refused the suggestion and ordered auto manufacturers to devote their entire resources to the needs of defense.[4] Car companies ran the last civilian cars off their assembly lines on February 10, 1942, and, barely missing a beat, began tooling for war production.[5] Before the war ended a little over three years later, the auto industry accounted for 20 percent of all US production, including half the airplane engines, a third of all machine guns, and every truck the military used. It also manufactured $11 billion in airplanes and related aircraft parts.[6]

While much of the manufacturing was done in automobile plants on repurposed assembly lines, some was done in plants built by the auto companies and by the federal government specifically for the purpose of building war machines. In its haste to build armaments, amid a confusing bureaucracy, the government overbuilt plant capacity. Some plants were not needed and some were simply too large or improperly planned. Truck shortages arose when truck plants were overhauled to build airplanes; locomotive plants were retooled to build army tanks at a time when locomotives were needed more than tanks.[7] The government even paid for building some brand-new factories when the production plans lacked the materials necessary for their realization. Some wondered what would happen to the extra manufacturing capacity when the war ended and there was no longer a need to be mass-producing army tanks and heavy bombers.[8]

Not only did the government control of the auto industry result in excess plants at the war's end, but with no new car production during the war, Americans had been forced to make do with whatever cars they had before the factories were commandeered. By the end of the war, America's car population was tired and ragged. Experts counted twenty-four million cars on the road, a third of them worth no more than a hundred dollars. If not for the lack of new cars, most would have been sold for scrap.[9] Automakers realized that this created a vast market for new cars, believing ten million Americans were primed to buy them once they became available.[10]

Preston Tucker was one of those who saw this opportunity, and he logically coupled it with his desire to create his own car. He decided to design an all-new vehicle from the ground up utilizing the latest technology available, particularly from the field of auto racing. And he would sell these cars to a starving consumer market.

7

The Pic *Article*

In 1944, as World War II was winding down, an automotive writer named Charles T. Pearson was one of many who speculated about what would happen in the auto industry when the war ended. What type of cars would be built, and when would new models be available to the public? Pearson poked around, and one day a source told him something intriguing: "Why don't you go and see Tucker? I hear he's got something."[1]

Pearson knew who Tucker was, having heard of his activities at Indianapolis with Harry Miller. He called and asked for an appointment to speak with him. Tucker invited him out to Ypsilanti Machine and Tool, where he was warmly received.

Pearson was impressed. Tucker was well dressed and confident, and his business was thriving. He owned a large home; the upper floor of the two-story building behind it, which housed his shop and personal office, was filled with draftsmen. The place was so busy "people were stumbling over each other." Tucker also had another large building a block away, filled with machinery and workers. Tucker's company was manufacturing something for the war effort; Pearson wasn't quite sure what, but the offices were a beehive of activity.

Pearson became a believer:

At first sight he was the typical small manufacturer so common around Detroit—well groomed, outwardly prosperous and self-assured. He talked readily and easily, but with reserve, in the manner of a man who commanded attention and expected it. From time to time he would refer to something important he had to hold back now but would reveal when the right time came. I caught no suggestion of the fanatic, yet in the animation of his expression, and the intensity of his brown eyes, I found the promise of a man who was going somewhere. Tucker acted as though he had something that would revolutionize the automobile industry, and his enthusiasm was contagious.[2]

Tucker told Pearson that he did, indeed, have big news about the auto industry, but he was not prepared yet to make an announcement. The two stayed in touch. A short while later, Tucker invited Pearson to his house for dinner. Pearson met Vera and sat down for a meal of meat and potatoes. After dinner, Tucker and Pearson retired to the den and talked about cars in front of the fireplace.

Tucker trusted Pearson and told him his plans for an all-new car. He was working on some deals that required secrecy for the moment, but he promised Pearson he could have the story once he was ready to announce it publicly. Tucker even gave permission for the reporter to see a man named George S. Lawson, who had made drawings of the proposed car, so long as Pearson kept the designs under wraps for the time being.

―――――

By enlisting Lawson to create the drawings of the revolutionary car he was dreaming of, Tucker had taken a step he would repeat many times while trying to launch his car: hiring men with extremely good credentials, as Lawson had spent the late 1930s at General Motors designing Buicks.[3] When Lawson made a quarter-scale model of the Tucker design in clay, the model was so realistic-looking that Tucker had admen photograph it outdoors.[4] With the proper background, the car appeared full-size and real. Photos of the model would soon appear in newspapers across America, and many readers would conclude that they were looking at a photograph of an actual car. For now, however, with the drawings and photos in hand, Tucker began recruiting people who might be able to help him launch his car company.

One was Abraham Karatz, who used the name Harold Karsten. Karatz, a former lawyer and financial promoter, had a criminal record. The details were sometimes hazy, but it was widely reported he had spent three years in prison for conspiring to embezzle $55,000 from a Chicago bank. He was out of prison by 1938.[5] Karatz was from Chicago and would be instrumental in helping Tucker start his car company, but his criminal record would haunt the project as well.[6]

It was not Karatz's legal background or financial dealings that led to his meeting Tucker, however. During the war, Karatz had acquired some government contracts to furnish the military with auto parts. One of the shops he hired to do the work was having trouble, and Karatz had been told to consult with Preston Tucker. When Tucker saw the blueprints Karatz was using, he spotted the problem: someone had made a mistake in the drawings and put down the wrong tolerances for the part. Tucker told Karatz to have the blueprints corrected, and when he did, it solved the problem.[7] Karatz was impressed, and the two stayed in touch.

By September 1945, the war was finally over, and Karatz had introduced Tucker to Floyd D. Cerf, a Chicago-based securities broker. Tucker showed Cerf the Lawson artwork and asked about raising money to launch a car company. Cerf liked the idea but told Tucker that mere ideas were unmarketable on Wall Street. It would be "necessary that he have a plant and organization and semblance of a product" before he could raise the necessary funds. Cerf would later say that Tucker seemed unfazed by the requirements and told him, "If that is what it took, he would go out and get it."[8]

While he was in Chicago, Tucker spoke to a reporter from the *Chicago Herald-American* and said he was going to launch a car company.[9] The paper ran a small story, but the news was buried in a flurry of other events of the day. Few people paid any attention.

Nonetheless, the time was right for an upstart auto company. As Tucker suspected, the existing car companies were hamstrung by years spent turning out army tanks and airplanes. Seeing the vast market before them and believing it would allow them to sell almost anything, the companies had decided not to invest much time or money in coming up with new models. Instead they planned to simply start churning out their prewar designs with little modification. As Tucker's car designer Alex Tremulis later wrote, "To meet the unprecedented postwar demand for product, automakers hauled out their prewar dies, and with little variation, turned out cars that were only mildly face lifted versions of the cars most people had just worn out."[10]

Tucker returned to Detroit. On December 26, 1945, he, Karatz, Lawson, and a few others signed an agreement to form a company. At the moment they had no funds and nothing more than a desire to go into business together, but they agreed that Tucker would control 20 percent of any stock they created, and the rest, although owned by the others, would be held in a trust controlled by Tucker. They also agreed that once the company began operating, Tucker would be paid a $75,000 annual salary.[11]

———

After the agreement was executed, Tucker called Charles Pearson back and told the reporter it was time for his big announcement.[12] Pearson interviewed Tucker and wrote an article that he sold to *Pic* and a few other magazines, which published variations of it. Titled "Streamlining That Car," it exploded into the public consciousness and set in motion one of the most astounding series of events ever regarding a consumer product in America.[13]

Pearson was mesmerized by his subject. He interviewed Tucker uncritically and wrote about Tucker's plans as if they were a fait accompli. The subhead of the article read, "Detroit's First Ultramodern Auto Already in Production—Designer of Rear-Engined 'Torpedo' Claims It Will Do 130 m.p.h. on Less Fuel." It was a tone for which he would not only be criticized later but for which he would almost be criminally prosecuted.

Pearson started with Tucker's credentials. "At 42 he has a recognized place in automotive engineering and is known throughout the industry, both here and abroad." He mentioned Tucker's "association" with Harry Miller and Miller's stellar record at Indianapolis. The "114-mile-per-hour combat car" was cited, along with a gyroscopic gun stabilizer and "the first fire control interrupter, a handy gadget that prevents preoccupied gunners from shooting off tail assemblies or chewing up propellers." The implication was clear: Tucker was an accomplished inventor, and now he had turned his expertise toward the automobile.

The writing flowed back and forth between what Tucker *would* do and what he *had* done. It was often unclear which was which. "The first super-super automobile job to get off the drawing board into the production stage is being put together at Detroit with only a little less secrecy as to exact mechanical detail than marked the early development of the Norden bomb-sight." How imminent was production? Or had it already begun? The article hedged. All it told the reader was that the car Tucker was building "may make models now in production obsolete almost over night."

The article featured a full-page rendering of the Tucker Torpedo by George Lawson and bold predictions dressed as facts. "THE CAR will cruise at 100 m.p.h., [and] get up to 65 miles per gallon of gasoline." The article lacked qualifiers; there was no language to suggest that the Tucker automobile was speculative or might never come to fruition.

Among the car's described features, some were quite outlandish. "The driver's seat is in the center," it said, to give the driver a better field of vision. The doors "will swing out and up to clear curbs when parked." The car would have a "Cyclops Eye" center headlight, and the car's fenders would turn with the steering wheel, allowing the fender-mounted lights to illuminate curves in the road. (Although unusual, this last feature was not entirely original to Tucker; steerable headlights were a popular aftermarket accessory on some prewar cars.)[14]

The article threw other features of the car at the reader, with hardly a hint they hadn't been tested or even built yet. The Torpedo was said to weigh only two thousand pounds, to be powered by a simpler but more powerful engine than those currently available, and to have an automatic transmission with fewer parts than its contemporaries. The power from the engine—placed in the rear of the vehicle—would drive the car through hydraulic torque converters, one on each wheel. It was a remarkably simple design—if it would work.

The Tucker automobile would also be streamlined. While the concept seems obvious today, domestic auto manufacturers had not focused on it previously. As John Heitmann, an automotive historian, wrote, "Drag and aerodynamics were for the most part ignored in the U.S. even after World War II, the one exception being the abortive Tucker of the late 1940s."[15]

Along with the drawing of the car, the Pearson piece featured Tucker sitting at his desk holding a piston. More photographs across the bottom of the article showed the car's components, including disc brakes and independent suspension parts, along with a photo purporting to show "HOW ROAD appears at 100 m.p.h. Note clear vision."

The article left the reader with the distinct impression that the Tucker Torpedo was going to turn the industry on its head. Since Tucker was not hamstrung by a legacy of building cars the old-fashioned way, he could start from scratch. His affordable car would be rear-engine, rear-wheel drive, with a sleeker outline, and have no obligation to follow rules laid down by anyone else.

But one additional piece of information overshadowed the rest of the article: the car would cost only $1,000.[16]

———

The *Pic* article hit newsstands in January 1946. Though it took up less than three full pages in a magazine few people had heard of, it sparked an immediate media frenzy. Some of this was calculated. Along with different versions of the article he sold to other magazines, Pearson rewrote the material as a press release for Tucker, who let news organizations know about the Tucker Torpedo and the excitement it was generating. Other media organizations reprinted the material as news.

Tucker had other ideas for attracting publicity as well. As the 1946 Indianapolis 500 approached, he decided to enter a car. He found one for sale that had been built by Harry Miller and was being driven by someone he knew, George Barringer. Tucker renamed it the Tucker Torpedo Special and told the press it contained some of the components planned for his new automobile: hydraulic disc brakes, independent suspension, and a six-cylinder engine, although it was a straight six. Tucker's entry was reportedly the only one that did not require special racing fuel. Barringer did a great job qualifying, but the transmission failed after only twenty-seven laps and the Tucker Torpedo Special headed for the garage. Pearson and Tucker wondered if a failure on such a prominent stage might lead to negative press, but journalists didn't seem to take note.[17]

Increasingly, however, they were taking note of Pearson's article. By the summer, the mainstream press was reporting Tucker's plans, with many details drawn directly from Pearson. "Tucker Visions New Auto to Cruise at High Speed," the *Milwaukee Journal* wrote.[18] *The Ottawa Citizen* explained, "Fenders and Headlights Will Turn on Preston Tucker's New Motor Car."[19] The *Pittsburgh Post-Gazette* announced, "Engine-in-Rear Auto to Buck Car Industry."[20] In November 1946 *Popular Mechanics* highlighted offerings from the auto industry for 1947; right alongside photos and descriptions of the latest Big Three offerings was a photo of the Tucker Torpedo. It was Lawson's scale model, but it looked real. The description made it even more believable: "Tucker Torpedo has six-cylinder engine in rear; curved back window extends into the top for full vision. This revolutionary car carries six passengers and will be in the 'medium price class'—$1500 to $1800." Nowhere was there any hint that the car did not exist yet.[21]

Years later, Pearson claimed that he had believed everything he wrote about Tucker and the Torpedo's imminent appearance. He had written stories on other companies and businessmen who told him they were on the verge of manufacturing something new, and they had always come through. He viewed the Tucker interview as business as usual.

So when I wrote "off the drawing board into the production stage" high in the first paragraph I assumed, by the time the story was published some months later, that Tucker would have the castings and other stuff he said had been ordered. Many of the stories I was handling at the time followed the same pattern—as soon as they got parts and materials they were in business, and the situation was getting steadily better. When I finally realized there weren't any castings or even patterns I was at first resentful, but later had to admit that, from Tucker's standpoint, there was nothing either dishonest or immoral at the time in referring to something that was still on paper as fact. In the year that followed I learned that to the irrepressible Tucker, with his boundless optimism and self-confidence, anything he had decided to do was already a fact, for all practical purposes, and there was no point in complicating things with a lot of tiresome detail and explanations.[22]

Pearson's faith in Tucker's plans was not unusual. Many who met Tucker noticed that he never used vague and uncertain terms when describing his intentions. A young designer named Philip Egan noted that Tucker was a "mesmerizing champion of all the concepts of his Tucker '48. [The] astounding description was not regarded by Tucker as a possibility; it was a fact. He was thoroughly convinced of it."[23] Tucker never actually said that he had built the engine; he just spoke of it with certainty, in the present tense.

Pearson was not even the only journalist to be enthralled by Preston Tucker's optimism. Tucker loved promoting his ideas, and soon other reporters were interviewing him and writing their own articles about his futuristic car plans. Depending on the editorial slant, a magazine would emphasize aspects of the car important to that magazine's readers. *Science Illustrated*'s article "Torpedo on Wheels" focused on the hydraulic fluid drive system Tucker wanted to use: "Hydraulic torque convertors provide a direct power-transmitting system that does away with the customary clutch, transmission, drive shaft, differential, and rear axle."[24] It was said that it would use eight hundred fewer parts in its drivetrain when compared to a typical automobile of the day. Again, much of the article was in the present tense, as if the car had already been built.

But neither Tucker's can-do attitude nor his PR machinations had prepared Pearson for the uproar that followed. When he sent his article off to *Pic* for publication, an editor at the magazine asked where he should send correspondence received in response to the piece. Pearson told them to forward it to Tucker, thinking he might enjoy the feedback. He later said that Tucker received 150,000 letters and telegrams in response to the article. Most simply asked when and where they could buy a Torpedo.[25]

8

The Tucker Corporation

Publicity may have come easily, but as interest in the Tucker Torpedo built over the course of 1946, Tucker was wrestling with the more practical elements of launching his new company. One of the most pressing concerns: he still had no money to fund the project. So in the spring of 1946 he held a meeting at the Detroit Athletic Club to discuss financing for the Tucker Corporation with the men he had met with the previous December. Some of the men present assumed they could become equity holders simply by agreeing to work on the project. But Tucker needed money before he could do anything further; he wasn't interested in giving away equity in the corporation. One man decided to end the arguments. He pulled out his checkbook and suggested that everyone put $5,000 into the project to get things rolling.

Several of the men stopped arguing when they realized it would take money to get a permanent seat at the table. No one else offered to contribute. So Tucker got up and walked out. "Good day, gentlemen," he told them. Charles Pearson, writer of the *Pic* article, said some of the men stayed behind to discuss launching the company without Tucker.[1] When those discussions proved fruitless, all the original founders—except for Karatz—left the project.[2] To proceed, Tucker would need to re-form the Tucker Corporation.

It was all for the better. Although Tucker was approached by scam artists and shysters, the current flood of publicity was giving him access to some of the most respected names in the auto industry. And his name was already known to them—if perhaps not as well-known as the *Pic* article had suggested—because of his work with Harry Miller. Many of the high-profile people in the auto industry whom Tucker approached agreed to come work for him. As a result, his new boardroom would be stocked with an impeccable group of executives.

Perhaps the highest profile belonged to Fred Rockelman, who had worked at both Chrysler, as president of the Plymouth division, and at Ford, where he had been general sales manager. In early 1946 he was frequenting the Detroit Athletic Club, where, as he later wrote, "all of the automobile men gathered—the old-timers, the newcomers, the experts and the novices, but all automobile men." An acquaintance in the industry, Robert Pierce of Briggs Body, suggested that Rockelman meet with Tucker. The three met, and Tucker explained the concepts behind his proposed automobile. The focus was on a rear-engine car with an improved automatic transmission. But the clincher for Rockelman was simply Tucker. "I was tremendously impressed with Tucker's 'sales pitch.'"[3]

Rockelman admitted he knew little about automatic transmissions or the other futuristic features of Tucker's proposed car. But he figured those were just technical issues that could be resolved later. Tucker's presentation convinced him, and he agreed to work for Tucker as soon as he had a plant. He would be VP in charge of sales.

By July 8, 1946, the Tucker Corporation had officially filed its papers of incorporation. The company authorized one million shares of stock with a par value of one dollar per share. According to company records, Preston Tucker purchased one thousand shares of the stock but did not pay for them at that time. Later, the SEC would note that the company, at the moment of its creation, "was financially sterile."[4] Nevertheless, Tucker had already invested much of his own money on the project, spending close to $100,000 on the endeavor by this point. Most of it had come from Ypsilanti Machine and Tool.[5]

The re-formed company held its incorporators meeting and elected a board of directors. Its members included Preston Tucker, Robert Pierce, and Fred Rockelman. Tucker was then named president of the corporation, Rockelman vice president of sales, and Pierce treasurer.[6]

Other high-profile auto executives joined Tucker as well. Hanson Ames Brown became executive vice president; he had been a VP at General Motors. Lee Treese was Tucker's vice president in charge of manufacturing; he had been similarly employed at Ford. K. E. Lyman had gotten his experience at Bendix and Borg-Warner. Herbert Morley had been a plant manager for Borg-Warner, and Ben Parsons was a recognized expert in the field of engineering consulting, particularly with fuel injection.[7] The Tucker Company was becoming an impressive organization. It would be even more impressive following its next acquisition: a monstrous manufacturing facility that would immediately grant credibility to Tucker's enterprise.

9

Tucker Acquires a Plant

Now that Tucker had assembled a team of auto executives to help him make cars, he needed the physical assets with which to build them. He discovered a plant in Chicago that Dodge had used during the war to build B-29 airplane engines. It now sat idle. As an asset of the government, it was available if Tucker could negotiate a deal.

The engine plant, located at 7401 S. Cicero Avenue in Chicago, occupied 480 acres. Completed in 1943, it cost the government $76 million to build. One of its structures was among the largest buildings in the world, covering 3.5 million square feet. Its basement held a cafeteria capable of feeding twenty-seven thousand people daily.[1] The sprawling complex contained a tool shop, aluminum and magnesium foundries, a heat treat facility to improve the material properties of metal, a die shop, light and heavy forge buildings, and administrative offices.

The War Assets Administration (WAA) was charged with disposing of surplus equipment and property that had been purchased to further the war efforts, so Tucker went to Washington, DC, and lobbied them to lease him the plant. He enlisted the aid of Walter P. Reuther, head of the United Auto Workers union; presumably, if Tucker got the plant up and running, he could employ a lot of UAW members. Reuther wrote to the WAA and carbon-copied his message to President Truman and other government leaders:

> We are extremely desirous that this plant be used as a complete productive unit for the manufacture of automobiles. We believe such use will provide maximum amount of employment and provide for maximum utilization of productive capacity both for the best interest of the workers involved and the nation. Our understanding is that Preston Tucker's proposal is the only one which appears to meet these objectives.[2]

Tucker could not afford to buy the complex outright. His powers of persuasion were at their peak, however. The WAA official with whom he was negotiating, Oscar H. Beasley, asked him how much cash he had available. Tucker told him $27,000 but explained that it wasn't the cash on hand that guaranteed the Tucker Corporation's success. It was the stellar group of automotive executives committed to the project. Tucker ran down the list of renowned auto executives who had come aboard. Beasley didn't even bother to ask Tucker to confirm the $27,000 figure—he didn't ask for financial statements either—and agreed to lease him the plant.[3]

———

Tucker gave the WAA a letter of intent to lease the plant dated July 1, 1946. The deal called for a $1 million payment to secure the lease. An initial payment of $25,000 was due July 3; $150,000 was due on August 1 and again on September 1. The balance of $675,000 was due on October 1, 1946.[4]

Tucker submitted a Western Union money order for the first $25,000, which he paid for with funds from Ypsilanti Machine and Tool.[5] That bought him until August 1 to raise more money. For reasons no one could adequately explain, the $25,000 money order from Tucker was never cashed. Oscar Beasley later claimed that someone had temporarily misplaced it but never said why he did not seek a replacement. "As far as I know it was an entirely honest deal," Beasley said, "and if Tucker benefited by the [payment] being lost for a while he was simply fortunate, because I don't believe there was anything deliberate on anyone's part. Something like this happening wouldn't have been all that unusual, with the amount of work they had in the financial section at that time." Tucker's critics later pointed to this incident, suggesting it must have been the result of corruption, but nothing ever came of the accusations. And since the transaction was in the form of a Western Union money order, which would have been paid for when it was issued rather than when it was cashed, he would only benefit from the mix-up if the money order were returned to him.[6]

While the parties ironed out the remaining details, the WAA allowed Tucker to move his key personnel into the plant to set up offices.[7] He chartered a plane to bring his new board members Fred Rockelman and Robert Pierce to the site. There was a sense of urgency, but also that money was not an issue, and for Rockelman, it was eye opening. "This was the way Preston Tucker did business," he said later. "When he was 'wheeling and dealing,' don't spare the dollars."[8]

Preston Tucker also moved his family to Chicago, to one of the most exclusive addresses in town on perhaps the most expensive residential block in the city. The apartment at 999 Lake Shore Drive was in a landmark district filled with important and historical buildings.[9] The ten-story structure had just been turned into a co-op, and Tucker acquired 9A for his family, a large unit on the highest floor occupied by tenants. He bought the apartment from Bror Dahlberg, who'd made his fortune as one of the founders of Celotex, a company that made building materials from agricultural by-products.[10] The reported sale price was $45,000.

Apartment 9A was about forty-three hundred square feet in size and provided views of Lake Michigan, Lincoln Park, and the mansions of North Lake Shore Drive. Floor-to-ceiling mahogany paneled the common rooms, consisting of the living room, dining room, den, and conservatory. The apartment had three bedrooms. Tucker also bought apartment 2C, which was a bit smaller than 9A, at perhaps twenty-six hundred square feet, for his mother.

———

Though Tucker spent lavishly on chartered flights and exclusive housing, his company, meanwhile, needed to raise money to make its upcoming lease payments. Floyd Cerf told the board that it would not be advisable to try a public stock offering yet. There wasn't enough time and the company had too little to show investors. The factory represented progress, but what they really needed was a car.

Even if they couldn't sell cars yet, though, they could sell dealerships. Tucker had saved all the letters he received after the *Pic* article, many of them from people eager to become retail sales agents for the Tucker Torpedo. Tucker sent the interested parties a letter signed by Rockelman, offering to let them invest in a Tucker dealership. The letter boasted of the company's recently acquired plant:

> One of the most important of recent developments has been our acquisition, by long-term lease from the Unites States Government, of the mammoth Dodge Airplane Engine Plant at Chicago. Thus we have established ourselves in the newest, finest and most completely modern factory in the world, with facilities and equipment unequaled in the automotive industry, and with a location in the very center of population, markets and sources of supply. We are now ready to accept applications for dealerships.[11]

The letter also made promises regarding the cars that had not been built yet:

> The man who acquires our franchise can be confident that he will be merchandising an automobile so far advanced and superior to competition, that sales are unlikely to present any problem whatever for many months, if not years, to come . . . . If any automotive dealer can be certain of a lengthy period of excellent profits, under conditions virtually made to order for success and satisfaction, the Tucker dealer would seem to be that man.[12]

The response was overwhelming. Letters flooded the company from potential dealers, and many of them went to visit the plant in Chicago. There was a sense of urgency, since only a limited number of dealerships were being offered.

Those who responded to the letter were told that they would have to front fifty dollars per car they were willing to commit to, and that the money would be held in escrow until the corporation was certain that the project was viable. The dealers would have to agree to two years' worth of cars to assure they would have enough on hand to succeed. Tucker hoped the offer would raise $15 million.[13]

But by the time the $150,000 lease payment on the plant came due on August 1, the Tucker Corporation had not yet raised enough money to make it. Preston Tucker did not have the money either.[14] He asked Oscar Beasley at the WAA for guidance. Tucker later claimed that Beasley told him to send a check and that he would hold the check until Tucker had secured financing. If need be, Tucker could try borrowing the money from the Reconstruction Finance Corporation, a government agency that loaned millions of dollars to American industries to prop them up, help the economy, and maintain the flow of consumer goods. Tucker told Beasley he'd mail a check.[15]

Someone else at the WAA called Tucker inquiring about the payment. Tucker told them the check had been mailed but if they had not received it, he would send a replacement, which he did. Wondering if Tucker had $150,000 to make the payment, someone at the WAA called Tucker's bank and found he had two accounts, one personal and one for Ypsilanti Machine and Tool. Each account held only a couple thousand dollars, far short of the payment they were seeking. The replacement check arrived and was accompanied by a note from Tucker asking the agency to hold it while they revisited the terms of the lease. Rather than complain, the WAA asked Tucker which terms of the lease they needed to revisit.[16]

The original lease agreement gave the plant to Tucker after the government had inventoried its contents, and the inventory had not been completed.[17] Though Tucker had begun moving into the plant, he could not complete the process until the issue was resolved. As a result, he said, the timetable for payment had been thrown off. Beasley accepted his argument and offered new terms. On September 18, 1946, Tucker signed a new intent-to-lease agreement with the War Assets Administration, by which the Tucker Corporation would simply need to have $15 million, either in cash or available credit, by March 1, 1947. If that hurdle was cleared, then lease payments would begin. Tucker had been told by several different stock underwriters that a public offering could easily raise that amount. Tucker had even brought a letter from one of them and showed it to Beasley.

The WAA returned Tucker's $150,000 bad check, along with his original money order from Ypsilanti Tool, which by this point had apparently been found.[18] The Securities and Exchange Commission would later point to these actions as evidence of someone's wrongdoing but could never explain how Tucker could have caused the payments to be held by the WAA.

———

Before long the Tucker Corporation had more reason to celebrate, as the dealer program became a huge success. In the last months of 1946, the company raised $240,000 for cars the dealers committed to buying. But the SEC in Chicago heard about the program and began investigating. It determined that the sales constituted a "security" under SEC rules. As such, Tucker Corporation should have filed a registration statement before embarking on the plan. No such statement had been filed.[19] More troubling to the SEC: it found that much of the money had not been placed in escrow as the dealer solicitation letter had promised. The funds were simply being placed into a Tucker Corporation account. And on one occasion, Abraham Karatz had deposited $15,000 directly into Preston Tucker's personal account.[20]

The SEC was unable to establish whether Preston Tucker himself knew how the funds were being handled, but it did notify the Tucker Corporation that the dealership sales agreements needed to be rescinded and reworked. Tucker agreed to do so; from that point forward, dealers would pay only twenty dollars per car they wanted rather than fifty, but they would be guaranteed nothing in return. There was no promise that the money would be held in escrow, and it was openly stated that the money could be used by the Tucker Corporation for any purpose.[21] One Tucker employee who sold franchises said of the new system: "Before we sign a franchise they have their lawyer in my office and I have my lawyer. I tell them if we do not build an automobile you don't get anything. You don't even get so much as one bolt.

There is no misunderstanding. They understood very clear that the only way they can win is for us to win."[22]

It was an astonishing thing to ask of franchisees considering how little they were being promised. But interest in the dealer program had been so intense that Tucker knew he would have no problem with people agreeing to it. Sure enough, when all the previous contracts were rewritten, the dealers overwhelmingly agreed to the new terms. Some sources said Tucker raised $6 million this way.[23]

For the moment, there was nothing else the SEC could complain about.

———

Meanwhile, however, not everyone in Washington was happy that the Tucker Corporation had gotten the Chicago Dodge plant. Word came from Washington that powerful forces were in league to take the plant from him and give it to another company called Lustron. Lustron wanted the plant to manufacture prefabricated housing, and the National Housing Agency (NHA) wanted to give it to them to help alleviate the postwar housing shortage.

Wilson Wyatt, the man in charge of the NHA, lobbied for Lustron.[24] In fact, he issued a decree giving the plant to Lustron and announced that the Tucker deal was off. Chicago news headlines shouted, TUCKER LOSES DODGE PLANT, much to the dismay of Tucker employees already working at the factory.[25]

The NHA demanded that the WAA cancel its agreement with Tucker. The WAA refused, and the matter became a political hot potato in Washington. The Reconstruction Finance Corporation supported the housing bid; it had lent $37.5 million to Lustron, while the company's promoters had only invested $36,000 of their own money in the business. Others in Washington wanted the Lustron deal sunk simply because it was a bad business proposal. In many respects, it had more potential drawbacks than Tucker's plan. When Lustron officials pitched the notion of prefabricated homes to the government, they hadn't even designed one yet. They believed they could build the homes, they just didn't plan on setting the architects to work until after they had gotten an assurance of government interest.[26]

Even so, Senator Homer Ferguson of Michigan announced that he would conduct hearings to determine "whether or not influence was used or claimed to be used" in the awarding of the Chicago plant to Tucker.[27] Ferguson's subcommittee began hearings in November 1946 and made Tucker and the men from the WAA defend the deal.[28] Soon, everyone became aware of the convoluted fashion in which Tucker had acquired a multimillion-dollar plant, by passing checks that were bad and money orders that were not cashed. Subcommittee counsel grilled Tucker on the $150,000 check for which he had insufficient funds. Tucker insisted he would have covered it by mortgaging the machine shop or his family home. "When the check got back there, it would have been made good."[29]

"Didn't you know it was an offense to issue a worthless check in the state of Michigan?" counsel asked.

Tucker replied, "I didn't think it was wrong. I was just trying to start a business and create some employment."

The hearing degenerated into unfocused mudslinging. Tucker said he had been approached by a well-connected attorney, whose name he did not provide at first, who offered to secure the plant for Tucker for "six figures."[30] Later, when he identified the attorney, the man took the stand and denied any such exchange.[31] One witness claimed Tucker's lobbyist, a man named Edward Gaffney, had been promised a 10 percent stake in the Tucker Corporation in exchange for landing the plant. Tucker denied it. When the subcommittee called the lobbyist as a witness, he disappeared.[32] Instead, Tucker testified that he had been strong-armed by another lobbyist who had said he could stop the NHA from taking away the plant in exchange for an 8 percent stake in the company. The individual denied this had ever happened.[33]

One WAA official gave his reason for giving the plant to Tucker: "Because I think he was a man with a plan, and he outlined his plan to us, and he had outlined a workable plan which called for finances, public financing. . . . This was the best proposal that was offered to the government for the disposition of this plant." On the other hand, the NHA representative testified that

Lustron would have made a fine tenant of the plant, particularly because the RFC was willing to lend the company the $52 million it needed.[34]

Eventually, the dispute ended up on the desk of President Truman himself, who refused to lend his support to the NHA's demands. This ended the threat to Tucker—and also helped end the political career of Wyatt, who saw this failure as an indication he was losing sway in Washington. He resigned his post during the fight.[35] Lustron did not lose out entirely. Before Wyatt left the NHA, he helped the company obtain a facility in Ohio and a new loan from the RFC for $12.5 million to get started.[36]

Though Tucker ended up keeping the plant, he was incensed by all the interference with his operation. Convinced that powerful people in the auto industry were lobbying against him, Tucker told anyone who would listen that Washington was being manipulated by Detroit.[37]

10

Before the Stock Offering

After negotiating the revised intent-to-lease agreement with the WAA, Tucker had contacted Floyd Cerf, and on October 2, 1946, they signed an agreement to allow Cerf to handle the sale of $20 million of Tucker Corporation stock to the public. Cerf worked out of Chicago's financial district and had never handled a job this big. But Abraham Karatz had introduced him to Tucker, and Tucker had always trusted Karatz's advice. Though Cerf agreed to handle the sale, he maintained his earlier precondition: before any stock was offered for sale, the Tucker Corporation must show a car to investors.[1]

Tucker agreed, and Cerf began preparing the registration statement to be filed with the SEC in May 1947. Although the original agreement with the WAA had called for Tucker to be fully funded by March, he was confident he would get an extension because of the time he had lost fighting over the plant with Lustron. Perhaps it seemed overly optimistic to some, but Tucker was right. At the eleventh hour, the March deadline would be pushed back to July 1.

Meanwhile, in his efforts to craft the prototype Cerf demanded, Tucker turned to a designer named Alex Tremulis, who would go on to become one of the most important people in Tucker's organization. A young but well-established car designer, Tremulis was known for drawing beautiful cars. He did not attend design school or college and simply taught himself to draw, and he had a reputation for taking chances and ignoring convention. He also had a big ego; he once told an interviewer, "I operate on the basis that the meek shall inherit nothing."[2]

———

Alexander Sarantos Tremulis was born in 1914 in Chicago and showed an early aptitude for drawing. As a child, he "loved toy automobiles, planes and rocket ships. Everything else bored me."[3] He often skipped school—he flunked an art class he found boring[4]—and spent time at local car dealerships, drawing the Stutz and Duesenberg cars in the showroom. Tremulis often modified the appearance of the cars in his drawings, showing different concepts and variations he imagined. In later years, he would call himself an "Imagineer."[5]

Dealership employees took note. In the 1930s Duesenbergs and other expensive cars often had custom bodies—coachwork—made to order, creating a demand for imaginative designers. Don Hogan, a Duesenberg sales manager, believed that Tremulis's concepts had potential and asked him to sketch some designs for customers. Hogan paid him $1.50 for a pencil sketch and $2.50 for one drawn in India ink. Tremulis often provided finished drawings the day after they were requested. In 1933 Hogan hired the nineteen-year-old Tremulis full time to draw car concepts for customers.[6]

His drawings soon caught the attention of others in the industry. Eventually he was hired by Auburn Cord Duesenberg.[7] At Duesenberg he got to feed his appetite for cars, with sometimes spectacular results.

In 1935 he test-drove a Duesenberg town car, hitting speeds in excess of 90 mph on country roads in Indiana. A car in front of him lost control—at least, that's how Tremulis told the story in 1988—forcing Tremulis to put the Duesenberg in a ditch to avoid a collision. The car tumbled three times and came to rest upside down in a cornfield. Tremulis climbed out, happy to be alive, unaware he had several broken bones in his neck. Tremulis then "called an engineer at Duesenberg's Chicago offices to tell him the test drive was running behind schedule."[8]

In 1936 he was promoted to chief stylist at Auburn Cord Duesenberg, and he stretched his stylistic wings. He worked on one of the most iconic designs the company ever built: the supercharged Cord 812, well known to car enthusiasts for its memorable "gleaming flexible metal exhaust headers," which ran from its hood to its fenders.[9] The car had been developed in secret and unveiled at the 1937 New York Auto Show. Its unusual design caused E. L. Cord, the car's namesake, to chastise Tremulis when he first saw it. Cord assumed that the exhaust pipes were tacky, nonfunctional ornaments. When Tremulis explained that the pipes were functional, an enthused Cord gave him a twenty-dollar bonus.[10]

Tremulis worked for several different car companies after that. His designs often looked futuristic. "The past is only history," he said. "I am more interested in the future."[11] He could clearly draw modern cars, but it took a while to find a place where he could fully explore his imaginative automotive vision.

Tremulis moved to Detroit after Auburn Cord Duesenberg ceased operation in 1937. At Chrysler, he designed the Thunderbolt, one of the earliest "concept cars" built in the city.[12] The car was fabricated by LeBaron, a custom shop, which Chrysler credited for the design, but Tremulis was the one who had created it.[13] He then did a stint in Beverly Hills, California, designing custom coachwork for Cadillacs being sold on Rodeo Drive to celebrities. The resulting cars were not futuristic, but it allowed him the opportunity to work more closely with the coach builders.[14]

Tremulis was drafted, and after sending drawings of aircraft to the War Department, he spent World War II at the aircraft lab at Wright Field in Ohio.[15] He helped with advanced aircraft design but also created drawings used to gain approval for new aircraft projects engineers were working on. His boss later said that Tremulis "put life into dull three-view drawings," which "helped to sell many an airplane design."[16] He wasn't designing airplanes so much as he was helping his bosses market them.

When the war ended, Tremulis returned to Chicago and took a job with an industrial design firm, Tammen and Denison. He found himself designing nonautomotive items such as bathroom fixtures.[17] But he badly wanted to design cars again.

Tremulis read about the car Tucker wanted to manufacture and believed he could rework the Lawson drawings into a practical design that could actually be built. He phoned Tucker and asked for a meeting.[18] Tucker told Tremulis he could have only fifteen minutes. Tremulis brought drawings of what he thought a Tucker automobile ought to look like. The drawings were based on the Lawson designs, but Tremulis had made them more realistic. For example, Tremulis eliminated impractical features like the curved glass windows in the doors.

Tucker asked to see more of his portfolio. Tremulis pulled out drawings of streamlined cars and airplanes, and the fifteen-minute meeting stretched into three and a half hours.[19] Despite the two men both having huge egos, they got along immediately. Tremulis understood Tucker's dreams, and Tucker believed Tremulis could create blueprints from them.

Tremulis was still employed by Tammen and Denison, but Tucker didn't want to hire the firm, just Tremulis.[20] He offered him what he called a "styling-study" contract, to develop the ideas they had discussed. Tremulis accepted.[21] Tucker then told Tremulis that his first order of business was to create final drawings for the Tucker sedan—that is, turn the Lawson drawing into a practical design car builders could start working from immediately—within six days. It was around Christmas 1946, and Tucker wanted to have them before the first of the year. The deadline seemed impossible, but Tremulis accepted.[22] Tucker agreed to pay Tremulis $700 per month with an eye toward a large raise once the car went into full production.[23]

———

Like others who interacted with Tucker, Tremulis found himself drawn to help him. Decades later, he recalled that Tucker was "a good boss" who had two pictures on a shelf in his office. One was of Jesus, the other of a Porsche automobile.

Tremulis's design background helped him dissuade Tucker from some of the more outlandish ideas for his car. Having designed practical objects both for cars and for household use, he had an understanding of what could be manufactured and what could not. But Tremulis also understood how to deal with Tucker: He didn't argue with him. Instead, he told Tucker how a design might be made better and still fit with his larger vision.

For instance, others had tried talking Tucker out of including features like steerable front fenders that turned with the wheels, because they increased costs and added little value. Tremulis—knowing of Tucker's desire for a safe car—simply told Tucker the design was unsafe. He reminded Tucker of Frank Lockhart, a famous racer who'd built a race car with fairings over the wheels, similar to Tucker's steerable fenders. The Stutz Blackhawk, as it was called, was designed for land speed records but had spectacularly crashed at Daytona and killed Lockhart. Tremulis told Tucker that they had later done wind tunnel testing on the car's configuration and determined that the fairings acted as rudders in the wind. As such, they would make the car dangerous to drive. Tucker agreed, and the feature was dropped.[24]

Tremulis liked the idea of a rear-engine, rear-wheel-drive car, because it wouldn't require running a driveshaft from the front of the car to the rear axle. Eliminating the shaft meant no tunnel—or "hump"—running the length of the car between the driver and passenger. Tremulis could design the car lower to the ground, playing to his preference for streamlined designs.[25] The Tucker automobile he designed sat five or six inches closer to the ground than its competitors. And Tremulis worked in other new ideas. In his drawings, the front seats and the rear seats were interchangeable and could easily be swapped. That way, if the front seats looked worn, the owner could rotate them like tires, putting the ones from the rear into the front, and vice versa.[26] Interchangeable parts would also lower manufacturing costs and make the car easier to assemble.

Tremulis struck upon another idea for making the car's parts more interchangeable. The pillar between the front and rear door on each side of the car cannot normally be switched to the other side, because door hinges for the rear doors are normally attached to them. If the doors on the car did not hinge on the pillar, however, a symmetrical pillar could be used on both sides of the car. The resulting car would have rear doors hinged toward the back of the car—other cars had been made this way—making the rear seat easier for passengers to enter and exit. Tucker liked it, and it became a design feature.[27]

Tremulis also knew he could work around some of Tucker's ideas without confrontation. Tucker had plans for a mammoth engine setup that the designer did not believe would be practical, so Tremulis designed the engine compartment to accommodate a more typical automobile engine in case the original build didn't come to fruition. Later in the process, when Tucker's preferred engine was indeed scrapped in favor of a more conventional engine, Tremulis's foresight would pay off.[28]

For now, however, Tremulis worried less about the engine and took his aerodynamic vision to extremes. Most cars of the time had small rain gutters running along the tops of doors, outside the car, to keep water from leaking into the passenger compartment. Tremulis designed *internal* gutters that let the rain enter the gap between the door and the roof and then channeled it out from inside the door frame. This design, as Tremulis proudly noted later, would result in a 1 percent improvement in aerodynamic efficiency of the shape of the car.[29]

———

On December 31, 1946, Tucker stopped by Tremulis's office to see what he had come up with. Tremulis considered his drawings unfinished but showed them to Tucker, who enthusiastically embraced them. Tucker chastised Tremulis for saying the drawings needed more work: "The trouble with you stylists is you never know when to stop."[30]

Tucker declared the drawings finished and gathered a group of intimates for the unveiling. Tremulis showed them one at a time. The audience was enthusiastic—after seeing Tucker's positive reaction—and the new drawings were approved.[31] With the car's shape now fixed, Tucker told Tremulis to build a prototype of his drawings within sixty days. Tremulis said it was an "utter impossibility."[32] Tucker told him to try anyway. He needed to have something to show investors to satisfy Cerf.

11

The Tin Goose

In January 1947 Tremulis set up shop at Tucker's Chicago plant and began building a live example of what he had drawn on paper. Most auto manufacturers would have begun with a full-size clay model first, but there was a shortage of modeling clay as the rest of the auto industry resumed production after the war ended. In addition, Tremulis did not have enough time to make a clay model. He decided to simply build the first model out of sheet metal, going straight from the drawings to an actual car. Tremulis still believed Tucker's sixty-day deadline was impossible but felt he could get the model built faster than most people thought possible. With a small group of elite craftsmen and metalworkers, they would build the first car in one hundred days. "With a great degree of affection," he dubbed it "the Tin Goose."[1]

Skipping the clay model was possible in part because Tucker had hired a friend named Herman Ringling, renowned for his ability to do bodywork with raw sheet metal. He was so adept that he worked the metal barehanded, telling people it gave him a better feel for the work. Ringling told the designers he could handcraft the sheet metal for the car as long as he had good drawings to work from.

For a basic framework, Ringling found a junked Oldsmobile roughly the same size as the proposed Tucker automobile.[2] He then fashioned fenders, a hood, door skins, and the other various body panels and put them on the Oldsmobile frame after removing the junked body panels. When he was done, the only original sheet metal on the car—that is, sheet metal that had been on the junkyard Olds—was the roof, and even that Ringling had reshaped. He just decided to recycle it rather than replace it. The finished prototype also retained some insignificant hardware from the donor Oldsmobile, like door handles and locks.[3]

The men at the Tucker Corporation knew that only a prototype could be handmade like this. They needed to tool up and mass-produce cars if the company was to succeed. In the auto industry, car manufacturers used clay models to measure the dimensions for production tools and dies. Since Tucker had skipped this step when the Tin Goose was created, his men needed to go back and create one.

————

On March 10, another young designer joined the team in Chicago. Philip Sidney Egan was born December 13, 1920, in Oak Park, Illinois. His résumé made it clear he was destined to design cars. His mother painted watercolors and his father was an art director at an advertising agency. The family car was usually a Pierce-Arrow. Philip studied aeronautical engineering before the war; after a brief stint with the army air corps, he spent some time designing airplanes and then moved to Lippincott & Margulies, a design firm Tucker hired to help with some of the detail work on the car.

On his first day, Egan met Alex Tremulis, who looked like a "debonair professor."[4] The two were kindred spirits. Tremulis had come a long way from sitting on the dealership floor, sketching cars while playing hooky. Now he led a team bringing his vision to life. Tremulis showed the young designer the workshop where Ringling was busy building an automobile in metal, the one that would become the Tin Goose. Tremulis then told Egan that Tucker still needed a clay model, something that Egan would be helping with. Egan knew they were doing things out of order, but for a good reason.[5] He soon realized that convention was irrelevant to Tucker and Tremulis.

The evening of Egan's first day, Tucker met with the design team, and Egan got a good look at the man behind the Tucker automobile. "Tucker immediately impressed me as the archetypal salesman who could not only sell refrigerators to Eskimos, but also have them liking the refrigerators after the purchase." Egan listened to Tucker and noticed he was unpolished in the way he spoke but it didn't matter. Tucker's enthusiasm for the project was contagious, and Egan admitted, "Before the night was over, I too shared the eagerness and enthusiasm of those who had chosen to follow him without reservation."[6]

Egan sat in on many early design meetings where the team discussed the finer points of the car's design with Tucker. While many major design features were settled, there were countless other details to work out. How would the bumpers look? Or the door handles, or the dashboard? Tucker loved ideas that made his car stand out—as if the rear-engine, rear-wheel-drive car with the cyclops headlight wasn't outlandish enough—and his designers were never shy about pitching them to him. Someone suggested that they design the exhaust with three pipes on each side, poking up through the top of the rear fenders. It would have been radical and it looked good on paper, but someone noted how impractical it would be: it would have been too inviting for children to drop things down the pipes, like small rocks, banana peels, or chewing gum. The idea was scrapped. But Tucker appreciated the suggestion and told them to continue being creative in their efforts.[7]

————

Fabricating the car body by hand was only one of the elements involved in building the car Cerf's public offering required. The body needed a chassis, and Tucker had promised a rather unusual drivetrain. He had publicly described his car as rear-engine, rear-wheel drive, driven by a six-cylinder engine that would lie flat in the trunk of the car, with two banks of three pistons each, sitting on opposite sides of the crankshaft. The "opposed" engine would be air-cooled, and put power to the rear wheels not through a transmission but through dual hydraulic torque converters, one at each wheel. Unlike the body, which Tucker's men could model with the junkyard Olds, the proposed chassis and drivetrain required the manufacture and assembly of parts and systems no one had ever before created for a consumer automobile. Many people told Tucker to skip the more radical components and simply use a standard chassis and drivetrain, allowing him to unveil the car on time. After all, who really cared about what was under the body of the car? But Tucker insisted on making the first car the way he had described it to the press.[8]

Since day one, Tucker had promoted his radical engine and torque converter setup, claiming it would allow the car to idle at a mere 100 rpm and to cruise at 100 mph with the engine only turning 1,000 rpm. Tucker's engine had some other unique features. For instance, it had a monstrous displacement of 589 cubic inches. This figure derived from its six cylinders, each with a bore and stroke of five inches by five inches. Tucker was asked from time to time why he had chosen such radical dimensions for his engine. He told people he had discussed his engine ideas with Harry Miller while he was on his deathbed. Miller had told him, "Pres, make it big!"[9]

Many critics of Tucker later claimed his fascination with the "five-by-five" engine showed he was impractical, wanting to build an engine so far out of the norm in the industry. Actually, Tucker had a very good reason for wanting to use those dimensions. The Chicago plant had made engines for the B-29 Superfortress bomber during the war, and those had been gigantic, with a bore and stroke of more than six inches by six inches. The machinery that carved the bores in the bomber engines remained in the plant, and Tucker hoped to use those machines when he began engine production. Since the machines were well suited to making huge engines, Tucker reasoned he was making good use of the available resources.[10]

The engine was worthy of note for more than just its mammoth proportions. Tucker admired the Miller racing engine, and one of its prominent features was monobloc construction: the cylinder head was cast integrally with the engine block, as opposed to being cast as two separate pieces. This single-piece "unit construction" configuration made the engine sturdier and eliminated the need for a head gasket. In that era, head gaskets were a common cause of engine failure.

The design complicated some aspects of the engine, however. Manufacturing would be more costly and access to some parts of the engine would be more difficult if the need for certain repairs arose.[11] In addition, Tucker ordered it built with hydraulically actuated valves. The hydraulic pump that powered them added weight to the engine, which he hoped to offset by using an aluminum engine block. The engine block would also feature brass cylinder sleeves, and would even use a magnesium oil pan to reduce acidity in the crankcase oil. Alex Tremulis noted that "on paper," the engine was "a masterpiece of simplicity."[12]

But once built, the engine did not perform as Tucker had hoped. Among other things, when the engine was not running, all the valves rested in the closed position. This made it almost impossible to start. It required a 24-volt starter motor powered by three hundred pounds of batteries.[13]

———

At the same time, the Tucker Corporation was in the midst of a publicity blitz, which had launched on March 2, 1947. Full-page ads in the *New York Times* and other prominent newspapers showed a drawing of the Tucker '48—the name Torpedo had been dropped—and heralded the story of the new car: "Now it can be told . . . How 15 Years of Testing Produced the Surprise Car of the Year." The ad urged readers to wait for the car, which was coming soon, and gave its history leading up to that moment. It related how Tucker had been associated with Harry Miller, had spent years providing armaments to the US government during the war, and now had put together an organization full of experienced automotive executives to build his car. The car was "Completely New" with engineering principles "Completely proved." The ad described a few of them, including the fluid-powered drivetrain, the aluminum disc brakes, a better balance, a rear engine, and independent suspension. Each feature was illustrated with an explanation of how it helped put the Tucker '48 "YEARS AHEAD" of the competition.[14]

One of the more unusual features was the "Safety Chamber." According to the ad, the driver and a front-seat passenger could "drop into" a spacious area beneath the padded dash on the passenger side of the car and be protected in a crash by "steel bulkheads." This action would take a "split second," according to the ad.[15] This feature was often overlooked, but Alex Tremulis later defended it, even though it never caught on with other auto manufacturers. In the 1980s he said the safety chamber had been borrowed from the race cars at Indianapolis, back when cars had both a driver and a mechanic on board. "Preston Tucker was very involved at Indy and the riding mechanics in the early days always had a hole to jump into—like that one—in an emergency. The race drivers called it 'the basement.' A place to go when you're sitting in the death seat."[16]

The campaign also included a beautiful six-page brochure extolling the Tucker '48, again named "the Surprise Car of the Year," with the Tucker family crest on the cover.[17] Inside, readers found an artist's rendering of "the Car You Have Been Waiting For." Early brochures contained a slightly less sophisticated drawing of the car. (Later, it would be replaced with a photograph of an actual Tucker '48.) "You've waited long years for a really new car. Here it is . . . completely new, yet with engineering principles completely proved in 15 years of rigid tests." The car would be available, the brochure optimistically promised, "later this very year."

While the *Pic* article and Tucker's earlier statements had touted engineering advancements and performance, the Tucker brochure focused on safety. Calling it "the World's Safest Car," the brochure spent a full page outlining the car's safety features. Better balance and suspension allowed for greater driver control. Disc brakes would stop the car more swiftly. The dashboard would be padded and the windshield would pop out but not shatter in a crash. The frame was rugged steel, and the cyclops headlight would illuminate around curves and corners.

Careful observers noticed that details of the production car differed from those in the *Pic* article. The cyclops headlight, for example, was now the one that would track the roadway by turning with the steering wheel; Tucker's initial plan had been to have the two headlights in the fenders turn and for the cyclops to remain fixed.

The advantages of the rear-engine, rear-wheel drive were spelled out over a full page. The car would have fewer parts, more interior room, and be quieter and simpler to maintain than the typical car of the day. Much of it was too technical for the average consumer, but the message was clear: "It is not simply an improvement on conventional cars. It is a completely new car based on engineering principles tested for many years, but never before used in mass production automobiles."

Another full page was dedicated to the Tucker Corporation's management and the plant. The brochure saved a full page for Preston Tucker himself, noting that his name was relatively unknown to the public but "in the most exacting field of automotive engineering—the designing and building of special cars—he is known as one of the nation's top creative men." This statement would eventually be touted by federal agents as a lie, perpetrated to commit a massive fraud on the public. But the statements that followed were certainly true. He did work with Harry Miller for fifteen years at the Indianapolis 500, he had designed devices under US military contract, and now he had founded the Tucker Corporation. The biography ended on a high note: "The Tucker '48 is completely new . . . unequaled for performance, safety and comfort by any car on the road today . . . yet with engineering principles completely proved in fifteen years of rigid tests."

In context, a typical reader would have caught that the fifteen years of tests coincided with the fifteen years Tucker had spent at the Indianapolis Motor Speedway with Harry Miller. Federal regulators would not see it that way, however.

12

Getting Ready

As the unveiling date for the Tin Goose approached, the Tucker Corporation prepared for its company's public stock offering. Harry A. Toulmin Jr., a patent attorney who was on many other corporate boards, was named chairman of the board. James Stearns, who had worked in the accounting department of Cadillac for twelve years, became the new treasurer and controller.[1]

On April 18, 1947, Preston Tucker bought another ninety-nine thousand shares of the one million shares issued when the corporation was formed, bringing his holdings to an even hundred thousand shares. Instead of paying cash, he exchanged the shares for debt owed to him by the company. The Tucker Corporation also owed Ypsilanti Machine and Tool some money, which was likewise swapped for 390,000 shares. The rest of the original shares were purchased by eighteen other founders and affiliates of Preston Tucker. At this point, Tucker's sales skills became paramount. He persuaded most of the other stockholders to put their shares in a trust controlled by VP of sales Fred Rockelman, executive VP Hanson Ames Brown, and him. This voting trust controlled 90 percent of the stock in the company.[2]

As Tucker took these steps to take the company public, he received what he called "another slug between the eyes."[3] On May 6, 1947, Cerf submitted the proposed registration statement to the SEC, the first step toward an initial public offering of stock. On June 11 the SEC issued a "stop order" in response. The SEC said the registration statement contained "untrue statements of material facts and omit[ted] material facts."[4] More specifically, it said promoters had made false entries in the corporation's books, which the SEC believed had been made to conceal payments received by promoters.

Tucker had already appeared on the Securities and Exchange Commission's radar when he launched his dealer franchise program. And in March 1947, a new man had joined the five-member commission: a Republican from Detroit named Harry A. McDonald.[5] McDonald had founded H. A. McDonald Creamery Company, "one of the largest distributors of dairy products around Detroit," the *New York Times* wrote later.[6] He also created McDonald, Moore & Hayes Inc., an investment firm, which led to a membership in the Detroit Stock Exchange. He was also very well connected in Republican circles. The Singing Milkman, as he was known later, led the 1940 Republican National Convention in song. Accompanied by a pipe organ, he took them through "God Bless America" and "Battle Hymn of the Republic," before ending with the University of Michigan fight song, "The Victors."[7] He was known as a friend of big business in Detroit,[8] home to three very big businesses, indeed: Ford, General Motors, and Chrysler. McDonald would go out of his way to make sure the SEC protected the Detroit interests to whatever extent it could.

The SEC's reach was quite limited in 1947, even according to itself. The agency was created to enforce the Securities Act of 1933, the law that required a registration statement to be filed in advance of a public stock offering. McDonald described the role his agency played in a talk he gave in Detroit in 1947: "The SEC merely serves as a repository for the information which must be filed, determines whether the registration statement meets the statutory requirements of full and fair disclosure, and enforces the antifraud provisions of the [Securities Act] through court injunction or criminal proceedings."[9] But even in this limited role, the SEC would cause quite a bit of trouble for Tucker.

Preston Tucker met with McDonald to see what could be done to resolve the stop order. Tucker later testified that the two met privately several times and McDonald complained about the pressure he was facing from the Detroit automakers. At his country club, apparently, executives of the Big Three followed him into the men's restroom and lobbied him to stop Tucker's stock offering. At one point, according to Tucker, McDonald told him he would face less resistance from the SEC if he modified his plans for the sedan and simply made it front-engine, rear-wheel drive like those made by everyone else.[10] Tucker replied that it would be a wasted opportunity not to go with the groundbreaking design he had chosen.

Tucker told Cerf to make whatever changes were necessary to the registration statement so that it could be refiled. In the meantime, he continued to stoke the public's excitement for the Tucker '48 ahead of its official unveiling.

———

Tucker tried again to drum up publicity for his automobile at the racetrack, enlisting the aid of race car driver Ralph Hepburn, one of the many friends he had made during his time at the Indianapolis Motor Speedway. Hepburn had competed at Indy fifteen times and was well-known, even though he never won there. He agreed to showcase a race car that Tucker dubbed the Tucker Special at the 1947 Indianapolis 500.

The fifty-year-old Hepburn was no longer racing himself but stayed involved in the sport; he was the head of the American Society of Professional Automobile Racers, a sort of union for the drivers. Shortly after the war, the drivers had felt they were being short-changed on prize money and banded together to demand more. When the Indianapolis Motor Speedway's owner balked at increasing payouts prior to the 1947 Indy 500, the ASPAR threatened a boycott. Not every driver belonged to the union, but enough did to make a dent in how many drivers tried qualifying. Some last-minute haggling netted improved pay for the drivers, and the ASPAR boycott was canceled.

Hepburn told the press he was headed to Indianapolis as captain of a "three car team," one of which was owned by the Tucker Corporation.[11] The Tucker Special, driven by Al Miller of Standish, Michigan, qualified at 124 mph, just 2 mph off the fastest qualifier.[12] Unfortunately, the car suffered "magneto trouble" and was dropped from the race on the thirty-fourth lap.[13]

It was announced that the Tucker Special would race in the Milwaukee 100 race the following week. The announcement gained Tucker quite a bit of attention, particularly because the car was the only one like it in the race: it was rear-engine drive. "Unique Rear Engine Car Will Run Race Here," the *Milwaukee Journal* announced. Their auto sportswriter called the Tucker Special "one of the oddest racing automobiles in existence," noting it was "the only rear engine machine to start the 500 mile race at Indianapolis" and was "similar in many details to the proposed Tucker '48."[14] But Tucker withdrew the car from the race before qualifying began a few days later. Race officials were told that the Tucker Special had suffered "motor damage which could not be repaired in time" for qualifying.[15]

Around this time, the Tucker Corporation also began preparing a more substantial publicity offering: a corporate newsletter called *Tucker Topics* that it would begin sending out to its dealers and distributors. A beautiful eight-page glossy magazine, the first edition showed a stylized rendition of the Tucker '48 on its cover. It opened with a letter from Preston Tucker describing the beginnings of the young company and the promise of the future:

> More than 100,000 letters from people wanting to buy a Tucker '48 is dramatic proof that the public is hungry for a completely new car—not just a pre-war car with new body styling, but one that is far ahead of any car offered today in performance, operating economy and value—a car based on engineering principles completely proved but never before seen in mass production autos.[16]

Articles in the newsletter explained progress made in creating a dealer network and the different ways in which Tucker dealers would be treated compared to those of other automakers. Since the Tucker sedan was designed to have major parts replaced rather than repaired, dealers would not need as many service personnel. The ones they did have would simply be swapping new parts for old rather than diagnosing and trying to repair broken parts. The article contained a group photo of sixteen men, dealers and distributors representing much of a territory in Illinois.

The second piece explained how the "World's Finest Car [will be] Produced in [the] World's Most Modern Plant." Impressive photos of the plant accompanied the article, showing engine parts being manufactured and employees at work. Then a write-up of the proposed Tucker engine explained the advanced design features, an aluminum block, hydraulic valves, and a sealed cooling system among them. *Tucker Topics* devoted a full page to the Tucker executives and their impressive credentials. The last page bore a reprint of two of the Tucker ads that the company had been running recently across America.[17]

Soon, however, the stylized renderings of the Tucker sedan would be replaced by photographs of the real thing.

The Tin Goose Unveiled

Tucker announced he would reveal the Tucker '48 sedan to the public at his factory in Chicago on June 19, 1947. Invitations went to dealers and distributors, investment bankers and other VIPs, and the media. Intense interest in the car pushed the factory showroom quickly to capacity. There was room for three thousand spectators, and it was clear not everyone could be accommodated. By nine o'clock that morning, the plant parking lot was full and extra police were soon needed to direct traffic. No one had been scared off by the SEC stop order on the Tucker Corporation stock sale, which was still in place.

Tucker arranged to keep the crowds entertained all day until the afternoon unveiling of the car. Visitors received name badges and a program and were then given a plant tour. Open-seat "motorized trains" trolleyed people around the gigantic facility. Catering to the largely male-dominated audience, young women who worked for the Tucker Corporation helmed the reception and information desks and acted as pages, guiding the visitors.

While many people were undoubtedly impressed by the vast Tucker Corporation complex, the star of the show would be the car, which remained hidden. Two stages had been constructed in the plant's huge assembly room, and one of them held a turntable obscured by silver and blue drapes. Finally, Rockelman took the stage. A band played a fanfare and a marine color guard marched in. The national anthem was performed and Rockelman made some quick introductions and a short speech. "We are all in this together and we are here today not only to see the car itself, but to learn of the progress that the corporation has made."[1]

Preston Tucker then took the stage and told the audience of the recent squabbles with Washington and the SEC. Then other officials of the corporation got up and gave their thoughts on the momentous occasion. The audience started getting restless. Was it all drama? Charles Pearson noted that the speakers "droning on and on until the crowd began to get restless" were stalling. Backstage, mechanics were frantically trying to make the Tin Goose presentable. They had been up all night, and the car was not ready by three o'clock as they had hoped. Now, several thousand people were just yards away, waiting to see it.[2]

The Tin Goose had several problems, most relating to its weight. When Ringling had hammered the body panels into shape, he had finished the uneven surfaces with solder. While this is a common practice with bodywork, Ringling had used much more solder on the Tin Goose than he would have on a car with properly formed body panels. Ringling's final product was beautiful but contained several hundred pounds of solder. Then, the Tucker engine with its hydraulically actuated valves needed a 24-volt starter motor and huge truck batteries to crank. At the time, the industry commonly used a 6-volt starter. The truck batteries normally used to start the Tin Goose were so heavy and cumbersome they had not been put in the car before. It would be unacceptable to jump-start the car now. The night before, engineers wedged two gigantic truck batteries—weighing 167 pounds each—into the car.[3]

Another nonproduction piece was the car's front bumper. It was made of wood. The designers had dithered on bumper designs and had not settled on one in time to have a front bumper stamped from steel. The designers painted the wooden bumper black and used metal inlays to give it the appearance of chrome.[4] To the untrained eye, it looked like steel.

The car's suspension contained arms made of aluminum. The specifications had called for steel, but someone had decided to replace them with aluminum at the last minute in an effort to shave some weight from the bloated car. This was an area where strength should not have been sacrificed. A mechanic making last-minute adjustments to the car slammed a door shut and one of the arms snapped from the jolt and the added weight of the solder and batteries.[5] Another broke a few minutes later. The first one had failed just a few minutes after a mechanic had climbed out from working under the car. He would have been seriously injured or killed if he had been there a few moments longer. The car could not be driven until the arms were replaced, but an identical set would certainly break also. A stronger set needed to be hastily machined. The machine shop produced arms using beryllium copper, a much tougher compound.[6] With the deadline approaching and the Tin Goose falling apart before their eyes, a couple of the mechanics began to cry.[7]

Bigger problems remained. Tucker had hoped to have fuel injection on the car, but the engineers couldn't get the engine to run with it. They installed a traditional carburetor instead. Even then, the engine ran rough. The hydraulic valve actuators operated too imprecisely for the engine to run smoothly. The engineers and mechanics found the problem—air in the hydraulic lines caused the valve timing to go out of whack—but could not possibly fix it in time. Instead, they tuned the car to run smoothly at idle and hoped it would keep running when displayed.[8]

The four suspension arms on the Tin Goose were replaced as the mechanics listened to the speakers stall the audience. Tucker ordered the band to play as loudly as possible, to drown out the noise of the work being done on the other side of the curtain.[9] Many Tucker employees wondered if anyone would be fooled. At four thirty the mechanics pushed the car up on the stage behind the curtain and told Tucker it was ready.[10]

Models in strapless gowns took the stage. Four of them held up trumpets and sounded a fanfare. Others pulled the curtains aside and revealed the Tin Goose—a maroon Tucker '48 sedan. The turntable began rotating to show the car from all angles. "People in the jammed assembly room went wild, shouting, whistling and cheering," Pearson later wrote.[11]

Preston Tucker's twenty-year-old daughter, Marilyn, walked out with a bottle of champagne in her hands. Tucker introduced her to the audience, many of whom thought the pretty blonde was simply another model, and she christened the car, smashing the bottle on the front of it. Champagne splashed all over her father and his double-breasted suit. It did nothing to dampen his excitement.

Another curtain was drawn back and models walked out onstage one at a time, carrying papier-mâché replicas of parts not needed on the Tucker. Each announced what she was carrying—such as a transmission—and the pile of unnecessary parts grew. Next, Tucker revealed a table piled high with correspondence, representing the telegrams and letters sent by 150,000 people seeking to purchase the car.

Then Tucker struck a serious note. "Let's get one point straight. I want to build cars and make money, of course. But there's something else. This country has been good to me, and I feel a debt of gratitude. I'd like to repay that debt, in part, by contributing something to America—something that will mean much to this country's future: an automobile that will be truly safe, economical, and comfortable transportation for millions of my countrymen."[12]

And with that, Ralph Hepburn got behind the wheel of the Tucker and drove slowly down a ramp and across the floor into a roped-off area where it would sit with guards keeping watch on it.

The launch had been a huge success despite the backstage chaos that preceded it. Many dealers and distributors later said they were moved to buy into Tucker's project when they saw the red Tucker—the Tin Goose—unveiled. Not many franchise sales were completed that afternoon, though, largely because people in the audience were too busy gawking at the automobile and asking engineers about the car's details.[13]

Tucker employees were relieved at how the launch went, knowing it had been an even closer call than they expected. The cooling system in the car hadn't been perfected and the engine began to overheat in the short time it had run at the unveiling. In the audience, Tucker's men detected a wisp of steam coming from the radiator, but apparently no one else did.[14]

14

The Stock Offering

The Tucker Corporation's ability to sell its stock had been in question at the time of the Tucker '48 world premiere. But then Tucker filed an amended registration statement that disclosed all the money received by the promoters, and the SEC dropped its stop order a week after the Tin Goose was unveiled, on June 26, 1947.[1] The corporation issued its prospectus for potential investors on July 7. The Floyd D. Cerf Company created the thirty-one-page document outlining the company's business plan.[2]

Among the boldfaced statements on the cover sheet was THESE SECURITIES HAVE NOT BEEN APPROVED OR DISAPPROVED BY THE SECURITIES AND EXCHANGE COMMISSION. Right below that: THE COMMISSION HAS NOT PASSED ON THE MERITS OF ANY SECURITIES REGISTERED WITH IT.[3] The SEC's cautions were not limited to the prospectus. The SEC issued a separate warning to the public that went much further: "The contrast between information contained in previous publicity and that in the prospectus, as it now has been amended, is so pronounced that we deem it necessary to warn the investing public of the danger of relying on any past judgment . . . in determining whether to purchase the securities of the registrant."[4] The SEC complained that Tucker's prospectus was "materially different" from "the prospectus as

72

originally filed"[5]—even though the SEC had approved the new prospectus. The SEC also wrote that "advertising" done in Tucker's name before the prospectus was issued had been "false and misleading."[6] Wondering what right the SEC had to issue such an opinion, Tucker's lawyers asked. An SEC representative said that the opinion had been drafted by a staff attorney named James P. Goode, who thought it would be a good idea to "cool off the enthusiasm on the Tucker deal."[7]

The SEC also complained that Preston Tucker had not invested any of his own money into the operation of the company. Yet its investigators later admitted that the entire operation up until December 1946 had been funded by Ypsilanti Machine and Tool.[8]

Though the SEC seemed to think its negativity was a necessary counter-balance, the Tucker Corporation's own assessment was hardly starry-eyed. The prospectus warned, "Attention is called to the fact that the proposed Tucker is a departure from the conventional passenger automobile built in the industry up to the present time." The pilot model had not been tested, and although Tucker hoped to build more models and test them, "these tests, which may take as long as three months to complete, may necessitate material changes in engineering design which may result in delay in attaining quality production."[9] As Charles Pearson later wrote, "The prospectus, as finally amended and cleared by SEC, painted a gloomy picture that would have scared the hell out of a wary investor."[10]

The prospectus laid out very clearly the "risks and difficulties" in the project. The car was "radically different" from others on the road and "present[ed] the possibility of problems with respect to performance and public acceptance." Some materials needed to build the car, such as steel, were in short supply. Competition with the rest of the auto industry was daunting. Other companies already had sales infrastructures and suppliers in place to provide materials and components. Thus, the shortage of new cars caused by World War II might be resolved by the auto industry before Tucker began mass production. And, to date, Tucker's operation had been "negligible."[11] Clearly, to compete it would have to grow exponentially. Who knew what kind of growing pains would be encountered along the way?

Having explained the risks and pitfalls facing the company—and investors—the prospectus described the product. The Tucker had been talked about for months, and various specifications had been given for it. Here, it was official. The car would be a four-door, six-passenger vehicle weighing just under three thousand pounds. It would have a 128-inch wheelbase. Since the *Pic* article had been published, two major changes had been made to the design of the Tucker automobile: the car's projected weight had increased to almost three thousand pounds from the previous two-thousand-pound figure, and the selling price had increased from $1,000 to "between $1,800 and $2,000."[12]

The main specifications for the car were laid out in a chart. The "tread"— referring to the distance between the wheels—in the front would be 62 inches and 65 in the back. The spec list contained many more unorthodox ideas. The car would use a 24-volt electrical system, rather than the industry-standard 6-volt. The transmission would not use a clutch or typical manual transmission parts; it would use hydraulic torque converters for "all forward speeds and a reverse." It would have independent suspension all the way around and four-wheel hydraulic disc brakes.

The prospectus described major features of the car in more detail, noting that some of them were departures from industry standards. For example, the engine installation would allow a quick replacement, with an eye toward simply swapping engines rather than tearing apart broken engines and waiting for replacement parts. If the system worked, the cars would have very little down time, even with major engine repairs. The old engines could be repaired at a more leisurely pace, or even at a central factory location, and then used again down the road in vehicles that needed replacement engines.

Following the early warnings in the prospectus it was clear: the Tucker Corporation was taking chances here, and the car they were designing was very different from anything anyone had previously tried building and selling.[13] The prospectus ended the description of the car with another caveat: "Some of the major features representing departures from the conventional automobile have not been tested sufficiently to demonstrate their performance characteristics."[14]

The prospectus then explained how Tucker had obtained the lease on the Chicago plant and had opened offices there in July 1946. It was not yet configured for manufacturing, but the corporation "estimated" it could be ready for production within six months.[15] "Production plans call for installation of an assembly line with an estimated capacity of 500 cars per eight-hour shift. Presently planned production contemplates two eight-hour shifts. The Company's projected production schedule calls for production of 200 cars the first month after commencement of assembly line production, with production gradually increasing thereafter."[16] Also included was an impressive full-page aerial photograph of the massive property.

A later section outlined the terms of the lease agreement with the War Assets Administration, which had recently been amended yet again. According to the latest deal, Tucker promised to have $15 million cash on hand by November 1, 1947. If he cleared that hurdle, the Tucker Corporation could then lease the property for $500,000 a year for two years and then $2.4 million a year after that, or 3 percent of gross sales of the company, whichever was greater. It would be a ten-year lease.[17] The corporation also had an option to purchase the property during the lease for $30 million.[18]

Throughout the prospectus, unlike in Preston Tucker's preferred style of speaking, all the corporation's statements and predictions were couched as "plans," and it was clear "it [was] impossible to predict the date when assembly line production [would] commence."[19] A couple pages later the prospectus stated, "The Company is unable to make any representations that the above mentioned volume of production will be attained or that facilities needed for fabrication will be delivered on schedule."[20]

The Tucker Corporation had already sold franchises to 49 distributors and 363 dealerships in the United States. The company aimed for 100 distributors and 2,000 dealers within two years of production. Clearly, Tucker had made progress on this front. The company had already raised over $4 million through these sales, more than half of it in cash and the rest in promissory notes. The prospectus also described the Tucker Export Corporation, an "unaffiliated company" formed to sell Tucker autos overseas.[21]

In addition, the Tucker Corporation revealed that it had 725 employees on its payroll in June 1947. It anticipated employing as many as 35,000 at peak production. Leading the way was Preston Tucker as president, with an annual salary of $50,000 (the equivalent of $540,000 in today's dollars). Hanson Ames Brown would receive $35,000 as executive vice president, while VP of sales Fred Rockelman and VP of manufacturing Lee Treese would each earn $25,000.[22]

The prospectus also laid out how much stock the founders of the company already had. Although it seemed pretty straightforward, some of the underlying math may have confused some investors. In later years, SEC investigators claimed the prospectus made false statements about the founders. The offering stated that Preston Tucker now owned 106,000 shares of Class B stock, of the million shares issued when the company was founded. Tucker paid for his shares, according to the prospectus, partially by extinguishing debts the company owed to Ypsilanti Machine and Tool, and that he had acquired through transactions with the company, which he ran at the behest of his mother, its sole shareholder. Ypsilanti Machine and Tool owned 390,000 shares. The prospectus noted that 90 percent of the Class B stock was held in a voting trust, controlled by Preston Tucker. Interestingly, the 10 percent he did not control was owned by Floyd Cerf.[23]

Several pages described other transactions Preston Tucker had been involved in before the prospectus was issued, including the purchase and sale of some race cars and associated parts. By the time the dust settled, Preston Tucker was paid $217,669.60 by the company for various things with which he had furnished it. At the time, no one objected to these transactions.[24] As for its finances, the Tucker Corporation had money in the bank. Against its liabilities of a little over $1 million, it held assets of more than $2 million, all from the dealership and distributor sales.[25]

———

With the prospectus issued, Tucker Corporation could sell stock—although it did not sell as quickly as Tucker hoped. The biggest hurdle came from two states that had banned the sale: Michigan, home of the Big Three automakers, and California.[26] Tucker assumed that the decision in Michigan had been the result of lobbying on the part of the Big Three, who presumably did not want more competition.

In California, the corporation commissioner, Edwin Daugherty, issued what even the press called a "blustering statement" railing against Tucker's proposed sale. It is unclear if Daugherty had actually read the prospectus. Daugherty claimed one of his reasons for the denial was that Tucker had not disclosed his relationship with convicted embezzler Abraham Karatz, even though it was fully disclosed in the prospectus, taking up almost half of one page. Daugherty also claimed that the proposed offering was unfair and cited, among other reasons, an unfounded claim that Preston Tucker already owned a million shares of Class B stock in the corporation.[27] The SEC later said the action in California was a direct response to the SEC warning about the difference between Tucker's publicity and the language of the registration statement.[28]

Preston Tucker approached Charles Pearson, whose *Pic* article had kicked off the initial wave of publicity for the Tucker automobile, and asked him what could be done to stimulate stock sales. The SEC frowned on overt promotion of stock during a sale, because the company was supposed to let the prospectus speak for itself. Pearson told him that the only thing they could legally do was to take the Tucker automobile out and show it off to the public. Surely that would help.

While the Tin Goose was drivable, no one at the Tucker Corporation believed it could be driven very far. The issues with the hydraulic valves in the engine had not been resolved yet, and the fluid drive transmission had not been tested well enough to trust driving the car any distance. Tucker decided to take the car on tour anyway. He just wouldn't drive the car to any of the stops.

———

The Tucker '48's next public exhibition was at the New Products Exhibition in Los Angeles, a fair put on by the United Inventors and Scientists of America at the Pan-Pacific Auditorium. Tucker flew the car to California in a large cargo plane. Shortly after it arrived, Tucker received a frantic message

from Chicago: the car had to be returned immediately. Tucker had been lobbying to get Robert McCormick, publisher of the *Chicago Tribune,* to go for
a ride in the car, believing he would be so impressed that the *Tribune* would
write a positive review like everyone else. McCormick said he was willing
to take a look at the car if it was available the next day.

Tucker called the airfreight company that had flown the car to California,
but the plane they had used had already been chartered by someone else, and
their other plane was likewise unavailable. Tucker told the man to name his
price; the Tin Goose had to be in Chicago regardless of cost. The man gave
an absurd price: $45,000. Tucker agreed, and soon the car was being rushed
from the exhibition hall back to the airport for a flight to Chicago.[29]

Back in Chicago, the car was delivered to the Palmer House hotel, where
it was brought inside through a freight elevator. McCormick walked around
the car and expressed a small amount of interest. Someone suggested that
the tall man sit in the car to see the spacious interior Tucker had been advertising. McCormick was wearing a hat and stood six feet four inches tall without it. He climbed into the car without removing his hat and sat up straight.
According to Pearson, the headliner crushed his hat down over his ears.
The publisher, known as "Colonel," found the incident a little off-putting.
Whether this incident was as important as Pearson believed mattered little;
the *Chicago Tribune*'s editorial stance would never be more than lukewarm
toward Tucker.[30]

The car was airfreighted back to Los Angeles the next day, where it continued drawing crowds. Its absurdly expensive round trip to Chicago had
amounted to nothing more than McCormick sitting in the car for a moment.

The Tin Goose traveled the country and caused a ruckus almost everywhere it went. In August 1947, at New York's Museum of Science and
Industry, the car was too big to fit through the doors. A large window was
removed so the car could be rolled in, and workmen set about constructing
its stage. A local newspaper mistakenly reported that the Tucker display
would start a day early. As a result, a mass of people showed up while workers were still constructing the display. Thousands stood on the sidewalk, and
the museum director worried what might happen if they were turned away.
He asked Tucker's men to hurry and finish the stage as best they could. The

spectators were then admitted without charge. Many didn't notice the half-finished display, which the workers completed later that night.

The exhibit continued to be a major draw, with spectators flocking to the museum to see it. Visitors were charged forty-eight cents admission, and some days the show drew fifteen thousand of them. The Tin Goose outgrossed several shows running nearby on Broadway. *Variety* reported, Tucker Auto, First Run. Gets Boff 42 G in N.Y. In fact, in its ten-day run, the car grossed a bit more than 42 G—$48,000 in total.[31]

As expected, many people left the Museum of Science and Industry with a burning desire to buy one of the cars. Carmine Coppola was one visitor intent on owning a Tucker. He had brought his son Francis with him, and as soon as he could, Carmine placed an order with a Tucker dealer for a Tucker '48.[32]

Another one hundred thousand people showed up to see the car at an exhibition in Chicago as the car hopscotched around North America.[33] It wasn't all smooth sailing, however. Some astute observers had noticed that while the Tin Goose was being shown everywhere, it was not being driven publicly. People had seen it drive a few feet at its world premiere, but no road tests had been allowed, and most people had only seen it on static display, sitting on a turntable or stage at a fair or an exhibition. Was Tucker hiding something?

———

Tucker may have believed he had bought Colonel McCormick's goodwill by bringing the car from Los Angeles to Chicago, but the *Tribune* publisher was one of those who thought that something might be amiss—and that there might be a story behind the Tucker car after all. He sent a reporter to the Tucker plant to investigate. The resulting article wasn't a typical piece celebrating the brilliant features of the car of tomorrow. It addressed whether the car was a fraud. The reporter, Frank Sturdy, was the automotive editor for the *Chicago Tribune* and insisted on going for a ride in a Tucker sedan. Tucker's people explained that the Tin Goose was the only complete car at the moment, and it was currently on display in Milwaukee. Sturdy pressed.

Finally, Treese told Sturdy he could ride a test chassis. It had no body, but mechanically it was identical to the Tin Goose. Sturdy agreed.

Sturdy drove the test chassis at the plant, and he seemed pleased. During the demonstration, Gene Haustein, Tucker's test engineer, noted for Sturdy that the chassis and the Tin Goose were still experimental. The revolutionary fluid drive system was still being developed, and as a matter of fact it had not even been made to go in reverse yet. It was a simple engineering question. They were still determining if the drive system would even work. If it worked, the reverse gears would be added. But if it did not work, the entire system would be scrapped for a conventional one. The reason they had not installed reverse gears was simple. The fluid drive system did not use any gears. Adding them may have turned out to be unnecessary, so why bother? Sturdy seemed to understand and went back and filed his story.

The fairly well-balanced story contained one section that stood out, titled "Test Chassis Can't Back Up." That detail spread quickly, leading many people to assume Tucker sedans were built intentionally without the ability to go in reverse.[34] The notion that Tucker sedans had no reverse gear would still be reported by the mainstream press two years later, in June 1949. For example, a story in the *Pittsburgh Press* that month described some of the features of the car and said, "There is a finger-tip electric transmission, with four forward speeds."[35]

———

Despite the odd rumors, car buyers were reacting positively to the Tucker sedan—and they weren't the only ones. Automobile parts manufacturers began calling on Tucker. Many of them already sold to the Big Three but were looking for new customers. In fact, the automobile supplier business was so competitive that they were excited about another manufacturer entering the field. A great majority told Tucker not only that they were anxious for his business but also that they would gladly extend him credit. Over the next few months, parts suppliers promised him the credit equivalent of millions of dollars. To take advantage of the opportunity, Tucker had to ready the cars for full-scale production.[36]

The initial stock offering had made available five million shares in the Tucker Corporation. By September 1947, much of it had been sold, but not all. Tucker told Cerf to end the sale on September 12.[37] After deducting commissions paid to others and to himself, Cerf had raised $15,007,000, which he gave to Tucker. As many as forty-four thousand people had bought Tucker Corporation stock.[38] The Tucker Corporation also had $2 million in notes from its prospective dealers, giving it assets of more than $17 million.[39] Tucker notified the War Assets Administration that he had raised enough money to meet the lease requirements, and the WAA wired back confirmation: the plant was officially his on November 1, 1947.[40]

15

Post–Tin Goose

The second edition of *Tucker Topics* was sent to dealers and distributors following the launch of the Tucker '48. The cover featured a photo (re-created for marketing purposes) of Tucker's daughter Marilyn christening the Tin Goose. Inside, Rockelman extolled the virtues of the company, and articles described Tucker's recent awards and the overflow crowds that had greeted the Tucker sedan wherever it was shown. The newsletter said that 170,000 people had viewed the car in Los Angeles and 192,000 more at New York's Museum of Science and Industry. One page was devoted to celebrities who came out to see the car, many posing for photos with it. Hollywood actor Adolphe Menjou brought his wife. Race car drivers and government dignitaries showed up as well. They expressed interest in buying the cars, and several even inquired about dealerships. *Tucker Topics* also showed more progress being made toward production, with photos of patterns for the body parts and workers inspecting fabric for the car's interior.[1]

The last page updated the progress of establishing dealerships, and brought back a name from Preston Tucker's past. Mitchell Dulian, whose car dealerships had employed the young Tucker as a salesman, became his old friend's "Eastern Sales Manager," with plans to establish offices in New York City.[2]

Other changes within the Tucker Corporation were less apt to end up in the company's marketing materials. Harry Toulmin Jr., the chairman of the board of directors, had resigned immediately after the close of the stock sale. Shortly after Cerf cut Tucker the $15 million check, Toulmin stepped down and issued a press release. He said Tucker had refused to commit to "written demands" that the money raised in the stock offering would be "spent and administered under the strictest regulation and controls normal to legitimate business."[3] While it seemed like a reasonable request, Tucker told reporters he had not agreed to Toulmin's demand because it was an attempt on Toulmin's part to exert too much control over the company. The stock sale had just closed the past Friday, and on Monday Toulmin was upset with how the money was being spent? Tucker laughed it off and noted that the money had simply sat in the bank over the weekend.[4]

If it had just been Toulmin exiting, it might not have mattered much. Shortly after, however, two more key executives, Hanson Brown and James Stearns, left the Tucker Corporation too. They claimed they were fired, but Preston Tucker said they had quit. Charles Pearson later wrote that the men did not fit in, since they had both come from the automotive industry, where things were done at a glacial pace. Tucker needed to get his car from the design stage to the production stage in a span of time these men considered impossible. These two represented the problem Tucker was trying to solve with his car. Some wondered why he had brought them aboard in the first place. The answer was simple: for the stock offering. With a group of established auto executives on the board of directors, the Tucker Corporation looked like a safe bet. With $15 million raised by the stock offering, Preston Tucker could go about business as he saw fit.[5]

To fill the void left by these high-profile departures, Tucker began hiring and promoting people he had known before he launched his business. Former employer Mitchell Dulian was one of them. Many others came from his days at Indianapolis, including Eddie Offutt, a mechanic who had also worked with Harry Miller. Tucker would eventually promote Offutt to chief engineer at the company.[6]

———

Another new hire had a history with a different member of the company's top brass. Fred Rockelman had worked with an adman from New York named Cliff Knoble who oversaw advertising campaigns for large corporations, including Chrysler. Shortly after the close of the stock offer, Rockelman had called Knoble and invited him to an expensive hotel, where Tucker was conducting business from his suite. Rockelman hoped Tucker would want to hire Knoble after he made his introduction. Knoble wasn't so sure if he wanted to join the venture. He had heard of Tucker but was unsure if he was a "wizard or charlatan, builder or opportunist, idealist or trickster, genius or fool."[7]

Knoble found Rockelman in the suite among a large group of people he did not recognize, and the two made small talk. When everyone had left the suite, the door to the bedroom opened "and a tall, well-built, smartly dressed figure emerged and strode across the room with extended hand and a hearty, 'Hello, Cliff.'"[8] Knoble was taken by surprise. So was Rockelman. Had they met before?

Knoble suddenly remembered he had worked with Tucker years earlier, when Tucker was managing a Chrysler dealership in Memphis. Even Rockelman hadn't known the two had met.

"Why, sure. We're old buddies," Tucker said. Knoble noticed how Tucker had exaggerated their relationship—but, after all, he was a salesman.[9] Tucker asked if Knoble was interested in handling the advertising for the Tucker Corporation. If so, Tucker wanted him to come work for the company directly. Knoble demurred, saying it seemed a little premature. Once a stock offering had been made and the company was financially viable, he'd be ready to join. Tucker agreed, certain that Knoble would be working for him soon.

Now, with the stock sale a success and the WAA lease secured, Tucker was clearly ready to make a go of it. Knoble joined the team on December 11, 1947.[10] But Tucker could only get so far with the Tin Goose. He needed to show investors and the public that the Tucker Corporation could produce more than one handmade car.

———

The Tucker Corporation's annual report, which it sent out to stockholders in early 1948, made the argument that it was prepared to do just that. The twenty-page document featured a beautiful cover graced with the Tucker family crest. Inside was a stunning rendering of a Tucker sedan. Preston Tucker opened the report with a heartfelt message:

> The greatest asset possessed by the Tucker Corporation is not to be found in a balance sheet. It consists of the confidence and good wishes of millions of fellow Americans, with which we are favored to a degree that has seldom been observed in business. In every executive of the corporation, this phenomenon has invoked feelings of humility, thankfulness and responsibility—and has confirmed in us all the resolve to give our utmost to be deserving of such trust.[11]

A studio portrait of Tucker, gazing at the camera with a slight smile, sat above the letter.

The document described the public clamor for the car and the honors various organizations had given Preston Tucker for bringing a new automobile to market.[12] A "Progress Report" recounted the months spent moving the company toward production and asserted that "automobile production at the Tucker Corporation is expected to become a reality in the near future."[13] The report did not give timelines or dates, but simply laid out what steps had been taken. Thus far, 1,394 dealers were signed up, along with 75 distributors to service them, an increase from the time of the prospectus, when there had been 363 and 49, respectively.[14] The company had raised $9,566,700 from just these two groups.[15] On a later page was a map of the United States covered with dots representing the locations of a dealer or distributor. It was clear that Tucker had covered the entire country with dealerships.[16]

According to the report, the Tucker Corporation planned to use many of the machines that were in the factory when it had been acquired and anticipated hiring three thousand employees shortly. While the company hoped to have several assembly lines operating eventually, it was currently gearing up for a single line, which could be operating by March 1948. Cars would be built and shown around the country. "Arrangements are under way for . . . first delivery to waiting Tucker owners later this year."[17] Again, no specific dates were given.

A description of the factory included beautiful photographs of the facility's highlights. Other pages featured portraits of the board members of the corporation; there were also, of course, several pages of balance sheets.

The report closed with a letter from the accounting firm of Peat, Marwick, Mitchell & Co., which had examined the corporation's books and annual report before it was sent to the shareholders. "In our opinion the accompanying statements . . . present fairly the position of Tucker Corporation and subsidiary at December 31, 1947 . . . in conformity with generally accepted accounting principles applied on a consistent basis."[18]

The report gave the distinct impression that the company was well positioned to kick off production of the Tucker '48. And it would spend the next few months doing just that. But eventually the SEC would find fault with the report's assertions—just one of many ways the agency was poised to make trouble for Preston Tucker's enterprise.

16

Gearing Up for Production

As Preston Tucker prepared to bring the Tucker '48 to the assembly line, he knew that the production model would have to be substantially different from the Tin Goose. His fluid drive transmission was not ready, and the 589 engine needed far too much work. But it wasn't just the drivetrain issues that needed to be solved. Tucker's men had not even finished designing the interior of the car. The Tin Goose had been finished with a Studebaker dashboard.

To design the interior, Alex Tremulis reached out to Philip Egan, who had returned to New York after completing his clay model of the Tucker '48. Egan was recently unemployed, having been let go by Lippincott & Margulies when the firm's business had slowed. Tremulis offered him a new role on the Tucker '48: designing everything within the driver's reach, the "driver control area of the car."[1] He met with Tucker and Tremulis to hear Tucker's vision of the car interior. Tucker's primary design cue was safety. The dash was to be padded. The controls should be within easy reach and simple to operate so as not to distract the driver. Tucker reiterated his desire for a "safety compartment" that the passenger could dive into in the event of a crash, certainly one of the stranger features of the Tucker automobile. It was unclear if anyone could actually use it in an accident.

Tucker also took an informal survey to see if he should install seat belts in his car. He consulted some of his racing friends and found that many of them did not use them in their racers. Rex Mays told Tucker he would rather not be strapped into an out-of-control race car, preferring to be free to get out on his own. As Tremulis later noted, Mays would die in a race the following year, thrown from his car while not wearing a seat belt.[2] After being ejected, he was run over by another race car. Had he been wearing a seat belt, he probably would have lived.[3]

Tucker spoke with airline stewardesses and even an airline executive, who told him, "If we put a parachute under each seat, this would imply that an element of danger existed and would so terrify the passengers that they would file out of the airplane and seek the closest railroad terminal in an exodus that would look like the evacuation of Dunkirk."[4] According to Egan and Tremulis, Tucker ultimately agreed with his marketing department that seat belts would imply that the car was unsafe. The Tucker '48 sedan would not have them.[5] Later, Tremulis said that Tucker had been in favor of seat belts but decided against them because "it was very unpopular at that time to talk about safety belts."[6]

Nevertheless, Tucker was so passionate about safety that to underscore his concerns, he took his entire engineering staff to a luncheon presentation given by a Detroit-area plastic surgeon who was a crusader for the cause. First, the doctor lectured about the need for auto safety in abstract terms while the audience ate lunch. Then, as dessert was served, he presented a slide show of gruesome color photographs of injuries taken in emergency rooms, as if challenging the audience to eat while viewing the shocking images. Tremulis noted "a lot of uneaten desserts," but the presentation had its desired effect. The Tucker engineers returned to their offices with a renewed focus on safety.[7]

Tremulis and Egan were privy to a variety of other issues that touched their department while they worked out the final details of the car. One problem was the cyclops headlight, which many considered the car's trademark. It only illuminated if the steering was moved more than ten degrees off center and the high beams were turned on. Otherwise, it stayed turned off.[8] Tucker had not considered what government bureaucrats might think of this. Fifteen states at that time had laws dictating automotive headlight configuration: each car was to have exactly two headlamps.[9] Tucker could lobby to overturn those laws, but that might prove difficult. The stylists came up with two possible solutions. The owners of cars in those states could simply disconnect the middle light. Or the Tucker Corporation could provide a stylish cover to snap over it. Tremulis and Egan designed one with a Tucker logo prominently featured.[10] They hoped to be able to offer the covers as a retail option when the cars were eventually sold to the public.

Tremulis often told Tucker that proposed design features were impossible or impractical. Tucker often conceded but reminded Tremulis of his mantra: "Just remember that we have a boss bigger than all of us and that's the automobile. Do what you have to do, but be sure it's right for the car."[11]

Typically, the designers had to work around the clock to meet fast-approaching deadlines. Tremulis said later that he and his crew often worked 110-hour weeks. To placate his wife, he promised he would take her out for a fancy dinner on Sunday nights. Inevitably, he would tell her to come to the factory and meet him there to save time. And then, after she had sat around on a grimy bench for a few hours, Tremulis would sheepishly ask her to order sandwiches and the two would eat them at the plant.[12]

As for Egan, his contributions to the Tucker '48 were understated but important. Automotive interiors were generally complicated; years later, a Tucker expert would note that "dashboards, certainly at that time, tended to be ornate. They tended to be spread out, they tended to be gaudy, they tended to be chromy."[13] The Egan-designed dashboard, on the other hand, was clean and elegant.

———

The company sent out another *Tucker Topics* in early 1948. The cover showed a massive press stamping out body panels with a caption indicating that at least some elements of production had begun; suppliers in Michigan were making parts for the Tucker '48. Fred Rockelman wrote the introduction, telling how thirteen hundred employees at the Chicago factory were assembling pilot cars. The first piece simply showed an aerial view of the massive Chicago plant, accompanied by an article saying the Tucker Corporation had fully moved into the plant, and although they were currently leasing it from the government, they fully intended to purchase it outright. Typically, Tucker was setting his sights quite high.

Pages were filled with pictures of the plant's huge interior and forklifts and tractors moving around giant machines. The corporation intended to use 70 percent of the manufacturing equipment that was in the plant when Tucker had taken it over. Further articles showed sales meetings held around the country, attended by hundreds of dealers and distributors in Chicago, Milwaukee, New York, and Los Angeles. A full page showed the thirteen hundred employees at a meeting, getting updates from Preston Tucker and other top management officials. The theme was repeated over and over again: full-scale production was just around the corner.[14]

Tucker Topics also described staff additions; it welcomed adman Cliff Knoble, along with a few others whose names would become important. Mitchell Dulian had been promoted to head the eight-man sales department. The department members all had impeccable credentials from their work with other big manufacturers like General Motors, Studebaker, and Chrysler.[15]

The magazine's final page was lighthearted. It announced the wedding of Preston's daughter Marilyn—she and her new husband were both attending school in Missouri—and included a picture of the bride and groom. Beneath that story was a photo of Prince Carl Bernadotte of Sweden sitting in a Tucker '48. According to the caption, he had visited the factory and discussed manufacturing methods with Tucker engineers.[16]

———

Behind the scenes, the growing pains continued. In February 1948 Preston Tucker called the first boss he ever had in the auto industry: D. McCall White. White had long since left Cadillac, where Tucker had been an office boy in 1916, and was now operating his own automotive engineering consultancy. The two had not spoken in thirty-two years.

Tucker invited White to Chicago and said he might be interested in hiring him to consult on getting production up and running. White flew to Chicago, where Tucker gave him a tour of the plant. They looked at the Tin Goose and some partially assembled cars. White asked to see the balance sheets: How much money did Tucker have on hand and how much had he spent so far? In his long career, White had worked in almost every management position possible at several different firms in a variety of countries. He had also worked for an aircraft manufacturer during the war, helping oversee wartime production. He was elderly now, but his mind was sharp. And if anyone knew what it would cost to begin mass-producing cars, it was D. McCall White.

White was not impressed by the car or by the plant. In his mind, the Tucker sedan was not completely engineered or ready for production. Tucker pressed him: What would it take to make it ready? White said it would cost between $50 million and $100 million to finish the design and engineering work and to tool up for the production figures of one thousand cars per day. Tucker was undaunted. In his mind White was saying it was possible. It would just take a lot of money.

Tucker asked if White was willing to come aboard and oversee the effort. White was not as optimistic as Tucker, but he said he would consider joining Tucker if the price was right. Tucker told him to name the price and said he could even draft his own employment agreement. White demanded an advance of $2,500 and a monthly salary of $5,000 along with living and traveling expenses. Tucker agreed.[17] Unbeknownst to White, Tucker intended to borrow more money to fund the operation as soon as they solved their engineering and manufacturing problems.

White arrived at the plant and began trying to get a handle on things. He found departments operating inefficiently, often unaware that their work was duplicating the work of others, along with people who were not following any chain of command.

The lack of centralized authority in the engineering organization resulted in an obvious lack of coordination, particularly since Messrs. Parson and Lyman disliked each other and refused to cooperate, which made a bad situation, since they both had some influence with Tucker.[18]

White complained to Tucker, who issued an order giving White "full and final authority on all matters pertaining to both engineering and manufacturing."[19] White was appeased until he discovered that none of the people in the dysfunctional organization followed Tucker's orders when he wasn't present.[20] Worse, he later claimed that Tucker would give orders contrary to White's and simply override White's ideas if he disagreed with them.

White later said that Floyd Cerf approached him and asked if White might be able to rein in Preston Tucker—that is, get him focused on making the car. White claimed that Cerf was concerned about Tucker's mismanagement of the company and had asked him if he might be interested in joining the board of directors of the corporation. He said he would not even consider it "unless Mr. Tucker's overall authority was taken away or substantially reduced."[21] White did not tell anyone these concerns at first, though. He simply did what he could to get the car ready for production.

————

Whatever infighting there may have been at the Tucker Corporation, the fourth issue of *Tucker Topics* painted a rosier picture. But even then, the message was toned down. Rockelman's letter to the readers noted how the Tucker Corporation had gained its financing only five months earlier and was attempting to do the impossible. While the big car companies put out new models yearly, those were merely updates of previous models. The Tucker Corporation was attempting to put out a whole new model in the same time the big companies would only need to redo perhaps 10 percent of a production model. Still, Rockelman was confident it could be done:

> Remember, we're not merely making a ten per cent change on an old model. We are building a wholly new car, a better car, and on a scale that will enable us to gain the economies of huge volume—and thus to offer the finest value to motordom.[22]

The magazine described progress securing dealers and distributors, noting that 1,637 retail outlets had now been signed. Six pages were filled with photos of body panels, stacked sheets of steel, and other car parts, along with photos of partially assembled cars rolling down a pilot production line. Other articles showcased more sales meetings and even the numerous letters the corporation had gotten with wacky offers requesting free cars. A woman had written Tucker and offered to drive a Tucker '48—if it was given to her for free—around the world at the equator in reverse. She did not explain what route she would take, but presumably this would help Tucker combat the negative press the company had gotten about the car's transmission.[23]

———

It fell to Tucker's men to actually resolve the issues with the vehicle's engine and transmission. Tucker had insisted that they iron out the bugs in the 589 engine, but many of its problems appeared to be insurmountable. Nothing they did made it easier to start, and the hydraulic valves never quite worked precisely enough for the engine to run smoothly. Tested on a dynamometer, the engine's output was horrible. The results were never officially announced, but word around the plant put the figure at a dismal 83 horsepower; Tucker had hoped for twice that. It took the seasoned veteran Gene Haustein to convince Tucker the engine had to be scrapped. He said it accelerated slower than the moon rose and sounded like a "barrel full of monkeys."[24] Tucker agreed to go with a different engine if one could be found in time.

Tucker sent Eddie Offutt to Ypsilanti and provided him a team, one member of which was Dan Leabu, Tucker's go-to man in times of emergency. Leabu was one of Tucker's longest-term employees. A University of Michigan graduate with a degree in engineering, he had spent more than ten years designing tools for Ford Motor Company. Tucker routinely gave his most important jobs to Leabu, and when he told the team to conjure a suitable engine, he knew Leabu would see to it that they got it done. Another member was Preston Tucker Jr., an engineering student at the University of Michigan. Tucker Sr. gave his team ninety days and the resources of Ypsilanti Machine and Tool to do it.[25] While most auto manufacturers would have considered modifying the engine compartment at this point, or even reconfiguring the car to be front-engine, Tucker told the men the engine had to go in the rear and fit in the space allotted by the Tin Goose's dimensions.

The men looked at various engine manufacturers that made six-cylinder opposed engines and focused on one in particular. Bell Aircraft in New York used an engine called the Franklin in some of its helicopters. H. H. Franklin had first made automobiles in 1902 with air-cooled engines that were simply constructed. The company struggled in the years immediately before the Depression but had survived by selling the engines to other companies such as Bell. Some were used in automobiles and some in aircraft. The company had changed names a few times—it was now known as Aircooled Motors—but the engine designs lived on.[26] One in particular, designed for helicopter use, was the right size to fit in the Tucker sedan. Being made to aircraft standards meant it was costlier but also better made and more dependable. At this point, cost was a lesser concern, so Tucker agreed to purchase four of the engines and had Offutt tear them apart, measuring all the parts and reconfiguring them.[27]

The Aircooled Franklin engine would need modification. The engine in the Tucker needed to be liquid-cooled. In a helicopter, the engine sat vertically; in the Tucker it would be laid horizontally. Offutt, Leabu, and the team worked night and day in the shop behind the Tucker family home in Ypsilanti reworking the engine. It needed a water pump and a block through which the water would run, a new exhaust manifold, and a different intake. The engine used a magneto, but Tucker would use a less expensive automotive distributor. And with the radiator in the back of the car, the air to cool it would come in through vents in the fenders, pass through the engine compartment, and be pushed by the engine fan out the rear of the car, through the radiator. Some of the work was done quite hastily. Many of the cars built later would have rough holes simply cut with torches into the rear fenders for the air intake grills to cover. The engineers never settled completely on whether the cooling system was adequate as they had set it up.[28]

After creating all the necessary new parts for the engine, the men put one together to see if it would run. Years later Leabu told a reporter that when they were done, "we hung a fuel tank from the ceiling, and hooked up a bat-tery, and it started. That was the most beautiful noise I ever heard."[29] They brought the first revamped engine to Chicago just fifty-five days after being given the task.[30]

Tucker had also relented on his desire to use the hydraulic drive, so his sedan needed a more conventional transmission as well. While he wanted an automatic, and assigned some men with the task of designing one, the company did not have time to wait for it to be developed and tested. They needed something else in the interim. Again, he sent Offutt to Ypsilanti with the order to come up with something, using whatever resources were nec-essary. Offutt and the others had realized that the placement of the engine in the rear of the car meant that a typical transmission of the time would not work. The system needed to fit in the rear of the car and deliver the power to the rear wheels. Someone noted that the now-defunct Auburn Cord Duesenberg had developed and marketed an unusual transmission a few years earlier that sat in front of the engine in a front-engine, front-drive car. If Tucker's men could locate Cord transmissions, they could place them in front of the engine in the sedan, and the whole assembly would fit snugly in the rear of the Tucker '48.[31]

Leabu went out and scoured junkyards and used car lots looking for Cords with the transmission they wanted. He found twenty-two, which were scavenged for parts, resulting in eighteen rebuilt Cord transmissions that would be placed in Tucker '48s.[32]

The configuration of the transmission in the Tucker '48s was unusual for its day and appears even stranger today. Shifting was controlled by a short aluminum lever on a small shaft on the right-hand side of the steering column. A shifting pattern cut out of steel showed where the lever would be pushed for each gear. The driver pushed the lever into the desired posi-tion and then depressed the clutch, activating electromagnets and a vacuum system to shift the actual gears. This "pre-selector" system was complicated, but it worked.

A Cord transmission was not designed to handle as much horsepower as the Franklin engine generated, however. Heavy acceleration from a dead stop in first gear could very well break gears inside the transmission.[33] It was simply another engineering obstacle they would have to deal with down the road.

Tucker cared little about the nuances of the car at this point. He needed one ready to show off at the first annual stockholders meeting on March 9.

17

The First Car off the Assembly Line— #1001

The first shareholders meeting was scheduled for March 9, 1948, in Chicago, and Preston Tucker would once again put on a show. This time it would be for people who had invested in the company. And a finished car would be his costar. At least, that is what Tucker told his men as the date approached. But at the moment they got the news, they did not have an engine or a transmission to put in it.

They rushed to finish a "production" car. The engine was finished in Ypsilanti the day before the meeting and driven to Chicago, where it was installed in the car overnight. The assembly room was decked out in flags, which probably made it look more like a political rally than a shareholders meeting. The unveiling was set for 11:00 AM, and the mechanics were putting the finishing touches on the car at 10:55.

Although there was still a last-minute rush to ready it, the event was not as frenetic as the launch of the Tin Goose. The stockholders waiting in the assembly area heard the rumble of an engine before the car appeared. Some said that Preston Tucker had told the mechanics to leave the mufflers off to make it sound more powerful, but it is just as likely that there wasn't time to install them. Tucker was behind the wheel, and according to some witnesses he raced across the floor of the plant at 60 mph. When he got in front of the cheering stockholders, Tucker stopped the car—dubbed #1001—and put it in reverse. It backed up, thanks to the twelve-year-old Cord transmission the men had just finished rebuilding and adapting to the car.[1] The audience roared with applause.[2]

Once the demonstration was over, Tucker conducted some corporate business. After some speeches, various resolutions were put before the stockholders, who now had a vote in the company's operation. Votes were conducted by voice, and the resolutions were all adopted with unanimous "Ayes!" from the crowd.[3] Chicago newspapers noted the festive atmosphere and how it didn't seem like a stockholders meeting. The seventeen hundred in attendance "asked not a single question about production, dividends, or other corporate matters."[4] Tucker did inform them that more cars were coming soon.[5]

The Franklin engine turned out to be perfect for the Tucker '48. Coupled with the rebuilt Cord 810 transmission, it created 166 horsepower. The engine only weighed 320 pounds and delivered an impressive 372 foot pounds of torque.

———

Tucker #1001 was not a mirage. The Tucker Corporation was gearing up for production. Body parts for cars are stamped on dies, and the Tucker '48 would have fifty-two pieces die-stamped in-house on dies made by die makers in Detroit. Many of them were made of Kirksite, a less expensive but less durable material often used for shorter production runs because it wore out faster than steel. With the arrival of the dies, sheet metal was being fabricated and the other parts of the car were being procured. A pilot assembly line had been put together and Tucker employees were working out the bugs of mass production.

With all the parts that went into the car, it was inevitable that there would be snags. Tucker had dithered on the steering wheel design, and by the time he made his decision, the vendor could not make them in time for the first cars made. Tremulis called some friends at Ford Motor Company asking if they had any quick solutions. Despite the obvious conflict of interest, a friend at Ford offered him a batch of slightly flawed steering wheels for the company's Lincoln Zephyr luxury cars. They had blemishes making them unsuitable for a Lincoln, but Tremulis's friend assured him that no one would notice. All he asked was that the steering wheels be replaced when the Tucker wheels became available. Soon, Tucker sedans rolled off the assembly line, steered by Lincoln Zephyr steering wheels.[6]

Tucker received great press coverage for his shareholders event, but some were beginning to question the progress being made toward mass production. Tucker had now only produced two cars. *Dealer News* noted that Tucker's "dream car" was still just a dream—and also pointed out that to make a profit, the car would likely have to retail for quite a bit more than its original promised price of $1,000.[7] In this last point, the *Dealer News* was being disingenuous; the Tucker Corporation's prospectus had clearly stated that the target price of the car had risen from $1,000 to between $1,800 and $2,000, not including shipping from Chicago.[8]

Money was an issue, though, and not just with the car's cost. The company was skimping on some of its purchases. When the first few models rolled off the line, they were made using some body panels made by vendors. If they were to hit the production figures they had touted publicly, they would need hundreds, and then thousands, of sets of body panels. Yet they had only ordered fifty.[9] Could Tucker raise more money? He applied for a loan from the Reconstruction Finance Corporation but was denied.[10]

A week later, Tucker announced that the company had lined up its steel supplies, one of the last pieces to the puzzle of mass-producing cars. The Tucker Corporation was attempting to purchase its own steel plant, but in the meantime it now had the steel necessary to build between 160 and 240 cars per day. In the same announcement, Tucker stated that the assembly line was being fine-tuned and there should be 125 cars completed by June 3, enough for each of the distributors to have one on hand by that time.[11] Newsmen noticed that Preston Tucker often gave dizzying, and varying, numbers for expected production. In February, a month before the shareholders meeting, he told reporters to expect two hundred cars in June, followed by twenty-two hundred in July, thirty-four hundred in August, and sixty-five hundred in September. By April of the following year, Tucker said, the company would be churning out cars at the rate of twenty-five thousand a month.[12]

———

In the April issue of *Tucker Topics*, Fred Rockelman wrote that the conveyor system for the assembly line was nearly complete. Production was not months away but mere days away. He used a baseball metaphor: "We're rounding third."[13] Home plate was in sight. Another piece in the same issue was a reprinted article from *Automotive News*, whose reporter had toured the plant and interviewed Preston Tucker. Saying it would be impossible for one man to successfully launch an endeavor of this magnitude, the writer said:

> However, there are notable exceptions. No. 1, of course, is Preston Tucker himself—ebullient, tall, good-looking—he gives the impression of a lone knight taking on the giants of the industry. At times he sounds crazy as a loon. After looking over the layout [of the plant], you wonder if maybe he isn't crazy like a fox.[14]

The article included photos of cars moving down the pilot assembly line, but the writer said that Tucker and his men were secretive about the finished product, not wanting to show any finished cars to the writer for fear of corporate espionage. Preston Tucker led the writer to believe that the Tucker '48s were being built with the torque-converter drives and that other manufacturers had been sniffing around, trying to find out the secrets behind them.[15]

Elsewhere in the newsletter were pieces on the annual stockholders meeting, the Tucker Export Corporation, and the hiring of Tucker's former boss D. McCall White. Also included was a notice that the company had purchased Aircooled Motors, the manufacturer of the Franklin engine used in the revamped Tucker '48. After finding out that Aircooled Motors was for sale, the corporation had bought it for $1.8 million on March 21, 1948.[16] This provided the company with engines, as well as a stream of income from those it sold to Bell and others.[17] It seemed a good investment even if the company hadn't needed a supply of engines: according to Tucker, Aircooled had made a $398,000 profit the year before.[18]

Finally, the latest issue of *Tucker Topics* reported on a weekly radio show Tucker would soon be presenting.[19] Always seeking new ways to get publicity, Tucker sponsored a program called *Speak Up America*, hosted by John B. Kennedy. It was a fifteen-minute-long talk show covering various issues of the day, and Preston Tucker read his own commercials during the show.[20] Broadcast by ABC Radio, it was heard on eighty-five stations across the United States on Sunday afternoons at 4:00 eastern time. Some people wondered if the show would do better if it gave away prizes. Listeners would submit fifty-word comments on different topics drawn from the show, and a Tucker '48 sedan would be given each week to the best answer received.[21] Fifteen thousand letters soon poured into the show's office.[22]

With production proceeding and the publicity machine humming along nicely, the Tucker '48 still had one major problem: it was far too expensive to build. The engines in the first few models built cost $5,000 apiece. Even if that were to be reduced dramatically—some thought a price of $1,500 was possible since Tucker owned the engine manufacturer—it still cost too much. And estimates for the cost of the rest of the car reached between $1,075 and $1,441.[23] Clearly, these costs had to be reduced or the retail price would need to be raised. The latter option was not preferable to Tucker, who had promised his cars would be affordable. Tucker continued to hope he could drastically reduce his cost of production when he began manufacturing on the same scale as his biggest competitors in Detroit.

18

The Accessories Program

Despite having raised $15 million in a stock offering and another $2 million selling dealerships, the rising costs of production meant that the Tucker Corporation needed another infusion of cash. So Tucker launched a program unlike anything else ever done in the automobile world. He would sell accessories to the car buyers before they took delivery of a car. It was hare-brained on every level, yet it worked beyond anyone's wildest dreams.

The idea had originated with Cliff Knoble, the adman Tucker lured from New York. Knoble knew the average car buyer bought $600 of options and accessories for each new car purchased. If that held true for the Tucker '48, perhaps there was a way to get that money sooner. Tucker could create a line of car accessories that customers could preorder and take delivery of before the cars were even built. Matching luggage, a dashboard radio, and seat covers would be made, sold, and shipped to customers right away. As an incentive, a control number would be assigned to each buyer giving him or her priority for delivery of a Tucker automobile. The earlier a person bought the accessory package from Tucker, the higher his or her name went on the list.[1]

Early in May, a *Chicago Herald-American* reporter came to the plant and test-drove a Tucker '48. He loved it. With Gene Haustein in the car with him, he got the car going 80 mph in the parking lot and hadn't put it in high gear yet. It started to rain before he could see it doing 100 mph, but he had no doubt it could have, noting that "the car loafs along at 80 with the throttle half open."[2] The writer also stated the car had gone through many "evolutionary changes" since it was first announced but he had no problem with them. The car met all his expectations.

In its May *Tucker Topics*, the company hinted that it had an exciting announcement for dealers. Fred Rockelman opened the issue with the story of how Preston Tucker had taken a production '48 for a drive in Chicago and had returned to the plant with a crowd of fans following him, hoping for a better look at the car.

"Details of one of the most important undertakings ever launched by the Tucker Corporation will be revealed in the next few weeks, a program which we are sure will be acclaimed by all our dealers and distributors."[3] The statement was attributed to Dulian, who noted that there were now 1,712 dealers and 80 distributors committed to selling Tucker automobiles.

The accessories program was announced on May 17 at a dealers meeting in Chicago.[4] The dealers were becoming anxious because they had no product to sell. They were invited to a hotel, where they heard updates on the progress of the car. Preston Tucker spoke and then turned the podium over to Knoble. Knoble outlined the accessories program to the dealers. He knew that many of the Tucker dealers had been used car dealers previously and that this would be their first new car franchise. At the time, used car selling was extremely competitive, and many dealers resorted to gimmicks and premiums to move cars. Knoble suspected the program would appeal to that segment of his audience, and he was right.

The dealers were given the opportunity to buy accessories on the spot, which they did in huge numbers. Preston Tucker was so impressed he pulled Knoble aside and put him in charge of the accessories program, offering him a 1.5 percent commission on sales. Knoble headed out and did similar presentations around the country, eventually selling $3 million in accessories. Tucker's net profit from the program was more than $1 million.[5]

Critics laughed at the program, particularly the concept of Tucker selling luggage. What did that have to do with the car? Knoble pointed out it had everything to do with the car. The luggage was designed to fit into the car's huge trunk—uniquely placed at the front of the car—and again Knoble was right. The luggage sold exceedingly well. Fifty thousand units were sold, raising almost $1 million.[6]

The accessories program may have attracted some unwanted attention, however. Charles Pearson later argued that the program, as successful as it was, may have drawn heightened scrutiny from federal regulators. The scheme seemed too far-fetched to be honest. Was it legal? Could it have been an indication that the entire enterprise was simply out to squeeze as much money as possible from unsuspecting customers?[7]

––––––

Elsewhere in the May *Tucker Topics*, readers were introduced to Alex Tremulis, who stood before a small model of the '48 accompanied by a story of the design team. Along with Philip Egan and a woman named Audrey Moore, Tremulis was credited with bringing the '48 to production in one-tenth the time it would have taken a traditional manufacturer. (Audrey Moore's credentials were as impressive as anyone's on the team: she had worked for the famed industrial designer Raymond Loewy when he designed Studebakers.[8]) Tremulis took the opportunity to point out the advanced state of the car's shape. "From one standpoint the Tucker is actually the first completely streamlined car ever built. Most manufacturers have succeeded in creating streamlined appearances only from certain perspectives. The Tucker '48 is streamlined from all angles."[9] The piece stated that the three—Tremulis, Egan, and Moore—were already working on the Tucker '50.

Tucker Topics also introduced its readers to Secondo Campini, an Italian engineer who had been working with jet propulsion during World War II. Campini designed a plane that flew with a form of jet propulsion during the war but never got much beyond the prototype stage. Unaware that the Germans had flown functional jet aircraft several years before he had, Campini told many people, including Tucker, that his was the first operational jet aircraft when it made a few test flights. It is unclear if Campini exaggerated or if it was the editors of *Tucker Topics*, but the article claimed that Campini's plane had flown in 1932 at a speed of 350 mph.[10] Neither fact was true. He was, according to the article, "the world's foremost authority on jet propulsion and the gas turbine." *Tucker Topics* hinted that the Tucker Corporation was toying with the idea of putting a turbine engine into a car in the near future.[11]

———

Preston Tucker would never be accused of thinking small. The previous year, as he laid out his plans for the infusion of cash from the stock sale with his staff, one of the first items he sought was a steel plant. His advisors said it was unnecessary, but Tucker was worried about raw materials. He had problems getting modeling clay for his first model. What if other automakers interfered with his supply of steel? The WAA, which had leased him the plant in Chicago, also owned some steel plants. Tucker wanted one. After the fight with the housing administration and Lustron, he knew it wouldn't be easy. Instead of a cushy lease arrangement, he'd have to buy the steel plant outright. This time, though, he had the money.

Still, in the months that followed, the acquisition process had bogged down once again. Originally the company had set its sights on a government-owned blast furnace in Granite City, Illinois, which had been operated by Koppers Company Inc. during the war. When the WAA announced it was seeking bids on the $2.5 million plant, the Tucker Corporation furnished a bid of $2.751 million; several other companies submitted bids as well. The WAA canceled the auction unexpectedly, announcing that the plant had been reappraised and its actual fair market value was $3.25 million. Rather than renewing the auction, the WAA simply announced that the plant was being sold to a corporation that had been formed just a week before the initial bid process had begun. The sale price was announced as $3.255 million.

Charles Pearson later wrote that Tucker was incensed. Litigation ensued, but the government got the case dismissed on the grounds of governmental immunity: the government can't be sued for doing its job. One judge who heard an appeal of the case said, "The transactions in this case are sur-rounded by a pervasive and most offensive odor of skullduggery."[12]

Another plant—reportedly the world's largest blast furnace, along with a coke plant—became available in Cleveland through the WAA shortly after. The WAA, probably because of criticism it had received from its previous disposal of plants, told bidders they needed to prove their ability to run the plant properly along with any bid submitted. Tucker purchased $100,000 worth of options on materials that would allow Tucker Corporation to begin operating the plant if it won the auction.[13] He also put up $100,000 earnest money. Tucker was the high bidder, over Republic Steel, another company that had bid on the previous plant and lost. But the WAA announced that it was not going to merely give this plant to the high bidder. It wanted further proof that the plant would be run appropriately. This gave the WAA license to investigate each suitor and then pick from among them based on criteria only they understood.

WAA representatives went to Tucker's plant to see what progress was being made with the car. Presumably they quizzed the other entities seeking the Cleveland plant. Soon, another hitch arose. Tucker once again came to the attention of Michigan senator Homer Ferguson, who accused the WAA of "gross mismanagement" for its disposition of government property.[14] Everyone knew that the biggest item on its list was Tucker's Chicago plant. Ferguson, of course, represented the state that was the home of Detroit's Big Three automakers. And now Ferguson was attacking Tucker indirectly, by going after the WAA.[15]

Later, Ferguson's critics would point out his direct connection to at least one auto company: Chrysler. Chrysler had developed air-conditioning for consumer use long before it was installed in automobiles, and their Airtemp division was a big moneymaker for them. Ferguson's wife was listed as the agent for Airtemp in Washington, DC, at a time when the company was negotiating lucrative contracts with the US government. Furthermore, one Airtemp franchise near Detroit had been awarded to Senator Ferguson's daughter and son-in-law, while his wife was awarded shares of stock to con-trol the franchise. These facts were publicized, but no action was ever taken against Ferguson since he, as far as anyone could prove, had never directly profited from these cozy relationships.[16]

On May 28, 1948, the WAA advised Tucker that his bid on the blast furnace was "inadequate," without further explanation. Eventually, the Cleveland plant would be awarded to the automaker Kaiser-Frazer, whose bid had been lower than Tucker's.[17]

19

The End of the Dream

By 1948, Preston Tucker had hired former race car driver Ralph Hepburn to be the western regional manager for the Tucker Corporation. Hepburn was more than just a trusted employee; he was a personal friend. And it was Hepburn whom Tucker had entrusted with the first public drive of the Tin Goose when it cruised off the stage at its world premiere.

In May, Hepburn decided to race one more Indy 500, even though he was fifty-one years old.[1] A car owner named Lew Welch had some of the fastest cars at the track, and one of his drivers, Cliff Bergere, almost crashed one during practice, losing control, leading to an argument between Welch and Bergere. Stories differ as to whether Bergere quit or was fired, but the vacant seat gave Hepburn a chance to race again. Just a couple days later he was out driving practice laps in the 550-horsepower car when he blew by an Italian driver named Luigi Chinetti. Chinetti said he saw Hepburn's car begin to "weave like a fish."[2] Hepburn never regained control and slammed into a wall, killing him instantly. Forty thousand spectators witnessed the wreck on May 16. Tucker was at the track that day but did not see the accident. He did, however, attend the funeral in Glendale, California, on May 22.[3] After Tucker returned from the funeral, his friends noticed his gloomy aspect.

Before he died, Hepburn was one of the most experienced drivers at Indianapolis. In his fifteen races he had completed 4,512 miles. His best result was a second place finish in which he lost by a mere two seconds to Wilbur Shaw in 1937. At the time it was the closest finish in the race's history.[4] Tucker said, "Ralph was a man of rare courage—one of the truly great figures in racing. His death is not mourned alone by us but also by the entire racing fraternity."[5]

Less than a week later, on May 28, 1948—the same day the WAA denied Tucker's bid on the blast furnace—the SEC told him that they were launching an investigation into his corporation.

———

The Tucker Corporation had come under increased scrutiny from the agency earlier in May, when it filed its annual report for the previous year with the SEC. Though the report covered a period of less than four months, since the stock offering had closed on September 12, the SEC contacted Tucker and told him there were problems with the report as it was filed. Usually, the SEC would issue a "deficiency letter" to a corporation, noting the problems with the report and allowing time for the corporation to make the needed corrections. Tucker traveled to the SEC headquarters with an attorney to see what the deficiencies were so he could correct them.[6] Several commissioners indicated they could simply put them together in a letter and Tucker could amend his report.

But while they were discussing the matter, SEC attorney James Goode entered the room and announced that a letter would not suffice. Goode said he wanted to subpoena the records at the factory and perform a full-blown public investigation into the company's operation. Tucker left not knowing which way the SEC was going to rule on the matter.[7] Then came the announcement that an investigation was underway.

On June 3, six agents of the SEC showed up at the Tucker Corporation and asked to see the corporation's books and records.[8] They did not explain what they were looking for or what had triggered their visit. One SEC representative told Tucker's attorney that the investigation would be confidential if the requested materials were furnished soon.[9] Tucker asked if the men could be more specific. What were they looking for? Tucker later said they would not tell him. He accused them of launching a "fishing expedition."[10] It was clearly related to the meetings he had had with the SEC after the corporation had filed its annual report. However, Tucker had one other thing going for him: Federal law strictly mandated that anything turned over to the SEC had to be kept confidential and closely held within the circle of officers, employees, and members of the commission. In fact, the prohibition was so strong it required officers and employees of the commission to defy subpoenas and court orders requesting the information. In those instances, the commission would go to court and fight such a subpoena.[11]

Despite the renewed government attention, the seventh issue of *Tucker Topics* had no trouble maintaining its optimistic tone. The cover showed a full-page photo taken from above of a Tucker '48 swarmed by a crowd on LaSalle Street in Chicago. According to the caption, the driver of the car spent an hour working his way through the crowd to get to the car.[12] Fred Rockelman's introduction noted the successful accessories program and the impending production of the Tucker '48, adding, "Let's go out and make ourselves some history!"[13] The first article was a reprint of the Chicago newspaper article describing the test-drive in a Tucker '48 just a month before the newsletter was published.[14] The future still looked promising.

But June 6, 1948, marked the end of America's love affair with Preston Tucker. That end was engineered by Drew Pearson, a radio broadcaster and newspaper columnist based in Washington, DC. His radio program, *Drew Pearson Comments*, was broadcast nationally and his newspaper column, Washington Merry-Go-Round, was syndicated nationally as well. Pearson's material often focused on bureaucratic and political gossip. He was well connected, and sources within the government furnished him confidential information, knowing he would broadcast it.

Historian Arthur Herman has written, "Pearson is hard to understand in terms of today's Washington media. A strong and fervent liberal, he was a political commentator, investigative journalist, gossip columnist, and political blackmailer rolled into one."[15] Pearson was a modern-day muckraker, but with a darker side. He had no qualms about smearing his targets with lies and destroying reputations. Some of his targets deserved the attacks—he was an active critic of Joseph McCarthy—while others found themselves in his crosshairs because Pearson didn't like their politics. Jack Anderson, Pearson's assistant, said that the truth to Pearson "was often a subjective matter."[16]

On his June 6 broadcast, Pearson announced that the Securities and Exchange Commission was about to launch a major investigation into Preston Tucker and the Tucker Corporation. Pearson boldly announced that the investigation would "blow Tucker higher than a kite."[17] Pearson did not identify his source, but he didn't need to for his listeners to believe him.

With that single broadcast, Tucker's good fortune was destroyed. In hindsight, Pearson's announcement can only be seen as a groundless and vicious attack. The SEC had only shown up at the Tucker factory three days before Pearson's broadcast. They had notified Tucker of an impending investigation but had not indicated it was any more important than previous occasions when the SEC had looked at Tucker's activities.[18] The investigation had not turned up anything damning yet. Pearson had nothing to substantiate his claim.

When trading opened the next morning, Tucker Corporation stock crashed. It soon hit 2⅜, less than half of its recent price of 5. Investors lost $10 million in value overnight.[19] But worse for Tucker, no one would extend the corporation credit with the cloud of a federal investigation overhead. This was particularly troublesome in the auto industry, where manufacturers expected suppliers to ship them components and materials on credit. Tucker would have to pay cash to most of his suppliers in advance.[20]

An irate Tucker did not know where to turn for help. He sent a telegram to the Justice Department, inquiring if it had been behind the leak, or to find out if Pearson spoke for them. The Justice Department ignored Tucker's telegram.[21]

Tucker's friends and allies suspected foul play: someone had set out to harm Tucker and his company. Cliff Knoble noted, "The 'leak' was too well timed—too shrewdly destructive—too immune to defensive counter measures—to have been accidental. Within twenty-four hours it practically destroyed the Tucker Corporation."[22]

Just in case anyone missed the broadcast, Pearson repeated the story in his syndicated newspaper column of June 10, read by millions nationwide: "The ax is now falling on Preston Tucker, the revolutionary automobile man, and falling hard."[23] Pearson explained how Tucker had lost out on the Republic Steel plant, and now "Tucker will have no steel to make his cars." Pearson did not explain why Tucker would not be able to simply buy steel on the open market. The meat of the article followed:

> Meanwhile, the Justice Department has 5 G-men investigating Tucker for alleged mail frauds. Likewise, the Securities and Exchange Commission is breathing hot on Tucker's back over his latest money-raising scheme. He has been trying to get his sales agencies to order accessories, even though he still isn't certain of even producing the automobiles to match. Tucker has over-subscribed his stock—a total of $25,000,000 being sold to the public—and has also sold out his franchises in advance, reaping in another seven million dollars. All this took a lot of promoting for a man who doesn't know where the steel for his first car is coming from.

Much of it was untrue. Among other things, the sale of the stock was in fact *under*subscribed: Tucker had ended the sale before selling all the shares he had offered in the prospectus. And Tucker did know where the steel for his first car would come from: car #1001 had been built three months earlier and shown to the press. Pearson was falsely telling his readers that Tucker had not built a single car yet when he had already built several.

On June 14 the SEC served a subpoena on the Tucker Corporation, demanding the surrender of virtually every record, letter, invoice, or other scrap of paper the company had in its possession. In a time before photocopiers, the reproduction costs for the requested materials, and the time it would have taken to make all the copies, were prohibitive.[24] When Tucker protested, he was told the investigation would be over in ten days and he would soon have all his paperwork back. Tucker refused to turn over the requested documents, and the SEC went to court. A federal judge ordered the Tucker Corporation to appear and explain why it would not honor the subpoena.[25]

—————

Through it all, Tucker's workers kept at it. They managed to assemble some cars, and those already finished still drew rave reviews. Tucker #1005 had been flown to Oakland, California, on May 25, and then driven to a local Tucker dealer. Later, Preston Tucker drove it east to Salt Lake City. More than fifty thousand people came through the showrooms to see the car when it was displayed on this trip, and the car's appearance on local streets caused a "near riot."[26]

And Tucker's engineers continued their work on outstanding design issues. Although Tucker had agreed to let the first Tucker sedans be built with manual transmissions, he still hoped to offer automatic transmissions in his cars. He asked Warren Rice, an engineer, to design a suitable one. Rice did so, assembling a working prototype of his "R-1" transmission. It was fitted into a test chassis, and it ran well. To see how it stacked up to others, Tucker's men installed it into a Buick they had bought as a test bed, and the Buick ran better with Rice's R-1 transmission. Tucker was so enthused he announced he would bring the transmission to Detroit and demonstrate it for the automotive press. He even gave Rice a $5,000 bonus, which incensed D. McCall White, who later told investigators the payment was "unwarranted and ridiculous."[27]

A demonstration of the new transmission was scheduled for a park in Detroit, where a crowd of people showed up to see the Tucker cars. People were allowed to walk around and examine them. One of the cars was merely a test chassis with the power train—using the R-1 transmission—installed. It had no body, but it could be driven. The other two cars were the Tin Goose and #1001 from the shareholders meeting. Rice invited journalists to go for a ride in the test chassis. Leo Donovan of the *Detroit Free Press* compared the ride favorably to the excitement of a "first ride in a roller coaster."[28]

Other reports were somewhat less enthusiastic. Working mentions of the demonstration into their coverage of Tucker's struggle with the SEC, newspapers pointed out that the cars did not contain all the features originally promised, such as fuel injection and disc brakes. But even they admitted that the test chassis with the automatic transmission worked perfectly, "operating in reverse as well."[29]

The R-1 transmission was a resounding success. But it was not ready for mass production yet. What the press did not know was that the R-1 transmission had a limitation that harked back to the scrapped fluid drive system: it could not be shifted into reverse without shutting the engine off.[30] It was a problem that simply required more time, but Tucker had been anxious to show off the car. Luckily, no one asked to see the transmission shifted from drive to reverse. While discussing the transmission, a Tucker representative told the press that the tooling for the car was 80 percent complete and that assembly lines would be able to turn out a hundred cars daily by mid-September.[31] Tucker said he intended to sell the '48s with automatic transmissions eventually, but for the time being, the cars would have pre-selector manual transmissions.[32]

Nevertheless, the "Tucker News Bureau" (Tucker's publicity department) issued a press release describing the automatic transmission demonstration. The release also laid out the current state of affairs at the Tucker Corporation. The release quoted Offutt as saying that the Tucker '48 had been modified slightly from its original configuration due to cost. "Our most important contribution, in our opinion, is increased safety, not only in design and construction of the body, but also in weight distribution for better handling and safer stopping in emergencies."[33]

The Tucker News Bureau also issued a press release announcing that permanent dies had been ordered and were anticipated in the plant no later than the end of July. Barring work stoppages at the die makers, or impediments from the SEC or the court, the Tucker Corporation could have cars rolling off its assembly line soon. "We are on the threshold of mass production."[34]

―――――

But Preston Tucker soon learned that the investigation was more widespread than the SEC had led him to believe. SEC and FBI agents traveled the country, interviewing investors who had bought dealerships, distributorships, or even stock. Tucker heard from stockholders who had been grilled by federal agents and, he later wrote, "it got so that even owning a few shares of Tucker stock caused a man more trouble and embarrassment than being accused of a sex crime."[35] In all, the SEC grilled at least twenty-eight investors who could be called as witnesses against Tucker.[36] The SEC never said how they chose the subjects of their interviews. Some reports placed the number of Tucker stock-holders at fifty thousand.[37] There is also evidence that the SEC found witnesses who were not favorable to their anti-Tucker case but ignored them and moved on, looking only for people who were willing to bash Tucker—as later interactions between federal prosecutors and Alex Tremulis would suggest.

The Chicago plant and Ypsilanti Machine and Tool were soon swarming with investigators, attorneys, and accountants. James P. Goode, Thomas B. Hart, and John R. O'Connor were the attorneys in charge of the investigation, while Sydney Orbach and Frank Corbin led a team of six accountants. The SEC even hired two engineers and told them to poke around the plant.[38] Then, although the agency had originally claimed to be following up on the recent annual report Tucker had filed, it decided to expand the investigation back to 1945, to what it called the "approximate date of formation of a scheme to defraud."[39] The investigation would take several months, and each side would blame the other for how long it took.

Preston Tucker decided he needed to fight back against the SEC. It was unclear what the SEC was up to, but a remarkable amount of damage was being done. And much of what the SEC had done did not appear to be above-board. Tucker wrote an open letter to the "Automobile Industry" that was published in several nationally distributed newspapers on June 14 and 15, 1948. The letter took up a full page, and Tucker was not coy:

Gentlemen: As you know, we are building a completely new motorcar—the rear engine Tucker. Being new-comers in the field we have had to start from scratch and work harder and faster than most of you. For example, instead of the 20 months you usually take to produce a new model of conventional design, my engineers have taken less than 10 to perfect a car which I firmly believe opens a new era in motoring.

★★★

But there is another group—a very powerful group—which for two years has carried on a carefully organized campaign to prevent the motoring public from ever getting their hands on the wheel of a Tucker.

These people have tried to introduce spies into our plant. They have endeavored to bribe and corrupt loyal Tucker employees. Such curiosity about what goes on in the Tucker plant should be highly flattering, I suppose. But they haven't stopped there.

★★★

When the day comes that anyone can bend our country's laws and lawmakers to serve selfish, competitive ends, that day democratic government dies. And we're just optimistic enough to believe that once the facts are on the table, American public opinion will walk in with a big stick.[40]

Tucker believed he was being attacked, but he did not name any suspects. "Most of the political pressure and investigations we have had to face these last two years can be traced back to one influential individual, who is out to get Tucker." Philip Egan and others believed Tucker was referring to Michigan senator Homer Ferguson.[41] Tucker had suspicions about the SEC's Harry McDonald as well but wasn't sure if Ferguson was pushing McDonald or if the SEC was acting on its own.

In court, Tucker's attorneys argued it would be impossible for the corporation to turn over everything the SEC sought and still operate. The subpoena demanded engineering drawings, blueprints, and paperwork the company needed to keep working. Finally, Tucker agreed to cooperate with the SEC but also announced he was temporarily shutting down his plant: "Tying up such records at this time will make it impossible to continue operating."[42]

For its part, the SEC claimed that the Tucker Corporation's registration statement, prospectus, and 1947 annual report "contained untrue statements of material fact"—all before they had obtained any additional documents from Tucker.[43]

Tucker told the press that the shutdown would not harm the company so long as it did not last longer than thirty days. If the plant remained closed for sixty days or more, the company would be "seriously jeopardized" and "might collapse."[44] "Whether its action is right or wrong, [the] SEC has effectively blocked our every corporate attempt at our most crucial point, when we are on the threshold of mass production with engineering and development completed." Ironically, the SEC action, ostensibly taken to protect shareholders, would almost certainly harm them by continuing to depress the value of their stock.

The closure of the Chicago plant idled 708 production workers. More than 800 had already been laid off for another reason a week earlier: workers at the company in Detroit making the dies for the Tucker automobile had gone on strike. Tucker's employees who would work with those dies had nothing to do until the dies showed up.[45]

Some employees, like Alex Tremulis, told Preston Tucker they would stick around and help as much as they could, even without pay. Later, Tremulis said, "It was Custer's last stand. We were dying. We just cut our salaries and kept the legend alive."[46]

Others, like Philip Egan, couldn't afford to wait around and see when they would get paid.[47] In all, Tucker Corporation laid off more than fifteen hundred employees. At its peak, the company had employed twenty-two hundred people with a payroll of $250,000 monthly.[48]

On July 14, 1948, a man who held a hundred shares of Tucker stock and two men who had bought Tucker dealerships filed suit in federal court, asking for a court-appointed receiver to take over the Tucker Corporation. The plaintiffs claimed the company's assets had been squandered, but as was becoming the norm in all things Tucker, the suit contained patently false allegations. While noting that Tucker had promised to build a "new and unusual" car, it wrongly claimed that "no car of any kind other than the experimental car, has been produced."[49] It also claimed, "He has no designs, models, plans or materials to manufacture a car."[50] The plaintiffs did not say where this incorrect information came from. They also made some outlandish claims, including that Preston Tucker had secretly built a home in Bogota, Columbia, presumably so he could abscond with the remaining assets of the company.[51] A federal court would eventually freeze the assets of the corporation, assuring it could not possibly conduct any further business.[52]

D. McCall White, the frustrated engineer who had been Tucker's first boss in the business, had one more month left on his $5,000-a-month contract. He went to the plant and told Tucker he was ready to work. Tucker found things to keep him busy, and he finished out his last month. White left and said that the men parted amicably, but he would later give a scathing statement to the SEC, accusing Tucker of being a liar, incompetent, and wasteful of corporate assets.[53]

But other plant employees got together and decided that they needed to do something to try to garner support for the company in its struggle with the SEC. They got permission to use six of the Tucker '48s that had been completed prior to the shutdown and held a parade in the streets of Chicago. They even added a Tucker chassis with no body to the caravan and invited others to drive their own cars along. The city lent a police escort, and Preston Tucker joined the event at the last minute. While driving one of the Tucker sedans, a motorcycle cop pulled alongside him and asked how the car handled. Tucker offered to let him drive the car. Did Tucker know how to drive a motorcycle? Of course. They traded, the police officer driving the Tucker '48 in the parade escorted by Preston Tucker on a police motorcycle.[54]

As Preston Tucker and a few faithful employees wondered what would happen next, it occurred to them that they had the parts to assemble more cars. Some assembly line workers were called back to work and given the job of assembling the remaining cars. Beginning in the third week of July, they built more, and by the time they were done, thirty-seven Tucker '48s in all had been completed.[55] Preston Tucker told reporters that tooling had been "progressing satisfactorily" to allow one thousand cars to be built daily when and if the company was left alone by the government.[56]

Outsiders speculated, however, that Tucker had shut down because he wasn't ready for production and was simply using the SEC investigation as an excuse. But a well-respected automotive writer, Tom McCahill, wrote an article that indicated otherwise. McCahill explained that he had visited the factory in Chicago and test-driven a Tucker '48 before the shutdown. His review wasn't published until August 1948, however, in *Mechanix Illustrated*. McCahill left no doubt what his opinion was regarding the car and the Tucker Corporation: "Tucker is building an automobile! And brother, it's a real automobile! I want to go on record right here and now as saying that it is the most amazing American car I have seen to date; its performance is out of this world. Why do I think so? Wait until you have had an opportunity to drive the car and you'll know what I mean."[57]

McCahill noted the "ballyhoo and attention" Tucker had received to date but then made it clear that it was well deserved. At the Chicago factory, he had seen a beehive of activity: two thousand employees and "cars in various forms of completion."[58] After the tour, he went for a ride in the Tucker and couldn't rave enough about it. After he dispelled the rumors—it did not have an engine from another automotive manufacturer in it and it could back up—he spoke glowingly of the ride. It was smooth and handled well. And the performance was amazing. "I soon knew I was in one of the *greatest performing passenger automobiles* ever built on this side of the Atlantic. This car is real dynamite!"[59] He compared it to other American-made cars. "The car is roomy and extraordinarily comfortable. It steers and handles better than any American car I have driven. As to roadability, it's in a class by itself."[60] The article was accompanied by half a dozen photos of the car and the assembly line, with a row of Tucker '48s in various stages of assembly. After reading this article, how could anyone doubt that Tucker's operation was legitimate?

But one question arises from McCahill's piece. He said he saw "nearly 200" cars being built, but his number was far too high. Tucker had ordered enough body parts for only 57 or 58 cars and 125 engines. It is possible McCahill miscounted or misestimated. It is also possible that someone gave him an incorrect number. We do not know, however, since McCahill did not identify his source, other than his own observations.

A writer for the *Chicago Daily News* named Phil S. Hanna also addressed the progress Tucker had made before he shut down the plant:

The first thing that strikes the eye is literally several acres of wheels, tires, body stampings, engines, frames and all the related parts that go to make up an automobile. You see hundreds of cylinder blocks, bell housings, radios, batteries and shock absorbers. I counted 58 finished car bodies in the assembly line. Work was stopped on these a week ago when the Securities and Exchange Commission moved in to investigate financing of the company.[61]

Elsewhere in the plant he counted ninety complete engines ready for installation and "mountains" of boxes containing spare parts. After touring the plant, where he saw men working "for free" to finish assembling cars, he rode in a Tucker '48 and was impressed. The test-drive included a demonstration of the sedan backing up, which had become routine for every test-drive involving a journalist. More important, the reporter was convinced of the viability of the operation. "The Tucker plant, according to what I saw, appears ready to start production of cars."[62]

Reviews and articles raving about the cars and the plant did little to counter the avalanche of negative press hitting Tucker. For every positive review there were a hundred negative stories about the SEC investigation or the federal court lawsuits.

———

On August 5 Cliff Knoble turned in his resignation to the company, in accordance with the ninety-day-notice clause he had agreed to when he was hired.[63] Knoble had grown discontent following the successful launch of his accessories program, as he wondered what the company had done with the proceeds. The money was intended to pay for the accessories, but there had been rumblings around the company that money was tighter than Preston Tucker was letting on. Knoble, who felt proprietary about the program since it was his idea, asked if the accessories money had been put into an escrow account, or at least an account to segregate it from the company's general operating funds. Everyone he spoke to—including Preston Tucker—told him that steps were being taken to ensure the funds were safe. But Knoble was tipped off that the corporation was using the accessories proceeds for general purposes. He confronted Preston Tucker, who told him there was a mistake and reaffirmed that the funds were safe. Shortly after, Knoble said, Tucker refused to meet with him any further.

Knoble's resignation was accepted, and he was told to vacate his office the next day. He hadn't received his most recent paycheck, and he never would. He was also never paid his promised commission for the accessory sales, despite bringing in more than $1 million in profit. Knoble filed suit to see what, if anything, he might be able to recover.[64]

One hope of saving the Tucker Corporation was that a big investor might give the corporation a cash infusion. Tucker may have even approached the enigmatic billionaire Howard Hughes. Newspapers had published reports of rumored meetings between Tucker and Hughes starting in August 1948.[65] Rumors swirled that Hughes considered investing, and a journalist asked Tucker about it. "I don't think I can comment either way. I'll admit certain deals are pending, but I won't deny or affirm that Howard Hughes is coming in." Hughes had little interest in the project. A spokesman for Hughes responded, "There never have been any negotiations. There's nothing to report."[66]

The rumors may have had some basis in truth. At the time, Hughes Aircraft employed a man named Tex Thornton. He had been one of the "Whiz Kids," a group of Army Air Force veterans who worked at Ford Motor Company after World War II, using efficiency techniques learned in the military to streamline the automaker's operations. Thornton later wrote to a friend in Detroit that Hughes had gotten a Tucker sedan, presumably from Tucker, and Hughes had run "some tests on it."[67] However, others within Hughes's organization did not think the project was worth an investment. Thornton did not indicate what opinion Hughes had of the Tucker sedan itself.

Meanwhile, Tucker pressed forward to get the Tucker '48 sedan built. He obtained permission to use the Indianapolis Motor Speedway in September to run endurance tests. Tucker, mechanic Eddie Offutt, and a few others drove eight cars to the track from Chicago.[68] One of the cars had the new automatic transmission in it that Rice had designed. At the track, they would drive the cars continuously, racking up thousands of miles on them to see how they held up to heavy-duty driving. One car was #1027, the car that would roll with Offutt at the wheel on September 24.

When #1027 arrived at the track, it had 280 miles on its odometer. The car was driven continuously at varying speeds until the odometer hit 1,002 miles. It was then brought into a garage for mechanics to inspect. The engineers installed a front sway bar and ran further tests. The car went back onto the track after being regreased and undergoing an oil change. It was then driven continuously for the next twelve hours, stopping only to change drivers and to refuel. It was during the last fuel stop that someone accidentally put aviation fuel in the car. The report documenting the accident described the cause of the stalled engine as "vapor lock," although the incorrect fuel could have caused the engine to stall in a few different ways.[69]

The report also noted that the windshield had popped out exactly as the designers had hoped it would in such an accident. Although fan blades had been bent, the car's engine still ran perfectly. The fenders and body had suffered cosmetic damage, but the interior of the car was unharmed. The transmission and the suspension likewise remained operable.[70] Overall, the crash was a success.

So, too, were the rest of the endurance tests, although Tucker discovered a few things that would need to be corrected in production. The car's suspension was unconventional; much of the car's weight was supported by a "torsilastic suspension" system with rubber components. The rubber did not hold up to the excessive wear and tear, and some of the cars rode a few inches closer to the ground on the drive back to Chicago. The engineers were certain they could speak to their suppliers and get a stiffer and more durable compound going forward that would solve the problem.[71]

About a month after the tests, Tucker's advertising department sent out letters to dealers describing Offutt's accident to show how safe the Tucker sedan was. Still, the letter told the dealers to be careful with the information. Just as they had been concerned that seat belts would suggest the cars were unsafe, they were now concerned that photos of a wrecked Tucker might imply the cars were dangerous.

———

Before the Tucker plant was completely idled, the remaining employees did what they could to assemble the remaining cars. On November 11, 1948, Dan Leabu composed a memorandum to Tucker and the others that two more cars—#1045 and #1046—had been almost completed. The cars only needed transmissions. The assembly line crew had also rebuilt #1010.[72] Eventually, people picking over the remains of the plant would find transmissions for #1045 and #1046 and even the parts to assemble a few others. The final number of Tucker '48 sedans produced would be fifty-one if the Tin Goose was counted along with the others.

Around Thanksgiving, Tucker announced that the plant would be completely closed for the long weekend and that he was looking for additional financing. He told the press that he had been talking to private investors who might invest $10 million in the company and that he had applied for a $30 million loan from the Reconstruction Finance Corporation.[73]

Tucker took the opportunity to identify for the press the person he thought was behind the attacks on his business. The *Milwaukee Journal* reported, "Tucker blamed Senator Ferguson (Rep., Mich) for many of his troubles. He charged Ferguson with 'aiding and abetting a definite smear campaign.' He said Ferguson had stated that he was 'out to get Tucker and put Tucker in jail if it's the last thing' he ever did."[74]

Less than a week later, it was reported that Tucker's loan application to the RFC was denied.[75] RFC officials would not give the press a reason for the denial, but most people assumed it was because of the controversy surrounding Tucker and his company.

20

Bankruptcy

On November 22, 1948, people who had bought Tucker franchises filed an "involuntary petition in bankruptcy." If granted, it would force the company into bankruptcy, taking control away from Preston Tucker and allowing it to reorganize under new management and continue operating if it was economically feasible to do so.[1] A flurry of other legal actions buried Tucker and the corporation in litigation. The cases were assigned to federal judge Michael Igoe.

The cases ran the gamut, from simple lawsuits for unpaid bills to a suit filed by an attorney asking that Tucker be restrained from leaving the country. One of the other cases before Igoe was the action filed back in July by several Tucker Corporation stakeholders, who made outlandish claims of misconduct against Preston Tucker. The original suit, which named only Tucker himself and the corporation as defendants, had been thrown out on a technicality, but the plaintiffs refiled it.[2]

The refiled civil action named Preston Tucker personally along with the corporation and sixteen other defendants. Among them was Tucker's mother, presumably because she was the nominal owner of Ypsilanti Machine and Tool. Again, this action sought to have the assets of the corporation taken from Tucker and the current management. To support their position, the filers made serious allegations about how Preston Tucker had conducted business. They charged that the 589 engine Tucker had initially promoted was a "myth" and claimed that the corporation was "in no position" to begin mass production of autos because it was too short of funds.[3] The action also asked for an accounting of how much money the company had at its disposal, presumably because they had no idea. Among the allegations raised a second time were that Tucker had a secret home in Bogota, Columbia. But this time, they alleged not only that Tucker had purchased the home to escape from the country but also that he had bought the home with funds stolen from the company.[4]

The plaintiffs also claimed that the Tin Goose had been nothing more than a "reconstructed 1942 Oldsmobile," slightly modified to fool investors, and that Tucker had never built an operating 589 engine.[5] In fact, the complaint suggested that the Tin Goose was not even capable of driving in any direction—forward or reverse—because its engine "was not equipped with mechanical abilities." It is unclear if the plaintiffs or their attorneys were aware that the Tin Goose had been driven at its world premiere in front of thousands of witnesses. Tucker told the press, "It is inconceivable that supposedly intelligent attorneys could file a suit so rampant with inaccuracies as this one."[6]

Judge Igoe consolidated several of the bankruptcy hearings for the sake of simplicity, and set the matter for hearing at a later date.[7] The parties pushing the bankruptcy asked the judge to order Tucker and the corporate officers to come and immediately testify about the company's financial condition, but the judge denied the request, noting it was premature.[8]

————

Even with all his legal problems, Preston Tucker still believed that if he raised a few million dollars he could reopen his plant and resume manufacturing cars. It was a long shot. Rumors abounded of "angel" investors, even after Howard Hughes had publicly stated his lack of interest in the project. On January 3, 1949, an attorney appeared before Judge Igoe and said he represented an "unnamed interest" that was "willing and ready" to help put the Tucker Corporation "back on its feet."[9] The attorney would not publicly identify the interest but offered to tell the judge in chambers. The judge considered the possibility and temporarily stayed the legal proceedings.

Automotive insiders thought the most likely suspect was the Willys-Overland Motor Company, whose president had visited the plant recently.[10] Nothing came of this overture, but more than one company may have been considering a partnership with Tucker. The Checker Cab Manufacturing Company had also done some serious investigation into the possibility. Checker sent an engineer on January 4 to examine the factory, and Preston Tucker had lunch with Checker's president a little over a week later. The deal fell through but was of enough substance to be reported by the *New York Times*.[11]

To give Tucker time to locate new funding sources, in early 1949 Tucker's attorneys asked the court for permission to reorganize the company with their client still at the helm while litigating the claims against it. Tucker's attorneys told the court that the company had assets of $14,434,380 against liabilities of $1,643,175.[12] These figures must have surprised some people, with so many people claiming that the Tucker Corporation was financially ruined. Preston Tucker explained the rationale behind the numbers. The Tucker Corporation owned Aircooled Motors, the company in Syracuse it had bought to provide the '48's engine. The purchase price had been $1.8 million, and the company produced a steady profit of $400,000 annually. Tucker believed Aircooled was actually worth closer to $5 million.[13]

The court granted the request and appointed trustees to oversee the reorganization. They wouldn't have to make their first report until May 2. All the civil actions were put on hold. Tucker had bought himself a reprieve, but the new arrangement caused other complications. The SEC had not yet returned the corporation's financial records, and now with court-appointed overseers in place, the agency turned the documents over to trustees rather than giving them back to Tucker. Tucker would never be given access to them again.[14]

One litigant whose suit was put on hold was adman Cliff Knoble. Although he had resigned from and filed suit against the Tucker Corporation, he remained entangled with the company. Because he had been the one sending information to the dealers, many of them continued calling and writing to him after his departure. He decided to publish a newsletter specifically for them, detailing the latest news and weeding out the rumors that were now overwhelming the Tucker story. The newsletter, *As It Looks to Me*, was published by subscription. He sent the first issue to dealers across America and asked them to send him four dollars if they wanted future issues. He promised to return their money if the newsletter was not continued.

In the newsletters, he distanced himself from Preston Tucker, even going so far as to suggest that Tucker ought to be removed from the leadership of the company. In the first newsletter, he said he was motivated by his desire to see the company succeed and that there were many others with similar motivation. "It can be stated bluntly that there is virtual unanimity of opinion among them that the corporation cannot progress under the management of Preston Tucker."[15]

Knoble would remain one of the people who stood on the sidelines waiting to see what would happen, hoping to return to the Tucker Corporation if it emerged under new ownership.

21

The SEC Report

The SEC investigation culminated on December 20, 1948, with a 561-page secret report. It began with a fourteen-page introduction, telling Preston Tucker's story in an extremely slanted fashion. From page one, it took the position that Tucker was a fraud:

> In the wake of an extensive newspaper advertising program which gave widespread publicity to Tucker Corporation's claim that, under the guidance of Preston Tucker (described as a recognized automotive inventor and designing genius), the company was about to mass-produce a revolutionary but completely tested and proved new passenger car, Tucker Corporation filed a registration statement . . .[1]

The notion that Tucker was not a "recognized automotive inventor" or a "designing genius" was a major theme throughout the report. The SEC writers never explained how one measured these things or determined if they were true or false. They spent more than five hundred pages, however, hammering away on these points.

The SEC investigators had not only removed all the records and documents from the Tucker Corporation to comb through for ammunition but also interviewed at least forty-three people they considered important witnesses in the case against Tucker and his associates. Their report listed eight people the commission believed should be charged with crimes and then five other "possible Defendants." Among the latter was Charles Pearson, and the only allegation against him was that he had written the *Pic* article that started the Tucker public relations juggernaut.[2] Pearson would ultimately not be charged with any crime, but it was a remarkable suggestion: that a man face prison time for writing a magazine article.

A critical reader would notice problems with the report and its allegations almost immediately. Cliff Knoble was named as one of the "possible Defendants" and would eventually be charged and tried along with Preston Tucker. What had he done wrong, according to the SEC? Despite its best spinning of the facts, the worst they could say about him was:

> He was active in the composition and dissemination of various letters and news releases which materially assisted Tucker Corporation's publicity program, apparently directed during most of that time at lulling its security holders, franchise holders, and the public in general into a belief that all was going well in the operations of the company and that production of Tucker cars was constantly "just around the corner." When the company's affairs had so deteriorated (Summer, Fall, 1948) that it was necessary to admit publicly the impasse which its operations had reached, Knoble was active in the accompanying campaign in which letters were sent to the distributor-dealer organization claiming that this result had been caused by many factors (including political pressure, government interference, opposition by the major automotive manufacturers, strikes, etc.) which actually had nothing to do with the situation.[3]

Amazingly, they did not even suggest that Knoble knew the truth to be different from what he described, nor did they take into account that his job involved taking official statements of the company and simply passing them along to others. The SEC assumed the "factors" Knoble described "had nothing to do with the situation." They noted he had received "benefits" from "the Tucker venture" in the form of a salary.[4] For this, the SEC suggested he ought to be prosecuted.

The SEC report also maligned the progress the Tucker Corporation had actually made, hinting that many of its successes had been somehow illegal. Broker Floyd Cerf, the report noted, had never handled a stock offering of more than $2.51 million and only had a net worth of $87,000 at the time of the Tucker offering. Yet he had been confident "that the issue could be sold merely on the basis of the widespread public interest created by prior publicity concerning the organization and its plans."[5] While some people may have found it admirable that Cerf successfully sold a stock offering under these conditions, the SEC believed it was a crime.

The SEC knew that some people would ask why they had decided to investigate Tucker in the first place. What had the corporation done to draw attention to itself? It had filed a registration statement with the SEC—as required by law—and the SEC had decided "to determine whether stop order proceedings should be instituted."[6] It is unclear why the SEC jumped to that step, rather than simply examining the statement to see if it comported with the law. The agency just assumed that the Tucker Corporation had probably done something illegal already.

After scrutinizing Tucker and the corporation's affairs, the SEC admitted that when Tucker had submitted the amended registration statement earlier, "there remained no legal basis for a refusal by the Commission to permit the registration statement to become effective." Then what was the problem the SEC had with Tucker? "The Commission, however, was shocked by the character of the extensive publicity which had appeared" and felt the need to render an opinion above and beyond merely allowing the Tucker Corporation to sell its stock to the public.[7] In other words, the registration statement issued by the Tucker Corporation was proper and contained appropriate statements regarding the company, but the SEC was upset about the publicity Tucker had been receiving:

Since January 1946, there has been extensive publicity concerning the Tucker organization and its plans to manufacture a modern automobile.

In many periodicals, newspapers, sales brochures and company advertisements, which are part of the record before us, there has been widespread
comment as to the radical features the Tucker car possesses, elaborate and
conflicting claims as to its expected accomplishments and performance, and
exaggerated statements as to the funds invested by the management. Many
of the statements that have been publicized in the past appear to be grossly
misleading and, in many cases, false.[8]

So the SEC felt the need to warn the public about investing in the Tucker
Corporation. In fact, the SEC appeared to have been upset that the stock-
buying public had ignored its warnings and bought the stock anyway: "Little
heed was paid by purchasers of stock and franchises to the amended registration statement or to the related prospectus. Far more importance was attached
by such investors to the Tucker literature, advertisement, oral addresses, and
exhibits, judged by the findings of the investigation upon which this report
is based."[9] Again, Tucker had done nothing illegal. The SEC faulted the legal
activities of the Tucker Corporation in getting good press.

The SEC report was filled with guesswork by SEC investigators. It
described the Tin Goose's debut and derided the fact that the car was a
one-off and not a production model. While most people at the time knew
this, the SEC wrote that the exact opposite was true: "Many, if not all, of
those present assumed from the display and from the comments of company
officials that this car was a perfected, finished automobile which contained
the various features which had been previously advertised and which was
'frozen' for imminent volume production."[10] The SEC did not address how
it divined what "many, if not all, of those present" believed to be true.

There was another common theme to the SEC report: that the Tucker '48
sedan "was not a tested, proved automobile of sensational and revolutionary
character, but, rather, an untested, unproved conglomeration of highly questionable engineering ideas in a very preliminary experimental state with no
reasonable prospect for perfection in the foreseeable future."[11] Today, it is clear
this SEC opinion was wrong—at least, the owners of the forty-seven Tucker
'48s still extant would disagree with it. More important, what right did the
SEC have to weigh in on how good an automobile the Tucker '48 sedan was?

————

The damning report would be the foundation of Preston Tucker's subsequent prosecution. Tucker would not be able to read it until long after his trials were over, but his prosecutors would use it as a road map, and others would use the report as ammunition in what would become an all-out assault on Tucker and his company. For a few months, though, almost no one would even know the report existed. By federal statute, the report remained protected from disclosure to anyone outside the SEC. The Code of Federal Regulations governing the "Commodity and Securities Exchanges" (section 230.122) specifically prohibited "any member, officer, or employee of the Commission to disclose to any person . . . any information . . . obtained by the Commission" during an investigation.[12]

Despite these safeguards, more negative stories about Tucker began appearing in the press, many of them sprinkled with facts and information from sources with access to the Tucker Corporation's records and books. Tucker wrote a letter to the head of the Chicago SEC office that included clippings and articles containing information that had obviously originated within the SEC. Thomas B. Hart, the agency's regional administrator, responded:

> This is to acknowledge receipt of your letter of January 11, 1949, together with two newspaper clippings. I wish to advise you that at no time has this Commission ever furnished or made available any information to any newspaper or to any other unauthorized person, nor has any information ever been made available to any attorney representing or purporting to represent any group of Tucker Dealers.
>
> Please be assured, as I have advised you in the past, that the Commission's investigation has at all times been conducted in a fair and impartial manner and in the strictest confidence and only for the purpose of ascertaining the true facts.
>
> Very truly yours,
>
> (s) THOMAS B. HART
>
> Regional administrator[13]

A family photograph from around 1904 shows many members of Tucker's family. Preston Tucker is the young child, sitting on the lap of his grandfather, Milford Preston. Milford was the father of Preston's mother, Lucille, who is on the far right. Shirley Tucker, Preston's father, is not in the picture. *Courtesy of TACA*

Preston Tucker as a young boy. His love of vehicles began with bicycles, then expanded to motorcycles and later automobiles. *Cynthia Tucker Fordon Collection*

Tucker sits on a Harley-Davidson motorcycle while visiting the Indianapolis Motor Speedway. Tucker attended the annual race there and often spent the days preceding the competition visiting the garages and speaking with drivers and mechanics. *Cynthia Tucker Fordon Collection*

Preston Tucker and his wife, Vera. *Cynthia Tucker Fordon Collection*

Tucker helped the Detroit-based Mundus Brewing Company with its fleet of delivery trucks. *Courtesy of TACA*

The innovative racers Tucker and Harry Miller build for Henry Ford in 1935 could have been much more successful, but Tucker oversold Ford on how quickly they could be built. As a result of their rushed production schedule, the cars suffered from a steering gear failure in the first race in which they were entered. Today, this Miller-Ford racer is on display at the Henry Ford Museum near Detroit. Tucker is not mentioned in any of the signage accompanying the car. *Author photo*

Tucker's prototype Tiger Tank made the news as World War II loomed, but the US government passed on buying the armored vehicle.
Courtesy of TACA

Tucker also designed and patented a motorized gun turret, but the military passed on purchasing it as well—despite persistent legends claiming that it was widely used during the war. It wasn't.
Courtesy of TACA

Tucker's earliest designs for a postwar automobile were less practical than what he eventually built. This model shows the Tucker Torpedo and its more pronounced fenders.
Courtesy of the Petersen Museum

From the patent for
Tucker's "Automobile."
The lines of this illustration
show the more practical
shape of the Tucker '48.
Author's collection

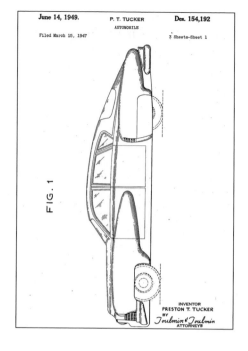

June 14, 1949.   P. T. TUCKER   Des. 154,192

AUTOMOBILE

Filed March 15, 1947   3 Sheets-Sheet 1

FIG. 1

INVENTOR
PRESTON T. TUCKER
BY
Toulmin & Toulmin
ATTORNEYS

Tucker hoped to
broaden his product
line once the '48 was in
full-scale production.
One item being
developed was this
unusual work truck.
Courtesy of TACA

Another rendering of
a Tucker concept car.
Whether drawings like
this were ever meant
to lead to production is
unclear. *Courtesy of the
Petersen Museum*

Preston holds a model of a Tucker automobile with Vera at his side. The model has no roof, even though Tucker never built a convertible. *Cynthia Tucker Fordon Collection*

Tucker always appeared impeccably attired, and very few people, even when visiting him at home, saw him wearing anything other than dress clothing. *Courtesy of TACA*

Tucker was the public face of the corporation, and his portrait was ever present in the company's advertising and public relations efforts. *Cynthia Tucker Fordon Collection*

Tucker surrounded himself with industry veterans when he launched his company. Many of them left after the company's public offering, amid controversy over how the company was being run. *Courtesy of TACA*

The Tucker factory in Chicago was impressive, and certainly led many investors to believe the company would succeed. Touted as the largest building of its type in the world, it had been built as part of the United States' massive armament efforts during World War II. *Courtesy of TACA*

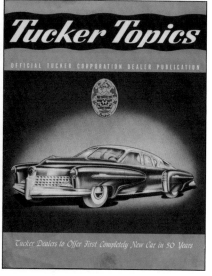

Tucker Topics was the company newsletter. A beautiful publication, its first edition carried a stylized artist's rendering of the automobile. *Courtesy of TACA*

At the unveiling of the Tucker automobile in June 1947, Tucker took to the stage along with some models the press dubbed the "Tuckerettes." *Courtesy of TACA*

Tucker's daughter christened the Tin Goose with champagne, spraying Tucker in the process. *Courtesy of TACA*

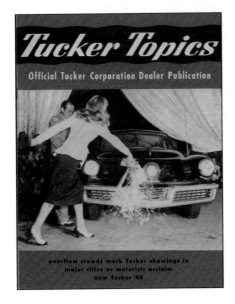

The second volume of *Tucker Topics* carried a picture of the Tin Goose's launch on its cover. Note that the image is not the same as the previous photo of the event: Tucker is standing in a different position and the curtains are different. The scene was clearly re-created for the purposes of marketing. *Courtesy of Mark Lieberman*

The Tin Goose in the factory. The easiest way to tell the Tin Goose from the production models is by looking at the rear doors. The production models carried "suicide doors"—the doors hinged at the back, meaning airflow might cause them to fly open if they were unlatched while the car was in motion. *Courtesy of TACA*

Publicity photos of the cars often showed the trunk or the hood open, to call attention to the car's unusual—especially for the time—placement of the engine in the rear. *Courtesy of TACA*

The doors also curved into the roof. This made getting into and out of the car a bit easier, especially in a day when so many people wore hats. *Courtesy of TACA*

The Tin Goose's B-pillar—the piece of metal between the doors—was different on the left and right side, because the rear door hinges attached to it. Alex Tremulis realized that by giving the production model "suicide doors" and hinging the rear doors to the C-pillar instead, the B-pillars could be interchangeable, saving a small amount of money on tooling costs. *Courtesy of TACA*

The Tin Goose was driven at a meeting of distributors and dealers. Critics claimed the Tin Goose was inoperable, but this was not the case. The car was not practical due to bugs in its experimental drivetrain, and it was not driven very far. But the car was drivable. *Courtesy of TACA*

The manufacturing process involved the creation of bucks, wooden models of the car's body and its various parts, on which the tooling for the car's metal panels would be performed. *Courtesy of TACA*

The passenger section of the car was assembled first; the front end and drivetrain would be added later. *Courtesy of TACA*

Technicians prepare to test the 589 engine. When the engine performed poorly, Tucker reluctantly agreed to consider an alternative power plant for his car. *Courtesy of TACA*

The engine eventually used in the production car was an opposed six-cylinder engine that had originally been designed for aircraft use. In the '48, the engine was liquid-cooled and carried the distinctive TUCKER insignia on its intake manifolds. *Author photo*

One view of the machine shop inside the Tucker factory. Many of the machines had been left over from the plant's days as a manufacturer of aircraft engines. *Courtesy of TACA*

Various parts manufactured for the earliest cars being built at the Tucker factory. *Courtesy of TACA*

A view of the engine shop. The blocks are distinctive in that each accommodates three pistons—with each engine containing two such blocks, sitting on opposite sides of the crankshaft. *Courtesy of TACA*

An engine assembly line was utilized to build and prepare the engines for installation in the cars. *Courtesy of TACA*

Once assembled, the engines were stored until they were needed for final assembly. At one point, the company had more than a hundred engines ready for installation in cars. *Courtesy of TACA*

Production '48s roll down the assembly line. Notice that the front three cars have had their front clips added, while those behind do not yet have their hoods or front fenders. *Courtesy of TACA*

A test chassis was often used for display purposes at exhibitions. It allowed people to see the unusual layout of the Tucker '48's drivetrain. The chassis was also used on occasion to give visitors test drives at the factory. *Courtesy of TACA*

The interiors of the cars were added on the assembly line before the bodies were fully assembled. *Courtesy of TACA*

An unfinished body shows how much work still needed to be done before the car was painted. The men looking at the car are not working on it; they very well may have been dealers, who were known to stop by the factory and check up on the progress of the business. *Courtesy of TACA*

Various pieces of sheet metal await assembly. Although Tucker often gave dizzying numbers to the press of how many cars he planned to build, he never had the parts to build more than about fifty cars. *Courtesy of TACA*

Unpainted cars on the assembly line. The man grinding metal on the second car suggests that some of the cars still needed a bit of bodywork at this stage before they could be painted. *Courtesy of TACA*

This car is clearly being used for display purposes, as it is roped off. The visitors could be dealers or distributors. Interestingly, this car does not have the stock bumper that was normally fitted onto a production car— its bumper does not have the cutouts for the six exhaust pipes. *Courtesy of TACA*

Tucker and some of his executives examine a partially assembled Tucker '48 as it moves down the assembly line. *Courtesy of TACA*

Even though dealers never got inventory to sell, many of them set up their stores in preparation. *Courtesy of TACA*

Another Tucker '48 is shown to a group of Tucker dealers, eager to receive their inventory. *Courtesy of TACA*

One of the better-known publicity photos of Preston Tucker, kneeling in front of his creation. *Courtesy of TACA*

Tucker demonstrates how well the Tucker '48 accommodates the matching Tucker luggage—in its trunk located at the front of the car. *Courtesy of TACA*

Tucker exits the courtroom of Walter LaBuy, the judge in the criminal case. Although Tucker was acquitted, the trial ruined him financially and drained him physically. *Courtesy of TACA*

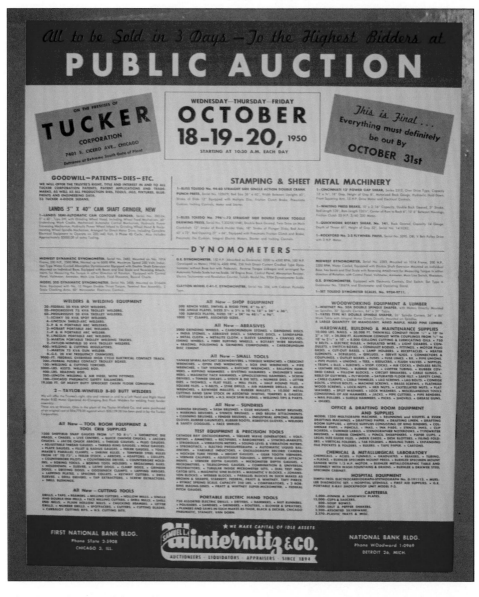

The physical assets of the Tucker Corporation were liquidated at public auction. The bulk of the assets were machines and equipment, but items up for bid also included Tucker automobiles, both assembled and in parts. *Author photo*

After the trial, Tucker moved back to Ypsilanti, Michigan. Behind his house were some other buildings, including a garage and his old machine shop. *Cynthia Tucker Fordon Collection*

Tucker in 1952. He still loved cars and hoped to launch another car company. *Courtesy of TACA*

Preston Tucker flanked by sons Preston Jr. and John, along with two grandchildren, Preston III and Cynthia. *Cynthia Tucker Fordon Collection*

The summer before he passed away, Preston and Vera hosted relatives at their home in Ypsilanti. By this time, Preston had been diagnosed with lung cancer. *Cynthia Tucker Fordon Collection*

Tucker #1046 is an example of a well-restored Tucker '48. *Courtesy of Mark Lieberman*

The rising prices of these cars guarantee that the remaining examples will be well cared for. *Courtesy of Mark Lieberman*

This Tucker '48 underwent a restoration to bring it back to the condition in which it left the factory the day it was completed. *Courtesy of Mark Lieberman*

The dashboard and driver controls in the Tucker '48 are simple and within easy reach of the driver. The gear selector is on the small shaft on the right-hand side of the steering column. *Courtesy of Mark Lieberman*

The area under the dash on the passenger side was described as a "safety chamber," into which a passenger could drop to escape injury in a car accident. The practicality of this feature was always subject to debate. *Courtesy of Mark Lieberman*

The only dial on the dashboard held the speedometer, along with four gauges. When the car was not moving, the speedometer needle rested at the 12:00 position. *Courtesy of Mark Lieberman*

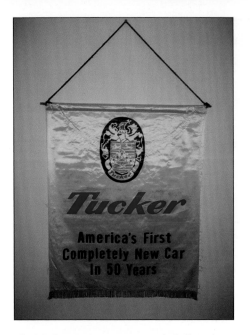

The Tucker Corporation provided all manner of advertising regalia for its dealers and distributors. Alongside the name of the company, these items often included a copy of the Tucker family crest. *Courtesy of TACA*

The family crest was also included as ornamentation on the car itself. *Courtesy of TACA*

This Tucker '48 resides at the Petersen Automotive Museum in Los Angeles. *Courtesy of the Petersen Museum*

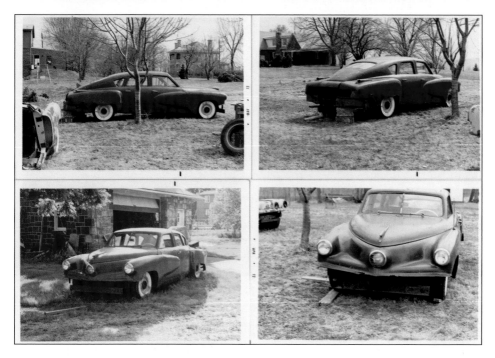

The Tin Goose in the early 1970s. The car had been sold at the liquidation auction and ended up parked in a field, partially resting on blocks. The bumpers had been removed, and nearby sat a piece of another Tucker '48, #1018. *Courtesy of Mark Lieberman*

One-half of Tucker #1018. This is one of the three completed Tucker '48s that are no longer intact. *Courtesy of Mark Lieberman*

The Tin Goose was eventually restored and is now owned by the Swigart Museum in Huntingdon, Pennsylvania. It has also been taken to car shows and even briefly visited Washington, DC, as seen here. *Courtesy of John Tucker*

The Tucker home in Ypsilanti. The house still stands, but the other buildings that were behind it are now gone. *Author photo*

A Tucker Corporation manufacturer's license plate. *Author photo*

Tucker did not know it yet, but Hart was lying. Still, there was no question that the press's information was coming from within the SEC, despite the federal statute that prohibited the disclosure of any of the information or documents uncovered in the investigation.

Tucker's own public relations staff attempted to counter the relentlessly negative publicity of the past few months. Around this time, the Tucker Corporation released a film, *Tucker: The Man and the Car*, a half-hour overview of the Tucker Corporation, its founder, and the Tucker '48. A narrator gushed about the futuristic car and its patriotic and visionary promoter. "But first, let me tell you a little more about the man, Tucker. Preston Tucker is a man who believes first, last, and always in the American way of free enterprise. Though there are those who believe there is no more room in this country for new industries or perhaps new competition."[14]

Tucker's life story filled the screen, from his first encounter with a car to his buying and selling cars as a young man. The narration was accompanied by film of Tucker at his desk and shots of his cars—several of them—driving on scenic country roads. A short section on his wartime efforts to create a combat car introduced the Tucker turret and may have been the origin of the myth that his turrets were widely used in the war.

The film walked viewers through the factory and down the assembly line, and made it very clear: the cars were real. The film also told of Tucker's fight to get his plant and even a little about the troubles of selling the stock. After taking the viewer through the production process and showing the tests at Indianapolis, the film made a sales pitch: "Now, just imagine. You starting a pleasant weekend in a Tucker. Put the suitcases in the front and away you go."

But the film ended with a comment about the obstacles facing Tucker: "If Preston Tucker and the corporation had not had to fight for their very existence, you, the great American public, would now be the proud owners of the first completely new car in fifty years." The music built to a crescendo as the camera focused on an American flag, proudly waving in front of the Tucker plant.[15]

22

The Grand Jury

On February 14, 1949, the *New York Times* reported that a federal grand jury was being convened in Chicago to investigate Preston Tucker and the Tucker Corporation for criminal activity. If Tucker had thought the SEC investigation had been intrusive, it was only because he had not known what the US Attorney's Office was about to do. That office served a subpoena on the Tucker Corporation that, according to the *New York Times*, "requisitions almost every conceivable Tucker record and paper dated from Dec. 1, 1946, to Jan. 31, 1949. Twelve to fifteen more subpoenas are expected to be issued before the end of the week."[1] At least publicly, though, Tucker remained optimistic; he said he was looking forward to the opportunity to "explain our side of the story."[2]

A *Detroit News* reporter, Martin Hayden, had recently visited the Justice Department in Washington to discuss the Alger Hiss espionage case. In a conversation with Alex Campbell, the chief of the criminal division, Hayden's hometown entered the conversation. Campbell said, "Incidentally, you are from Detroit. We are going to prosecute a lot of people from your hometown." Hayden asked the nature of the prosecution. Campbell said, "The Tucker automobile fraud."[3]

Hayden knew little about Tucker and did not follow up at the time, but after hearing about the grand jury, he asked Campbell for more details. According to Campbell, Tucker had pulled a fast one at the annual shareholders meeting, setting up a "fake assembly line" to fool investors. Campbell told Hayden that Tucker would be prosecuted, but there was another problem: the SEC was aware of Tucker's fraudulent activities and had done nothing about it. It was because of the SEC's inaction, Campbell said, that the Justice Department was being forced to act.

Hayden knew Harry McDonald at the SEC very well and was surprised to hear that the SEC had failed to act on such an obvious violation of securities law. The next day he met with McDonald. "What is the matter with the SEC?" Hayden asked. "You are supposed to be protecting the investors of the country, and now it takes the Justice Department to find out what is going on?"

Taken aback by the accusation, McDonald told Hayden the SEC had done a thorough investigation of Tucker. "Why, the whole Justice Department action is based on a report that we prepared for them. We gave them all the evidence." To prove his point, he made an offer: "I will show you the report, and you can see it for yourself, that we have not been lacking in diligence in our duty."

———

The grand jury convened on February 21, 1949. The investigation was led by US Attorney Otto Kerner Jr. The panel had a copy of the monstrous SEC report to use as an outline.

The grand jury subpoenaed what amounted to several carloads of documents. Preston Tucker decided to make good use of the opportunity for some free publicity. To underscore his operation's legitimacy, Tucker loaded all the requested documents into eight Tucker sedans and drove them to the courthouse,[4] where he gave an impromptu press conference from the front seat of one of the cars. He noted that he had not been personally called to testify but would be happy to if asked. "I have nothing to hide."[5] "I don't know of anything we've done that's wrong. We can account for the $27 million which we collected. We have $15 million in assets, including $7 million in current assets. We've run a total of fifty or sixty cars through our assembly line and we have 100 cars in various stages of production." The *New York Herald Tribune* said Tucker expected the investigation to clear his name and allow the corporation to get back to business. The paper also, however, noted Tucker's other problems, including a "flock of lawsuits."[6]

The grand jury called ninety-five witnesses over three and a half months and created a ten-thousand-page transcript.[7] Eddie Offutt recounted the Indianapolis tests and was grilled about whether they had actually driven the cars to the track under their own power.[8] The testimony was taken in secret, but rumors abounded as to what others had testified to. At least one person was said to have told the grand jury that the SEC's prosecution was driven by Senator Homer Ferguson's desire to "get Tucker."[9]

On March 3, 1949, SEC commissioner Harry McDonald spoke to a meeting of stockbrokers in Chicago. He did not mention that his organization was busy attacking the Tucker Corporation on the other side of town, but he did address the role the SEC and its people played in the business. "May I make this one observation? After having served two years on the SEC, and having come daily in intimate contact with not only the other commissioners but the directors and staff members of the various divisions, I am satisfied that they have only one, sincere purpose—and that is to be constructively helpful."[10]

Less than a week later, McDonald contacted Martin Hayden again and offered to make good on his promise to prove that the SEC was doing its part in prosecuting Tucker. He asked Hayden to meet him at the Statler Hotel, where McDonald was living. There, McDonald handed Hayden a copy of the SEC report, telling him he could read it and write a story based on its contents, as long as he kept his source a secret.[11] It was important for McDonald to ensure Hayden's discretion, as the commissioner was breaking the law by sharing the report.

Hayden studied the document and drafted a story that ran on the front page of the *Detroit News* on March 13. Hayden simply parroted the charges raised in the report without examining or questioning any of them. The headline read, GIGANTIC TUCKER FRAUD CHARGED IN SEC REPORT.[12] Hayden did not bother to check any of the story's facts, nor did he talk to Preston Tucker. He later claimed he did not need to. Whether the report was accurate was irrelevant: he was reporting on the report's existence, not its contents.[13]

After the *Detroit News* ran its piece, other newspapers around the country ran similar pieces, savaging Tucker and his business. Hayden could not prove it, but he was certain that McDonald had shown the document to the other reporters as well. Many of their stories contained information he had not reported which could only have come from someone else with access to the report.[14]

———

On June 10 the grand jury issued indictments against Preston Tucker and seven of his associates on charges of mail fraud, conspiracy, and SEC regulation violations.[15] Indicted alongside Tucker were Mitchell Dulian, Floyd Cerf, Robert Pierce, Fred Rockelman, Otis Radford, Abe Karatz, and Cliff Knoble.[16] Knoble learned of the charges against him while on a visit to his hometown, when a friend showed him the story on the front page of a newspaper.[17] Of the eight men charged, only six had been proposed as defendants in the SEC report. Amazingly, the SEC had not suggested prosecuting Karatz, the financial promoter with a criminal record. The SEC might have thought he would be more useful as a witness. The grand jury indicted him anyway. Likewise, Otis Radford, who served as the company's treasurer, had not been mentioned by the SEC as a possible defendant.

Tucker's response to the charges was firm: "The only crime I have committed is starting a new business."[18] He told reporters that the prosecution was being driven by sources with ulterior motives. "The government put me into business, and now it's trying to wreck me."[19] One paper quoted Tucker blaming the prosecution on "a few people in high places who are tools of vested interests. . . . The auto tycoons of Detroit are behind it."[20]

At least one stock exchange suspended trading in Tucker Corporation stock, which had fallen from five dollars to forty cents a share. Newspapers unanimously clamored for Tucker's hide, reporting on the "flop" of his company and all but saying he was guilty of a massive fraud. Most articles stressed how much money Tucker had raised and compared it with how few cars had been produced. And even those, according to the slanted reporting, were "unable to run backward."[21]

Time magazine's report on Tucker's indictment reflected the new spin:

> The indictment made no attempt to set forth the complex schemes by which Tucker had raised—and spent—$28 million collected from the sale of stock and dealer franchises for his Torpedo 8 [*sic*]. The grand jury merely totted up Tucker's statements and labeled each one "false." Said the jury: Tucker & Associates, "seeking to capitalize on the unusual demand" for autos, falsely "represented [Tucker] as an automotive inventor and designing genius" and obtained money "for [their own] personal benefit and profit" by "payments of excessive salaries and expense accounts to themselves, by the creation of fictitious experimental and development projects."[22]

The magazine left readers with no doubt that Tucker was guilty. "The investors in Tucker had only themselves to blame; the Securities & Exchange Commission had said practically the same thing when it blew the whistle on Tucker's initial effort to sell stock."[23]

The article noted that each defendant faced a possible 155 years in prison and $60,000 in fines.[24] It also threw in some "facts" that were simply untrue, such as that the Tucker '48s were built with "motors lifted from the cars of other manufacturers."[25] Tucker had said the grand jury indictment was "the biggest rape of free enterprise ever perpetrated on this country"; *Time* told its readers to wait for a jury to "decide who had been raped."[26]

Collier's *and* Reader's Digest

On June 25, 1949, *Collier's*, a magazine with a circulation of over three million,[1] published a negative piece about Tucker.[2] To boost readership, the magazine ran ads in the *New York Times*, *New York Tribune*, and the *Cleveland Plain Dealer* with the header HOW TUCKER MADE A SUCKER OUT OF AMERICA.[3] *Reader's Digest* would republish a shorter version of the piece in its September 1949 edition, for which the publication paid $2,000.[4] The *Collier's* article, in one form or another, would be read by millions.

"The Fantastic Story of the Tucker Car" reminded readers how Tucker had promised a futuristic car with so much fanfare. But "behind the glamour the Torpedo looked a little different," the article's description of the Tin Goose's failings began. It had taken seven hours of frantic work to prepare for its debut. It needed auxiliary batteries to start. It had no reverse gear. It was nothing more than a reworked Oldsmobile. Much of the story was inaccurate, but that was of little importance. The real gist of the piece was that Tucker's car was a facade to allow him to rob innocent Americans. The subtitle of the *Reader's Digest* version was "Preston Tucker's 26-Million-Dollar Bubble."[5]

Major portions of the article were clearly taken verbatim from the SEC report. But other elements were more inventive. At one point, Lester Velie, the *Collier's* writer who received $1,750 for writing the piece, referred to the carmaker as "P. Tommy Tucker" and "P.T. Tucker," associating Tucker's name with the circus man P. T. Barnum.[6] He repeatedly referred to the Tucker sedans as "handmade" and wrote that the Tin Goose "had no reverse gear," "could not back up," was "non-reversing," and, in a later passage, called it the "hand-made car, the nonreversing, seldom-driven Tin Goose."[7]

Still, the most defamatory portions related to Tucker and those around him:

> Tucker's people at this time were a mixed group. Shuttling with him between Chicago, Detroit and Washington were Karatz and another contact man described in a pamphlet of the William J. Burns International Detective Agency as a "check passer and confidence man" wanted by police of two cities. In his entourage also was a Countess Consuela Talalla, of piquant accent and vivacious manner, who had met Tucker in a New York night club. Divorced later, she was seen much with Tucker and once sought to intervene with Chicago police when they jailed another Tucker aide for passing a bad check.[8]

Velie never gave his source for the information on Tucker's dark associates. Interestingly enough, it was not in the SEC report; even the SEC never sank so low as to accuse Tucker of founding his corporation with help from wanted criminals and future divorcees. Some of Velie's information may have come from Homer Ferguson's 1946 hearing into the awarding of Tucker's plant by the WAA.

Velie also never mentioned that he had lifted major portions of his story *verbatim* from the SEC report.[9] He misled his readers into thinking he had interviewed SEC officials and others mentioned in the report. In retrospect, it seems clear that Lester Velie condensed the agency's monstrous volume into a shorter piece that he could sell under his byline and sensationalized what he could.

Velie ended by suggesting that the SEC needed more authority to enforce security laws and that the laws needed improvement. "Perhaps if the SEC had required the prospectus in the Tucker case to be written in simple

English, and in four pages instead of 15, the facts might have trickled down to the public." Nowhere in his article, though, does he give examples of any of the "stilted and tortured legalistic English" he claimed was in the prospectus, nor does he name any facts that were omitted.[10]

Velie admitted he went for a long drive with Tucker in one of the cars he ridiculed. "This writer drove with [Tucker] from Chicago to Detroit in his handmade, pearl-gray Tucker Torpedo. We paused for lunch near Lansing, and a crowd gathered about the sleek, dashing car. 'The only car in town,' said one admirer. 'No other car can touch it,' said another. 'Why don't those fellows in Washington and Detroit let you build it, Mr. Tucker?'"[11] Velie did not address the irony of having ridden in a supposedly sham automobile.

Tucker and others wondered if *Collier's* had been motivated to publish the article by its many advertisers with ties to the auto industry. In 1949 alone, *Collier's* sold $4,341,955 worth of advertising to sellers of automobiles and automotive accessories.[12]

More periodicals piled onto the story. *Coronet*, a general interest magazine with a circulation of two and a half million, ran "Good-Bye to Tucker's Dream Car" in November 1949. The article was a mishmash of the negative things people were saying about Tucker, most of it unsourced. Many of its facts were wrong. According to *Coronet*, Tucker's advisers told him he needed a factory before he could raise money, when in fact they insisted that he needed a car. The magazine also claimed that Tucker's dream car would have a periscope through its roof allowing the driver a better view. The body would be aluminum and the car would be able to stop on ice. The engine could be replaced at any service station, "just like a battery." The Tin Goose needed to be pushed by hand because it did not run. The inaccurate description of the Tucker sedan was so outlandish, readers would believe any investor to have been a fool to invest in the venture.

What few facts the story got right were garbled, misstated, or given out of order. At this point it was clear: the American press felt it could print anything it wanted about Tucker, the uglier the better. The piece ended with: "At his trial in Chicago, Preston Tucker will confront a new job of supersalesmanship when he tries to disprove the government's charge that his 'Dream Car' was a fraud."[13]

24

The Trial

As the media uproar grew throughout mid-1949, Preston Tucker's trial was getting underway. The proceedings were held in the Chicago Federal Building, famous for being the site of the trial of Al Capone.[1] It was the same courthouse where the corporation's bankruptcy proceedings were being held.

On June 23, Tucker and six codefendants voluntarily appeared in court to answer the charges and posted bail. Karatz was in California and the prosecutor indicated he could appear later. News reports that reported his plea—"Preston Tucker Pleads Innocent"—also noted that "Tucker drove to the courthouse in his gray Tucker."[2] Tucker, Karatz, Cerf, and Pierce posted a $25,000 bond each. Dulian, Rockelman, Radford, and Knoble had to post $10,000 apiece.[3] Some defendants had moved out of the area after the plant closed and now needed to find ways to pay for a legal defense and a place to stay, and still support their families. Even though the SEC had spent a year preparing its case, the defendants had to prepare their defense in only ninety days.[4]

Those who could afford to hire good attorneys did so. Cerf hired Floyd Thompson, a former Illinois Supreme Court justice who was one of the nation's most respected attorneys. Thompson had successfully defended Samuel Insull, the man who ran Commonwealth Edison before its stock crashed during the Depression.[5] Insull was tried three times on charges that included mail fraud, and Thompson guided him to acquittal each time.

The defendants were working on their defense as the nation's news outlets released more and more pieces bashing the Tucker Corporation, based on information that could only have come from the "secret" SEC report.[6] Yet the SEC still refused to share the document with Tucker and his codefendants. The prosecution insisted to the court that in accordance with the law, the SEC report had been kept strictly confidential—that it had never been shown to anyone outside the SEC or the US Attorney's Office—and thus it was not something Tucker was legally entitled to see. It was clear that the agency was going out of its way to try the case in the media, and the report was its biggest weapon.

Albert Dilling, Robert Pierce's defense attorney, was so frustrated by the negative pretrial publicity he asked Judge Walter LaBuy, who was overseeing the criminal trial, to hold the publishers of *Reader's Digest* and *Collier's* in contempt and order an adjournment of the trial, hoping something could be done about the negative press. The judge said he would take the request under advisement. But jury selection began the next day, October 4.[7]

———

The prosecution hoped to get many of Tucker's friends and associates—the ones not charged with conspiracy—to testify against him. Many of them knew they had dodged a bullet when they weren't charged, since the prosecution's net had caught some people whose only possible sin was an association with Tucker. If the prosecutors asked you to turn on Tucker and you didn't, would you be charged next?

Before the trial, prosecutors had contacted Alex Tremulis. Would he come in and talk with them before the trial? He met with Robert J. Downing, an assistant prosecutor, who asked him about the Tin Goose. Wasn't it true that the name Tin Goose was given to the car because it was "hodgepodge . . . built from an old Oldsmobile"?[8] Tremulis explained to him that the name was a term of endearment and was not meant to denigrate the car. He told Downing that the Ford Tri-Motor airplane was also called the Tin Goose, likewise in a positive fashion.

As for the Oldsmobile, it had been used as a buck—a frame upon which to assemble the parts as they were fabricated—when Tremulis was given the task of building the prototype in sixty days. The alternative would have been to make the framework out of wood, but the Tucker Corporation did not have a pattern shop at the time. It was faster to make one out of metal because they had an excellent team of metalworkers. Tremulis sensed that the prosecutor did not care to hear his explanation. Later he said, "Had I known that the name Tin Goose would be used as an instrument to pound nails into the coffin of the Tucker Corporation, I would have personally carved the automobile out of marble."[9]

Interestingly, even though Tremulis would be called as a witness at trial and was a major figure in the design of the Tucker '48, the SEC gave no indication that it had interviewed him during its own investigation. His name is absent from the list of "Supporting Witnesses" in its report.[10] One wonders if his supportive attitude toward the company led to him being omitted. How many other unfavorable witnesses did the SEC leave out?

———

As the trial date approached, a group composed of Tucker dealers, stockholders, and distributors announced they wanted to reopen the Tucker plant and manufacture cars without Preston Tucker. To do this, they proposed a stock offering to raise $20 million. Then they would seek more funding from the Reconstruction Finance Corporation.[11] It was similar to the path Tucker had been on when he was sidetracked by the criminal charges. Anticipating that some might wonder what would be different about this effort, they said the money raised would "be used only in the process of manufacturing automobiles."[12]

The parties seeking to take over the company hired an engineering firm to assess the corporation and its assets and determine what it would take to begin mass production of the Tucker automobile. After two months of study, the firm announced it would cost no less than $71 million to accomplish the task. The cars would have to be sold for almost $3,300 to make the venture worthwhile. They recommended scrapping the Tucker design. Gone would be the Cord transmission, which Tucker had planned to discontinue anyway. They would eliminate the center headlight, use a conventional suspension and frame, and redesign the body panels and bumpers. Some changes were purely cosmetic, hinting that they simply disliked Tucker's car because it was different. One headline said, PRESTON TUCKER WOULDN'T KNOW HIS OWN AUTO.[13] The matter was set for a hearing.

———

The criminal trial started on October 5, 1949, before a jury of eight women and four men.[14] The previous day in bankruptcy court, Judge Igoe had canceled the Tucker Corporation's lease on the Chicago plant,[15] so headlines announcing the opening of the trial often mentioned the loss of the plant— for example, TUCKER LOSES AUTO PLANT; TRIAL OPENS. The loss of the plant likely meant the end of the endeavor,[16] but the parties seeking to take over the operation without Tucker continued fighting. They told the court that if they were allowed to proceed, not only could they begin profitably manufacturing Tucker autos, but the first ones would be rolling off the assembly line within ninety days.[17] The judge did not appear to be convinced.

At the criminal trial, opening statements laid out the legal arguments for the jury and the press, who would report daily on the proceedings. US Attorney Otto Kerner Jr. said that the defendants "obtained money by means of untrue statements of material facts and that the defendants conspired to violate the laws of the United States."[18] Millions of dollars had been raised with "false and misleading advertisements" and then squandered through "misuse of the funds."

Defense attorney Frank J. McAdams responded that Tucker had encountered "innumerable obstacles" and still "missed by only a few weeks attaining mass production."[19] He told the jury how the announcement that the SEC was investigating the company in mid-1948 had begun a chain of events that doomed the enterprise. "That very same day, the War Assets Administration

rejected the Tucker Corp.'s bid for a steel blast furnace. The SEC investigation continued up to the time of the indictment. It destroyed all credit of
the corporation. The investigation was the fatal blow. It blocked the small
amount of additional financing which was needed to put the Tucker automobile into mass production." He said the company had only needed another
$3 million when the SEC actions shut down the plant. He summarized by
telling the jury that the defendants had all acted "in good faith" and that the
statements made in Tucker advertising "were and are true."

Entering and leaving the courthouse became an ordeal for Tucker—a bit
more than for the other defendants, who were not as recognizable. Tucker
had appeared in the press so much in previous years and had been so willing to talk that now reporters often mobbed him as he entered or departed
the courthouse. Tucker's son John explored the building and discovered
a circuitous route that took his father away from the reporters by taking
an elevator the wrong direction, crossing a floor, and then taking another
elevator. By doing this, Tucker evaded the press on days he didn't want to
be bothered with them.[20]

Tucker was understandably concerned about his financial well-being. Not
only was he spending a fortune on attorneys, he worried about creditors coming after his personal assets. Around this time he approached management
of the co-op where he owned the two apartments and sought to have them
transferred into his mother's name. If he had thought of it when he moved in,
he could easily have put his mother's apartment in her name, but he hadn't.
Now, the management refused.[21] Their reasons were never made public, but
it seems likely they viewed his request as an attempt to hide his assets. Tucker
would be forced to weather the legal storm and see what happened.

Among the first witnesses called was Charles Pearson, author of the *Pic*
article, which had started the buzz for Tucker. Pearson admitted writing
the article, and the prosecution asked him to read the entire article to the
jury. Some reporters wondered what the purpose of Pearson's testimony
was, speculating that the prosecution "apparently planned to try and prove
that the article was part of a conspiracy on the part of Tucker and his codefendants."[22] If that was the case, why wasn't Pearson charged?

Pearson later wrote about his time on the stand:

I was one of the first witnesses, and when I got back to Chicago to take the stand and saw Tucker again, I could see that he had taken a terrific beating since I had seen him a few months before. His nerves were on edge and he was depressed, and bitter against the forces and men who had put him out of business before the trial even started. Yet he was at the same time confident that he would be vindicated. No matter how events were against him, nothing could shake his confidence in himself.[23]

The prosecution ran into trouble with their fourth witness—of more than seventy planned. Mark Mourne, Tucker's cousin, had been one of the corporation's founders and testified about the early days of the company. At the time he was called to testify, Mourne was an attorney in Colorado.[24] The prosecutor asked him if he had discussed Abe Karatz with Tucker, and the defense attorneys objected. The jury was sent out and the court warned the prosecution to steer clear of Karatz's criminal history, which had been ruled inadmissible. After the judge made his point, the jury returned, and the prosecution asked the witness what he had talked about with Tucker.[25]

"I told Mr. Tucker that Mr. Karsten [Karatz] had a criminal record."

Attorneys for the defense immediately objected and demanded a mistrial. US Attorney Kerner, of course, opposed the suggestion. Kerner argued that Karsten's criminal record—conspiracy to defraud a bank more than fifteen years earlier—was "similar in character and related in time" to the charges for which Karsten and the others were now on trial.[26]

The judge disagreed and declared a mistrial. The court told the parties they would start over after picking a new jury.[27] While a new trial might seem extreme, it was the correct decision in this instance. The defendants were being tried together, and the court had ruled that one defendant's criminal history—a single conviction fifteen years earlier—was irrelevant, particularly in the case against the other defendants. If the court had not granted a new trial, the other defendants would have been able to argue on appeal that their cases were tarnished by the jury hearing that a codefendant had been convicted of fraud.[28]

Later, Mourne denied that he had brought up Karsten's criminal record on purpose, saying it "'popped out' under prosecution questioning."[29]

———

A second jury was selected by October 18, consisting of six men and six women. The second trial began with US Attorney Kerner telling the jury the government would prove Preston Tucker had set out on a massive fraud scheme and that the Tucker Corporation was a sham, its only purpose to bilk investors and "to prey upon the public, the dealers, and distributors, and the stockholders."[30] In all respects, it was the same story as at the first trial.

The second trial's first witness was George Lawson, the man who had drawn the original design for the Torpedo. He told the jury he had only been paid $10,000 for his work even though he believed he was owed $45,000.[31] Almost all the early witnesses were former employees or associates of Preston Tucker around the time he launched the company. Prosecutors knew it had problems when not all of them were friendly to their side. It appeared that many of Tucker's former associates still were fond of him and felt he had done nothing wrong.

Mark Mourne was called again to testify. This time, the court admonished him to steer clear of the topic that had caused the mistrial. His testimony was uneventful.[32]

———

People following the Tucker trial in the papers may have caught an intriguing story playing out in Washington with another car company. Kaiser-Frazer had recently run into financial trouble. It had approached the Reconstruction Finance Corporation and asked to borrow money, explaining that it would not be able to continue operating without the infusion of cash, much of which would be used to finance cars being sold wholesale to dealers. When critics questioned whether this was a wise use of taxpayer funds, the RFC responded by releasing details of the loan to the public. The RFC agreed to lend Kaiser-Frazer $34.4 million with the repayment to be made within eighteen months.[33]

Kaiser-Frazer, before receiving the first dollar of the $34 million, then went back to Washington and asked for another $15 million loan.[34] Less than a week later it was reported that a second loan was approved, but only for $10 million. To secure the funds, the company simply pledged the assets of the company. Kaiser-Frazer said it needed the tens of millions of dollars "to finance dealers who handle the firm's automobiles."[35]

Kaiser-Frazer most likely received preferential treatment from the federal government because one of its cofounders, Henry J. Kaiser, had been instrumental in helping the US war effort. Kaiser had overseen the group of companies awarded the contract to build Liberty Ships and was greatly admired in Washington. When the war ended, he had turned to building cars, teaming up with Joseph W. Frazer.

———

Alex Tremulis was the thirteenth witness in the second trial, and the prosecution tap-danced around the issue of his Tucker prototype. Knowing that he admired his creation, they did not ask him if it ran well or if it was a real car. They asked him a few questions about how cars are marketed and then asked him what the prototype was called. Tremulis told the prosecutor, "the Tin Goose." With that, the prosecution's questioning ended.[36]

The defense cross-examined Tremulis, who was obviously a friendly witness. He explained that while they had indeed used some parts from a junkyard as a starting point, the Tin Goose was largely a unique creation. And further, what had been done to create it was common in the industry. The men at Tucker were no guiltier on this point than any other auto manufacturer. Everyone did it. And there was nothing wrong with it.[37]

Tremulis was mortified when he read the local newspaper coverage of the trial. An unhappy Tucker employee had testified the same day that the Tin Goose was a "monstrosity" and the newspaper had confusingly put that statement next to Tremulis's in the headline. Later, Tremulis recalled that the headline "read, in effect, 'Tucker Car Called Monstrosity—Stylist Labels Car Tin Goose.'"[38]

The prosecution resumed its disparaging line of questioning with manufacturing VP Lee Treese. Wasn't it true that many of the Tucker '48's features were borrowed from other auto manufacturers? Yes it was—and, he pointed out, some of those same auto manufacturers had since borrowed some features from the Tucker '48 for their car designs. Again, it was a common industry practice.[39] After each witness, courtroom observers became more and more convinced that the prosecution team knew very little about the auto industry.

Unusual as it was for government witness testimony to be so helpful to the defense on direct examination, many witnesses provided even more help for Tucker and his codefendants on cross-examination. On cross, Treese told the court that the die program for making the Tucker body panels was near completion when the plant shut down. He swore they were on the verge of mass production. When asked why they failed, Treese told the jury it was outside interference. Asked for an example, he told of being kicked out of his own office so SEC investigators could set up shop in it and dig through company papers.[40]

One of the most highly touted pieces of evidence the prosecution seized upon was an engineering report. An engineer named Robert Walder had been paid the handsome salary of $1,000 monthly by Tucker to critique the company's progress. Walder's report had not been optimistic, and neither was Walder's testimony. He testified Tucker's men were exhibiting "just plain dumbness and inexpert engineering."[41] He called the Tucker engine project hopeless and "still-born," and said it would never get the mileage Tucker hoped for. He told Tucker he had a better chance of "flying to Mars on a broomstick." He continued, "It seems fantastic that personnel charged with the guidance of your development program should make so many flagrant mistakes. You nonscientific and green experimenters mean well, but for a man's work, hire a man." The critical report, portions of which were read to the jury, had been created at Tucker's request. If he wasn't trying to actually build cars, why would he hire someone to evaluate his car-building process? And lost in the shuffle was the fact that the report was created in August 1947 and addressed only problems with the 589 engine and dual torque converter setup.[42] The report was not critical of the car itself. After receiving this report, Tucker took Walder's advice and scrapped the 589 and torque converter configuration. Even so, Walder had resigned from the Tucker Corporation after only two months.[43]

Despite his testimony seeming favorable to the prosecution, Walder provided another avenue of attack for the defense. Though they were barred from discussing Abe Karatz's criminal record, they often played up the fact that he used an alias, calling him "Abe Karatz, a.k.a. Karsten." During Walder's testimony Karatz's attorney noticed he had a heavy German accent. Suspecting that Walder may have changed his name, he asked him, "What was your father's name?" The family name had indeed been Braunwalder, and Robert Walder had been known much of his life as Robert Braunwalder. The attorney asked him how he was identified on the subpoena issued by the government. Was it, "Robert B. Walder, alias Robert Braunwalder"? No, it was not.[44] Clearly, the defendants were being held to a different standard than everyone else.

Some testimony consisted of former Tucker employees describing the ineptitude of Preston Tucker or others in the organization. William Stampfli told of how the suspension arms broke in the hours leading up to the Tin Goose's world premiere. On cross-examination he was asked if it wasn't true that the specifications had called for steel suspension arms and the ones that had broken were aluminum. A flustered Stampfli clearly did not know much about what went into the car. How much time did he spend working with the Tucker Corporation research department? "I didn't even know they had one," he admitted.[45]

It was because of witnesses like Stampfli that a copy of the SEC report would have been a gold mine for the defense. He was one of a number of prosecution witnesses who made contradictory statements to the SEC. In the report, Stampfli swore that in May 1947, the Tucker Corporation "had nothing" ready by way of an engine or drivetrain for the Tin Goose.[46] Yet, just a month later, the Tin Goose was unveiled with an operating engine and drivetrain. Surely Stampfli knew that those components were not created in just a month. Stampfli was so uninformed he told the SEC the Tucker Corporation never "road tested" any cars: "As a matter of fact none of the cars had even reached the stage where such tests would be in order."[47] He was either lying or unaware of the tests at Indianapolis. Regardless, the defendants had no way of knowing that Stampfli had made the statements to the SEC, which kept them from cross-examining him about them.

Other testimony was so bizarre it made observers wonder if the prosecution was encouraging witnesses to perjure themselves. Paul Wellenkamp, a former Tucker Corporation engineer, testified that he found no evidence that any Tucker cars or their parts were tested at Indianapolis. The prosecutor pointed out to the jury that Tucker had claimed in advertisements that the cars' components had been tested at the famous racetrack. Therefore, Wellenkamp's testimony was meant to demonstrate that no such testing had taken place.[48] It was a misguided argument, as Tucker's ads were simply pointing out that various items like disc brakes and independent suspension had been successfully used on cars at Indianapolis for years. But Wellenkamp was wrong about the road tests, as well; he'd only worked for Tucker for three months and was not an employee when Tucker and Offutt took the fleet of Tucker sedans to Indianapolis for testing.[49] Presumably, one of the reasons he parted company with Tucker is that Wellenkamp had advised Tucker to scrap everything unique about his car "and (start) substituting standard equipment."[50]

Even so, not everything Wellenkamp said was bad for Tucker. On cross-examination he was asked, "Do you think it was an honest effort in good faith to produce that kind of an automobile?"[51]

He answered: "Yes, sir, I do."

The prosecutors seemed focused on arguing that the Tucker Corporation was inept when it came to building cars. But was that criminal? At one point the judge chastised the prosecutors. He reminded them that the case was not about whether Tucker or his associates knew how to build a car. The men were on trial for fraud and conspiracy. Perhaps the prosecution should start moving in that direction?[52]

Elsewhere in the courthouse, the stockholders committee in the civil case got their hearing and announced they had a deal that would save the corporation and allow them to continue operation. They proposed a new stock issue to be offered to then-current Tucker stockholders. An SEC attorney told the judge that the group had not registered any stock offering with the

SEC, so at that point what they were proposing was illegal. The committee then told the judge they would raise another $20 million by borrowing it from the Reconstruction Finance Corporation. It is unclear if the committee knew that Tucker had applied for RFC loans to save the company but had been denied. The judge denied the committee's request.[53]

———

The rest of the Tucker family continued to live their lives as best they could while their patriarch was on trial. John Tucker had attended Chicago Latin School, a local private school, and had met Mary Jane Dodman, who was a year younger and a student at a nearby school. The two began dating, often ending the evening at the apartment on Lake Shore Drive for hot chocolate. Years later, Mary Jane recalled that Preston Tucker would sometimes allow himself to be seen not wearing a suit and tie, occasionally dressed in flannel pajamas when the young couple returned in the evening.[54]

Mary Jane and John decided to get married but thought a low-key ceremony would be best in light of the trial. The two discreetly went to Waukegan, about forty miles from Chicago, assuming the matter would stay under the radar. When the newly married couple returned to Chicago they saw their marriage reported in the newspaper: TUCKER SON MARRIES. They later found out that the judge who had officiated their wedding was the brother of an attorney involved in the Tucker trial.[55]

———

Despite the government's best efforts, prosecution witnesses continued helping Tucker's cause and did very little to prove the fraud and conspiracy case. One witness mentioned the Kaiser-Frazer company, which allowed a defense attorney to ask follow-up questions. Wasn't it true that Kaiser-Frazer promised to produce a front-wheel-drive car that they never followed through on? And wasn't it true that, rather than prosecuting them, the government had lent Kaiser-Frazer another $44 million to help its business? Yes, it was. At this point, the jury knew that the government was playing favorites. (Some in Congress likewise wondered why Kaiser-Frazer was receiving so much money from the government. One of the directors of the Reconstruction Finance Corporation appeared before Congress to explain the department's loose purse strings. He said it was part of the RFC's attempt to help struggling "small companies." When a congressman noted that Kaiser-Frazer was by no means "small," he backpedaled: "It is a small business in the automotive field.")[56]

Several witnesses were called to discredit Tucker's advertising claims. Had he designed and built race cars with Harry Miller? Fred Offenhauser, a famous race engine builder who had worked with Harry Miller, said that Tucker did not do any engineering work, and Miller's son and widow both said they thought Tucker's relationship with Miller was minimal. Preston Tucker's attorney simply asked the widow who had paid for Harry's funeral. She quietly admitted it had been Tucker. Many observers thought this answer erased everything she had said previously about her late husband's time with Preston Tucker.[57]

The prosecution scored some points when they called Herbert Morley, onetime vice president of the corporation. He had angrily confronted Tucker when he and Rockelman became concerned about $800,000 that had been spent without proper authorization. It was this argument that had led to his departure from the company.[58]

But the next witness hurt the prosecution's case. Emery Hughett had been a bookkeeper at Ypsilanti Machine and Tool and presumably could shed light on the odd relationship between that company, owned by Tucker's mother, and the Tucker Corporation. He testified that an IRS agent named "Mr. House" showed up at his office and started taking records even though he had no subpoena or court order. Hughett stopped him and took the papers back, at one point slamming a drawer and telling the agent he would not be taking anything without legal justification. The IRS agent became livid. He told Hughett that Senator Homer Ferguson would "get Tucker."[59] After the IRS agent left empty-handed, Hughett was in a local restaurant and saw two men he did not recognize looking at records taken from Ypsilanti Machine and Tool. He later came to know them as SEC representatives

James Goode and Frank Corbin. Hughett raced back to the office and saw that records were missing. He found some of the records stashed in a desk placed behind the building for trash pickup, leading him to believe the agents were planning to come back and get them later.[60] Goode and Corbin were both working on the SEC report, which would play such a major role in Tucker's downfall.[61]

Hughett was called as a prosecution witness, but he told the judge he was scared of the prosecutors. The prosecution asked Hughett to identify records of the Tucker Corporation that he had not created. He offered to identify any records he recognized but protested that he could not vouch for documents with which he was not personally familiar, implying that they could have been altered or even fabricated completely while in government hands. At one point he turned to the judge and said, "I've been threatened so many times I don't know what to do."[62] He wanted to testify truthfully but was worried he would be harmed by the government if he didn't perjure himself and testify falsely about Tucker.

His testimony became more interesting on cross-examination. Hughett had been summoned to testify before the grand jury. There, he said, SEC agents pulled him aside and threatened him. They would have him indicted if he told the grand jury about the illegal searches of the Ypsilanti Machine and Tool offices.[63] When he left the grand jury room after testifying, an SEC official was waiting for him. "You told them about the scrape at Ypsilanti, didn't you?" When Hughett denied it, the SEC man replied, "You'll be indicted if you do." Curious as to what charge he could be indicted for since he had done nothing wrong, he asked. The man replied, "We can always drum one up."[64]

Cliff Knoble found the trial fascinating, beyond the notion that he faced decades in jail if he was convicted. He wrote limericks and took notes to occupy his time. He found one exchange particularly enlightening. The prosecution called a witness, a former engineer who had been hired by Tucker and given the task of redesigning an engine to use in the sedan. The witness told of how the project was a failure and that, when he had finally quit, the engine he had been working on had been a dead end. His conclusion was that Tucker, as a result, had no engine to put in the sedans, if they were ever to be built. Smugly, the prosecution turned the witness over to the defense for cross-examination.

The witness admitted he was unaware that Tucker had three separate engine projects going at the same time and had told each one to work in the strictest secrecy. As a result, each group thought it was the only one working on an engine for the Tucker sedan. Preston Tucker had thought this would be a fine way to see if the different groups could come up with novel solutions to the problems they faced. The witness's project had flopped. The second and third groups' projects, however, had succeeded. The second group had gotten an engine to run and the third group had come up with the engine that Tucker had ordered into production. The witness was unaware that a competing group with the Tucker Corporation had not only built a successful engine but that when the factory was shuttered, more than a hundred engines had been manufactured and were sitting in the factory, ready for installation. It had never occurred to the witness, or the prosecutor, that in an organization that large, someone else might have been working on the exact same problem and reaching different results.[65]

Many government witnesses suffered from a similar lack of knowledge. The prosecutors apparently asked witnesses if they knew about various aspects of Tucker's business and if the answer was negative, jumped to the conclusion that there was no evidence to support the contention. One point the prosecution kept returning to was that "Tucker had no connection with any development of racing cars for the Indianapolis speedway."[66] If Tucker had no such connection, then the advertising and promotional materials issued by Tucker contained false and misleading statements. The prosecution called a directing engineer of Gulf Oil Research and Development to the stand in mid-December and asked him about Tucker's role at Indianapolis. R. J. S. Pigott testified he was unaware of any work done by Preston Tucker on any automobiles at Indianapolis. Presumably, the witness would have known of any connection, as in 1941 Gulf entered cars at Indianapolis that had been designed by Miller.

The defense attorneys then cross-examined Pigott, who quickly admitted he had no idea what role Tucker played in Harry Miller's enterprise. All he knew was that he had not dealt with Tucker in 1941. What happened before or after that, the witness could not say. Pigott's testimony was so pointless it drew objections from the defense, who accused the prosecution of "always wanting to waste and spend more time, more time."[67] Reporters who had stuck around to this point noted that the courtroom had long since lost its appeal to spectators and was even wearing on the defendants. One news report even included a mention of Cliff Knoble's entertaining scribbles.[68]

———

In early December, SEC commissioner Harry McDonald spoke at the thirty-eighth annual convention of the Investment Bankers Association of America in Hollywood, Florida. His introductory remarks described the range of activities policed by the SEC, including "the crackpot schemes to the Tucker dream-car which cost American investors $26 million." He also said, "I want the public, and particularly you in the industry, to get the best treatment possible, fair—courteous and expeditious."[69]

During Tucker's trial, various witnesses referred to material contained in the SEC report, and it was clear that the report was the prosecution's road map. Although work product of an attorney may be privileged and not subject to disclosure to the opposing side, the SEC report clearly did not qualify as work product or privileged material. In fact, the report had already been shown to enough third parties—journalists in particular—that the prosecution was certainly foreclosed from raising that argument when the defendants asked the court to order the prosecution to produce the report. The prosecution objected. Judge LaBuy said:

> As to the objection of the government on the ground of secrecy and confidential nature of the report, the government is in an anomalous situation. Confronted with evidence of dissemination of the report to the public press by the [SEC], the District Attorney finds himself on the horns of a dilemma when duty requires him to plead the confidential nature of the document sought to be protected.
>
> To permit the SEC to expose the report to the public press and have the District Attorney deny the same right to the defendant shocks the Court's sense of justice, fairness and right.[70]

Although the court's conscience was shocked, Judge LaBuy refused to order the prosecution to turn over the report at that time. Presumably, he did this because the release of the SEC report could only be ordered by the SEC itself. And they continued to tell the court that they had never released it to anyone. Tucker and his codefendants would have to wait until the trial was over to appeal this issue.

———

As the end-of-year holidays approached, some defendants began suffering dire financial problems because of the trial's length. Though the prosecution planned to call more than seventy witnesses, they had only gotten through a third of them. Most of the defendants did not have much money to begin with, and some had actually found part-time jobs to perform while not in court. Mitchell Dulian worked nights and weekends selling cars. The defendants asked if the court could shorten the holiday break to make the trial end sooner. But the court took a two-week break for the holidays.[71]

When the trial resumed after the New Year, the prosecution turned to investors who had bought Tucker stock or dealerships. Dan J. Ehlens testified he had done both.[72] He had been grilled by SEC investigators for four days before Tucker was indicted.[73] In 1946 Ehlens had read the *Pic* magazine article and became interested in becoming a Tucker dealer. He already owned a used car dealership in Minnesota and traveled frequently to Chicago on business. Rather than writing to Tucker, he went to the plant and introduced himself. He then made several more trips, convincing Tucker that he deserved a franchise. He met with Rockelman and A. R. Peterson, a regional sales manager for the Tucker Corporation.[74] In this respect, Ehlens's experience was typical. Many who bought dealerships did so after taking the initiative to go to the plant in Chicago. Some went to see if the project had substance; others went to make an impression on Tucker.

Ehlens fulfilled the dealership requirements and signed a contract with the Tucker Corporation on February 18, 1947. He committed to buying fourteen hundred cars over two years and paid $14,000 in cash up front. He signed a note for another $14,000. Ehlens was so enthusiastic about the project that he convinced the Tucker Corporation to let him be a distributor and set up dealerships around his area. He did that with gusto and found himself swamped with requests from others.

On cross-examination, Ehlens testified that he ran a credit check on the Tucker Corporation, but not until after he had gone to Chicago several times seeking his own franchise. He had met with Rockelman and signed a contract before he sought a Dun & Bradstreet report on the company. The report showed nothing remarkable at the time, but the defendants wanted the jury to see that Ehlens had not been particularly vigilant in how he had entered this transaction—otherwise, he would have run the check earlier.

On May 20, 1948, Preston Tucker brought a blue Tucker sedan to the Golden Valley Country Club near Minneapolis, where Ehlens saw it. The car received a "tremendous reception."[75] In July, a black Tucker '48 sedan was driven to Minneapolis by a Tucker representative, where it was displayed and loaned to journalists for test-drives. Ehlens himself drove the car three thousand miles during that time and noted it ran well, although it only got 20.8 miles per gallon. When prompted by the government, he noted the car had a manual transmission, not the automatic that Tucker had promoted. Still, he admitted, "I was greatly pleased with the performance of the automobile."[76]

Ehlens became disillusioned with the Tucker enterprise when cars were not forthcoming to sell, but he managed to acquire one for himself. After he recounted his story for the prosecution, defense attorneys talked to him about the Tucker '48s he had driven. There were the two brought up to Minneapolis as demonstrators and the one he owned. How did the car treat him? While he had been almost vitriolic on the topic of Tucker the man, he spoke lovingly of his Tucker '48. At the time of the trial, he had driven his own '48 thirty-five thousand miles and at speeds exceeding 90 mph. "It was the finest car he had ever driven," one newspaper reported of his testimony.[77]

Ehlens also damaged the prosecution's case when he described visiting the Tucker plant many times. He saw the assembly line in action. He did not know its length, but when pressed, he said it was "plenty long." Workers were assembling cars on the line, but he did not know how many. Each time there, more cars were being produced.

"When was the next visit you made there?"

"About another thirty days."

"What did you see on that visit?"

"More cars."[78]

The government presented its numbers, derived from the SEC investigation of the Tucker Corporation books and papers. In its existence, the company had taken in $28,491,652. Expenditures totaled $28,309,280.[79] The largest budget item had been employee salaries and wages. Another huge expense was the rent and operating costs of the plant, including taxes.[80] While the sides wrangled over whether the money was spent or earmarked properly, one fact came out loud and clear: the money had not been stolen and it had not disappeared.

Joseph Turnbull, an SEC accountant, was the final prosecution witness.[81] He found a series of "questioned transactions" while scrutinizing the Tucker Corporation books. According to his calculations, Tucker had received $500,000 from the venture and the various defendants had received close to a million dollars combined. Yet he could not point to any fraudulent or dishonest transactions. It was simply his opinion, as an accountant, that the transactions were questionable. He hadn't even investigated any of the items beyond seeing them listed in the company's books.

On cross-examination, defense attorneys took turns attacking his testimony. Broker Floyd Cerf's attorney grilled Turnbull regarding his claim that Cerf had made $2.443 million dollars in commissions selling Tucker stock; the witness apparently did not understand that more than six hundred security brokers had sold Tucker stock, each of them deducting a sales commission. None of that money ended up in Cerf's hands. Many of Turnbull's other numbers—for instance, suggesting Preston Tucker skimmed half a million dollars from company coffers—were likewise shown to be unsupported. Tucker had sold the corporation two cars, one for $3,394.78 and the other for $1,763. Turnbull described the transactions as profiteering, not knowing Tucker had bought the cars at exactly the same prices at which he sold them. Turnbull, the "accountant investigator," had not bothered to determine what the cars had cost in the first place.[82]

As the withering cross-examination continued, Turnbull's answers became less and less specific. After noting how Turnbull's numbers conflicted with each other, an attorney asked, "You, yourself, have arrived at several figures of benefits to Mr. Tucker from your worksheets, depending on the way you figure it?"[83]

"Yes, it depends on what you call it," the accountant replied. "Some of the things you can treat one way and sometimes you can treat them another."

Scrambling, Turnbull said he had only made a "partial investigation" of the finances in question. The defense attorney asked if he had been told to make "only a partial investigation of what the books and records show?"[84]

"I was not instructed to make a full investigation, if that is what you mean."

For the prosecution's final witness—the seventy-third overall—Joseph Turnbull was not the grand finale many had expected.[85] Nevertheless, after he was excused, the prosecution rested its case.

———

It was now the defendants' turn. On January 16, 1950, the parties assembled in the courtroom and the judge told the defendants to call their first witness. The attorneys stood, and each announced they would not call any witnesses. As far as they were concerned, the case presented by the prosecution was so flimsy, it didn't need to be defended against. "You cannot put up a defense where there is no offense," attorney Dan Glasser told the judge.[86] The defense attorneys offered to move directly to closing arguments. The spectators were stunned, as were the prosecutors, who had assumed closing arguments would not be made for a month or two. The judge gave them two days to prepare.[87]

On January 18, the prosecution gave the jury a five-hour argument explaining why Tucker and the others should go to prison. They "knowingly committed one of the largest frauds that has ever been perpetrated upon the public of these United States."[88] The prosecution had long since given up on seeking convictions for violations of securities law in the strictest sense. They tried to aim the jury's attention at the company's advertising and publicity. "It doesn't make any difference what their intent was when they started out. They made misrepresentations of what they had. Read the pack of lies in their ads and remember what they had and what they didn't have in the way of an auto."[89]

The defense attorneys each spoke with a common theme: Either these men had set out to build a car or they had set out to defraud investors. It couldn't be both. And in case the jury was curious which it was, a Tucker '48 sedan was parked outside the courthouse at that very moment. One defense attorney suggested the jurors go for a ride in the car before reaching a verdict.[90]

The judge instructed the jury on the law: "The fact that the defendants and those associated with them failed to mass-produce an automobile and accomplish what they undertook is not of itself proof of fraud. Erroneous judgment may be as consistent with good intentions as with bad intentions."

———

It was a Saturday morning at 11:00 AM when the case was given to the jury. A little over twenty-four hours later they had a verdict. They found all defendants not guilty on all counts.

"Tucker and the other defendants cheered wildly and a few wept openly yesterday when a Federal court jury of seven men and five women cleared them of 31 counts of mail fraud, Securities and Exchange Commission violations, and conspiracy," reported the United Press. After thirty minutes, quiet and order returned to the court. Tucker spoke to the press: "I'm ready to help in any way possible in a reorganization of the Tucker Corp. or anything else. My immediate plan is to get my wife, Vera, back on the road to health. She is in this courtroom now against the doctor's orders. [The jury's verdict was] a victory for all dealers, stockholders and distributors. My interest has, of course, always been second to theirs."[91] As for Vera, she was merely exhausted. She was worried sick and insisted on attending court every day even though she clearly needed rest. Now that the trial was over she could finally get some.

One juror told the press it wasn't even a close call. William Zacher said, "It wasn't so hard to reach a decision. From the beginning, only two jurors voted guilty." A few ballots later, those two agreed with the rest and the not guilty verdict was unanimous.[92]

On January 22, 1950—a Sunday—Preston Tucker walked out of the federal courthouse in Chicago a free man.[93] Tucker invited the jurors outside, where he gave them a demonstration of the Tucker '48.[94] Later, he said, "It's been like a bad nightmare. This is a victory for the stockholders and dealers as well as free enterprise."[95] He told reporters he would do everything he could to reorganize and revive the corporation.[96]

The US attorney called some of the jurors into his office, asking them to "explain" their verdict—something they did not have to do. One juror was so upset by the confrontation he called Tucker's attorney William Kirby and told him about it. Kirby told him he didn't need to explain his verdict to anyone.[97]

―――

Considering how much time and effort the SEC and the prosecution had expended accusing Tucker and his associates of criminal activities, the acquittals represented a colossal failure on the part of the government. The result vindicated Tucker on the grandest scale. And the defendants' actions in not even bothering to mount a defense showed that everyone in the courtroom knew the government's case had been bogus. But would that matter? Tucker's career was in tatters. Government officials could move on as if nothing happened. And they did.

SEC officials gave little thought to the acquittals. On February 21, 1950, Harry McDonald spoke in Detroit before a home crowd audience of Detroit Stock Exchange members. He updated them on "some of the cases which were at that time much in the limelight."[98] Specifically, he noted "the Tucker case" and how "everyone" wanted to know about it.

"The Tucker case is history."

He then moved on to another topic. Less than a month after Tucker and all his codefendants had been found not guilty on all counts, this was

McDonald's complete statement. He then addressed the American Light and Traction Company, Detroit Edison, and how some other utilities might be affected by recent changes in securities law. He did not say another word about Tucker. He closed his talk by saying, "The invitation to come here as your speaker was most flattering, and it has indeed been satisfying to be with you, people I have known so well for so many years. I salute you all as friends. I thank you for your kind attention. Good night."[99]

The SEC had lost the trial but had won the war. They put Tucker out of business and assured he could never do business in America again.

Reflecting years later, Alex Tremulis noted another tragic aspect to the trial. By refusing to present a defense, Tucker's attorneys had made a bold decision that ultimately vindicated Tucker the man. But it also meant that the Tucker automobile had gone undefended. A robust defense—though it had proved unnecessary from a legal perspective—would have been a great opportunity to showcase the car's merits and confirm the legitimacy of the Tucker Corporation's operations.[100]

———

Preston Tucker was ruined when the trial was over. He was broke and his company had been taken from him. On January 26 he was arrested—"detained" by a court officer—for failing to honor a $3,567 judgment against him in an unrelated matter. Tucker had bought a farm but failed to make final payment on it. Though the seller had obtained a judgment, Tucker didn't have the money to pay it. His attorney negotiated with the creditor to reduce the figure, and Tucker's friends raised the money. Another attorney pitched in a thousand dollars. Papers told the story nationwide of Tucker, the man who had raised $28 million but found himself briefly in the equivalent of debtor's prison.[101]

Meanwhile, the bankruptcy court had appointed a receiver for the Tucker Corporation, and Preston Tucker and his management team had lost control of the company. It was clear from the civil proceedings that the judge did not like Preston Tucker. On one occasion, Judge Igoe listened to Tucker's lawyers describe Preston Tucker's efforts to find an eleventh-hour investor to save the company and said, "I don't have the least bit of confidence in the statements of Mr. Tucker." Later, news organizations reported that he said, "That is the difficulty in this whole case and the sad situation presented by the whole case is that the persons who have been defrauded are the poorest and smallest people in America, five or ten dollar people, those are the people we have to protect around here." He said this on January 27, 1950—five days after Tucker had been acquitted of such fraud.[102]

The legal wrangling over the carcass of the Tucker Corporation raised an interesting question: Why didn't someone simply buy enough of the outstanding shares to take over the company? Tucker only owned a small portion of the Class B stock, and Class A stock held the same voting rights. With five million shares in the corporation outstanding, someone could have simply bought 2,500,001 shares of the stock and taken control. When the stock crashed after the Drew Pearson broadcast, the shares could have been bought for pennies on the dollar. The only issue, it seems, was what the new owners would be inheriting. Simply changing management of the company did not guarantee smooth sailing for the corporation.[103]

———

Tucker sold his apartment in Chicago to Raymond E. Dodge, an Olympian-turned-entrepreneur whose company made the Oscar and Emmy statuettes.[104] His mother's apartment had been sold the previous year. Tucker returned to Ypsilanti, to the family home on Park Street, along with his wife, mother, children, and the grandchildren who were by now in the mix. Some of the family members lived in apartments in the shop behind the house where Preston had met with Charles Pearson years earlier. Preston Jr. and his wife lived in one apartment, John and Mary Jane in the other.[105]

All the family members would often gather for meals in the main house. Without a business to run, Preston found more time to spend with his family, often calling for the grandchildren to be brought into the house when he saw them in the yard. When they were a little older, he would load his Cadillac with the children and take long drives on country roads around the area.[106] He still enjoyed listening to his music. He had even wired his television room with special speakers so he could hear Lawrence Welk better when the bandleader was on.

One day Preston took his granddaughter Cynthia for a walk. He spotted a penny on the ground and showed it to her. "Don't ever be so lazy and not bend over to pick up a penny." The man who had raised more than $25 million handed the penny to her. Decades later, Cynthia still stopped to pick up pennies when she saw them on the ground, always thinking of her grandfather when she did so.[107]

25

The Civil Suits

Though Tucker had been vindicated in the criminal trial and was settling back into life in Ypsilanti, he was not prepared to simply give up on the legal concerns his company's destruction had raised. Believing that he had been targeted unfairly by the criminal action, he filed suit for malicious prosecution against US Attorney Otto Kerner Jr. and two of his assistants, Lawrence J. Miller and Robert J. Downing. He also named Harry McDonald, Thomas Hart, and some others involved in his case.[1] He also filed lawsuits against various news organizations that he believed had defamed him, including the *Detroit News*, *Collier's*, and *Reader's Digest*.[2]

Among the suits was *Preston T. Tucker v. The Evening News Association*, the publisher of the *Detroit News*. Preston filed the case in federal court in Michigan, asking for $3 million in damages. All the civil actions against the media outlets hinged on one simple theory: Tucker had not defrauded anyone, so when the press said he did, that constituted libel.[3] Through the lawsuits' discovery phase, Tucker could subpoena evidence and compel witnesses to answer questions under oath in front of a court reporter. Who was behind the investigation? Who leaked the SEC report to the press? This endeavor was made more difficult by the fact that even as he pursued discovery, Tucker still did not have his own copy of the agency's report.

Attorneys for the defendants in the suits demanded that Preston Tucker appear for a deposition, where they would be allowed to question him under oath about the claims he was making. Very early on, the *Detroit News'* attorneys pulled out a copy of the report and began questioning Tucker about it. His attorney and he were both shocked. The attorney objected: "May the record show that so far as I know, Mr. Tucker has never seen the SEC report. Mr. Tucker repeatedly tried to get the report and was turned down by the commission."

Opposing counsel found that hard to believe. Tucker spoke up: "Well, what I can't understand is that the SEC report, by the congressional act itself, is supposed to be a secret report . . . and I am amazed to find the report in the hands of the *Detroit News* attorneys."[4]

In a subsequent deposition, Martin Hayden, the *Detroit News* reporter, testified that he had hinted to Harry McDonald that he would write a story critical of the SEC unless McDonald revealed details of the previously unreported confidential investigation. It was then, Hayden said, that McDonald invited Hayden to a hotel and handed him a copy of the 561-page report.[5] Tucker's attorney asked Hayden what steps he took to verify the facts he had taken from the report to use in his story. Hayden hadn't bothered. He admitted he simply parroted the report, assuming it was all true.[6]

Tucker's attorney questioned Hayden at length about the report, even though he and Tucker did not have a copy to work with. Halfway through the day, Tucker's attorney said he was going to adjourn the deposition until a later date so he could subpoena a copy of the report to allow for better cross-examination. After a brief discussion, Hayden's attorney offered to give a copy of the report to Tucker's attorney as long as they could finish the deposition that afternoon. Tucker's attorney would be given an hour to study it before they resumed after lunch. This copy would be the first that Tucker had seen.[7]

Hayden had not gotten this copy from the SEC; when he had been shown a copy to write his damning newspaper article, he had not been allowed to keep it. The new copy had come from the Tucker Corporation's bankruptcy trustee. When asked why he didn't ask McDonald for the report, Hayden said he didn't want to "cause Mr. McDonald any more trouble."[8] It was the first indication by Hayden that he knew his receipt of the confidential report was a violation of federal law.

This was not the only instance in which the bankruptcy trustees provided aid to the parties Tucker was suing. Before depositions were taken of the SEC members who had swarmed the Tucker factory, their attorneys were given access to the Tucker records for three weeks so they could prepare. The documents were not, however, made available to Tucker or his attorneys.[9]

Tucker's suit against *Collier's* revealed similar bias on the part of the US Attorney's Office. Lester Velie had written the *Collier's* article after he was likewise shown the report in Chicago, in the office of Otto Kerner. Later, when he asked to see it again, he went to Washington, where the SEC lawyer Thomas B. Hart gave him the report, along with an office to work in while he took notes.[10] Hart had been the one who wrote to Tucker and assured him that the report had not been shown to anyone in the media. (During the litigation, a representative of *Collier's* swore under oath that the magazine did not have any editors or managers fact-check the article before it went to press; the magazine trusted the writer to keep the facts straight.)[11] Velie's and Hayden's testimony directly contradicted the prosecution's assertions in the criminal trial that the SEC report was confidential and had never been shown to anyone outside the prosecution.[12]

Tucker filed his case against Kerner and the others for malicious prosecution in Illinois state court, and the defendants had the action removed and heard by the federal court. The case was sent to the courtroom of Judge Igoe. Tucker's attorneys asked the judge to disqualify himself, noting the various prejudicial things he had said in previous proceedings. Igoe denied the request and threw Tucker's case out of court. Tucker appealed and the court of appeals wrote that it could find nothing improper in the handling of the case. As for what Igoe had said about Tucker? The court of appeals said the statements were hearsay, and perhaps *Collier's* and the other news organizations had simply made some of them up.[13]

———

In October 1950 the bankruptcy trustee auctioned the Tucker Corporation's remaining assets. It was an interesting exercise. The plant was filled with valuable car-making equipment, along with quite a few cars in various stages of assembly. The auction took place over three days at the end of the month. Among items auctioned were "title and interest in and to all Tucker Corporation patents, patent applications and trademarks, as well as all production dies, tools, jigs, fixtures, blue-prints and engineering data . . . . [and] 23 Tucker 4-door sedans."[14] Auction flyers detailed the more valuable equipment, like a new Landis camshaft grinder, six dynamometers, stamping and sheet metal machinery, cutting tools, welders and welding equipment, and more. The auctioneer admitted that the poster-sized auction flyers lacked room to list everything. "Due to the urgency and magnitude of this sale, a completely detailed and itemized description of all of the items to be sold could not be compiled prior to going to press and will not be available in published form as is customary in such sales."

On October 30 the auctioneer sent the trustee a report of items sold, amounts raised, and buyers' names. The highlight was the list of Tucker sedans and their selling prices. Tucker sedan #1039 sold for $2,200 while #1011 sold for $2,000. Several sedans without transmissions sold for $1,050.[15] Remarkably, the cars sold at auction for around Tucker's suggested retail price, even though buyers received no warranties, there would be no source for replacement parts, and buyers had no place to take them for factory service.

The public's fondness for the cars seemed to help owners overcome such obstacles. A few months before the auction, a Seattle Tucker sedan owner had written directly to Preston Tucker, now back in Ypsilanti, with questions about a particular Tucker '48 he'd purchased in an earlier sale. Tucker did not have access to the records but remembered it: it had been a factory display car taken around the country as a demonstrator. While the company owned the car, it had been driven 150,000 miles. Its new owner was curious about the transmission slipping out of gear. Preston Tucker told him he was not sure which transmission was in this particular car, but the high mileage certainly meant the transmission was worn. He told the man to contact Dan Leabu for further help with the transmission.[16]

With the October 1950 auction, the corporation's assets were disposed of, the plant was emptied, and the Tucker Corporation ceased to exist. While the machinery and equipment drifted anonymously back into the stream of commerce, the Tucker '48 sedans would remain a vivid reminder of Preston Tucker's accomplishment. The company had bought the materials and parts to build fifty of the cars after the Tin Goose, and astoundingly, all fifty of them would eventually be assembled. Before the assets were liquidated, thirty-seven had been completed. The parts for the other thirteen were bought at the auction and later assembled.[17]

———

Along with disposing of the physical assets, like the tools and parts to build the cars, the trustee also had the power to resolve any legal claims the corporation may have been entitled to make. The trustee chose not to do so, simply telling the court that any claims the Tucker Corporation may have had against the government were being abandoned. Presumably, the trustee did not believe any of the corporate legal claims were worth pursuing. Several stockholders became upset upon hearing this. Why not sue the government for shutting down the Tucker Corporation? After all, the trial had exonerated it of wrongdoing.

A stockholder named Schmidt filed suit in the federal court on behalf of the stockholders of the Tucker Corporation, seeking $50 million from the US government for its malicious prosecution of Tucker.[18] Characterizing the Tucker trial as an "inquisition," the plaintiff pointed out what had by this point become apparent to anyone who followed the case: The SEC had surreptitiously leaked information about the investigation to broadcaster/columnist Drew Pearson, knowing that he would publicize it nationally. It had conducted an investigation that shut Tucker down and started rumors that it had uncovered fraud and corruption at the company. It had then handed the top-secret SEC report to journalists in Detroit, knowing that it would be the basis of national news stories bashing Tucker.

The US government was again defended by Otto Kerner Jr., and he convinced the district court to throw the case out. The court ruled that the plaintiffs had failed to state a claim upon which relief could be granted, agreeing with the government's defense that, in essence, the allegations of the suing party would not constitute a viable lawsuit even if determined to be true. The court noted that the law giving the SEC its mandate specifically empowered it to make investigations and to "publish information" concerning its findings.[19] Since the SEC was merely "publishing information" when it leaked the SEC report to journalists, it was doing exactly what it was supposed to do.

The stockholder appealed, but the court of appeals agreed with the lower court, leaving the stockholders with nothing to pursue. Neither court addressed the notion that the manner in which the confidential report was leaked violated federal law. Presumably, if that was an offense worth pursuing, the government itself would have to bring a case against the agency in criminal court. It was not something for which an individual could bring a legal action.

But it seems particularly disingenuous for the court to claim that the SEC was within its rights to "publish" information about Tucker by leaking information to Drew Pearson. At that point it had not even begun its investigation yet. What was it "publishing" when it told Pearson it was going to investigate Tucker and that the investigation was going to blow his operation sky-high?

———

Meanwhile, the federal government continued lending money to Kaiser-Frazer. In December 1950 another $25 million loan was announced. The government attached a few conditions: Kaiser-Frazer had to freeze the prices on its new cars, and it had to cut its production in half.[20]

By July 1951 some congressmen again began questioning the generous Kaiser-Frazer loans. In all, the company had borrowed $69.4 million and had paid back only enough to reduce the debt to $62 million. When the RFC tried to tell a congressional subcommittee that the loans were necessary to save the car company, they were rebuked: "Notwithstanding this, the sub-committee believes that the RFC should not have made the original loan."[21]

In early 1952, President Truman nominated a new administrator of the Reconstruction Finance Corporation: the SEC's Harry McDonald. Normally, such a nomination would have breezed through the Senate, but a House subcommittee had said it would hold hearings into McDonald's tenure at the SEC. The hearings were held behind closed doors, and Tucker made the trip to Washington to tell the panel about his dealings with McDonald and the SEC. He didn't gain any sympathy from them, however. After he told them about how he had been treated by the SEC, McDonald testified that he had simply done his job. He had investigated Tucker and his business and turned the results of the investigation over to prosecutors.

As for the release of the SEC report? He admitted he had done it and said he saw nothing wrong with his actions. "My purpose was to protect the com-mission against unjustified criticism and to maintain public confidence in the commission," McDonald testified. "I would unhesitatingly do the same thing today under similar circumstances."[22] He never explained why it was all right for him to violate federal law in the process while pursuing his "purpose."

The subcommittee was impressed by McDonald. Rather than dig too deeply into the legality of his actions, it announced that there was "no credi-ble evidence reflecting adversely upon the honesty and integrity of" McDon-ald. The members unanimously agreed to close their investigation, clearing the way for McDonald's nomination to be approved in the Senate.[23]

Later in the year, Kaiser-Frazer sought an extension on its repayment of the RFC loan. Harry McDonald didn't seem too worried, even though Kaiser-Frazer had only reduced the debt to $49.7 million.[24]

The following March, Kaiser-Frazer would purchase Willys-Overland Motors, the company that manufactured the Jeep. By that point Kaiser-Frazer had only reduced its outstanding RFC debt to $48.4 million, yet the Willys transaction had cost the company $62.3 million, suggesting that it could have paid back the RFC if its directors had wanted to. The loan had actually been due in full two years earlier.[25] Kaiser-Frazer simply chose not to pay it off, and no one in Washington did anything about it.

While Kaiser-Frazer's loans appear to have been a bad investment on the part of the RFC, they were not unique. Lustron, the company that had almost ousted Tucker from the Chicago plant in 1946, obtained $35 million in RFC loans that was not repaid.[26]

————

Though Tucker's suit against the government had been dismissed, his other lawsuits continued to work their way through the court system. As the discovery process in the *Detroit News* case went on, Tucker learned how the news organization worked. His attorneys served interrogatories on the defendants, written questions that litigants must answer in writing under oath. Tucker asked the *Detroit News* how it checked the truthfulness of the story written by Hayden. Just like *Collier's*, it hadn't: "No regular procedure is employed for checking the truth or falsity of facts reported in an article based upon an official report of a branch of the United States Government."[27]

Were *any* of the statements contained in the report true? The *Detroit News* admitted it had no idea. Tucker's attorneys laid out each allegation from the *Detroit News* article and asked if the *Detroit News* believed they were true. The paper responded to each one the same: "This defendant is without personal knowledge of the matter inquired about in this interrogatory, with the result that it is unable to answer the same." The verbatim answer was repeated thirty-nine times. The paper admitted that it received $940,000 in advertising revenue from automobile and automotive concerns in 1949, the year it ran the article attacking Tucker.

In his own sworn affidavit to Tucker's attorneys, Harry McDonald again admitted to disseminating the confidential SEC report. He said that he had "made available" the report to Hayden "shortly before March 13, 1949." To insulate himself from personal liability, he swore that he had done it "in his capacity" as a commissioner on the SEC. His affidavit was not provided to the litigants until April 1952, after the lawsuit against him had also already been dismissed and he had been sworn in as administrator of the RFC.[28]

All parties stipulated that at the time McDonald made the report available to Hayden, doing so was a violation of federal law. The parties included the full text of the statute McDonald had violated, "Section 230.122 Nondisclosure of Information obtained in the course of examinations and investigations," and filed it with the court. The circle was now complete. The *Detroit News* claimed it was not liable because McDonald was the one who broke the law. The courts had said McDonald could not be sued because he was a government agent. Again, the only apparent remedy lay in the government itself sanctioning McDonald for what he had done.

26

Preston Tucker Speaks Out

Perhaps frustrated by the fact that his legal actions were making little or no headway, Preston Tucker decided to finally speak publicly about what had happened to him and his car company. In March 1952, he wrote an article for *Cars* magazine titled "My Car Was Too Good,"[1] in which he answered the questions he said everyone was asking: Was the Tucker sedan a good car? And if so, why wasn't it being put into production? But first he wanted to clear the air:

> Sure, we made mistakes. Lots of them. So has everybody who ever tried to accomplish anything important. But the biggest mistake I ever made was building an automobile that promised so much in appearance and performance that it gained the greatest public acceptance in automotive history. It was for that mistake I paid and paid heavily—almost with my freedom.[2]

Then came the short answer to the first question: yes, the Tucker sedan was a good car. He noted how the few finished Tuckers had been driven more than one hundred thousand miles and were still going strong. Tucker challenged readers to put his car side by side with any car on the road in 1952.

He believed the Tucker would stack up in styling and performance. In fact, many features he'd wanted to include in the Tucker were now becoming accepted by the auto industry, like padded dashboards, safety windshields, and disc brakes. Certainly, time would prove him right on his vision for the car of tomorrow.

He told of how he started the company and of its troubles with the War Assets Administration, then of its conflict with the SEC and the trial. Tucker laid most of the blame on Harry A. McDonald. He suspected that McDonald was being prodded by Michigan's Senator Homer Ferguson, but it was McDonald who "threw the big punch."[3]

Tucker countered many of the SEC report's allegations and thanked the public for their support. He even apologized—"I regret that a lot of people lost money because they had faith in me and the Tucker car"—but made sure the readers knew that the corporation had not been "broke" financially when the government shut him down. "I feel if we had been left alone we could have pulled out of it. When we closed the plant, the Corporation had assets of $12,800,000." It was the government and their appointed trustees who were bad managers:

> The trustees sold equipment in August of that year at public auction for $156,000—18 per cent of the original cost and 45 per cent of the trustees' own appraisal of $345,000. Efforts on the part of stockholders were ignored; all they asked was holding it until September 22 when the court had scheduled a hearing on reorganization of the Corporation. But the trustees took no chances. They went ahead and disposed of assets on the basis of 18 cents on the dollar.[4]

Tucker believed Aircooled Motors alone was worth $5 million. Even the court-appointed trustees said the company's net worth in 1955 was $1.6 million with assets of $2.48 million against liabilities of only $412,503. And when the trustees gave that report, Aircooled owed its parent, Tucker Corporation, $905,000.[5]

Tucker ended by stating that if he was to get back into the automobile business it would not be to revive the Tucker '48—that car was now outdated in his mind. "If there is ever another Tucker car, I can promise that it will be as far from accepted, conventional design as is necessary to give the public the safety and performance I built into the original Tucker and which I believe sincerely the motoring public wants and deserves. I will never again be associated with an assembled automobile."[6] Instead, he would sell a build-it-yourself automobile in kit form.

———

Tucker's legal actions against the various news agencies languished in court for years after he filed them in 1950. The defendants and witnesses were scattered around the country, and they were in no hurry to see the lawsuits heard in court. It wasn't until July 13, 1954, that Preston Tucker gave his own deposition, allowing the *Detroit News* attorney to cross-examine him about his allegations.

The attorney asked Tucker who had instigated the attacks against him and his company. Again, he laid the blame with the SEC. The attorney asked him why the SEC would do that, and Tucker stated his belief that the Big Three auto companies—Ford, GM, and Chrysler—were behind it. Tucker believed the Big Three had influenced Homer Ferguson, Harry McDonald, and SEC attorney James Goode into putting undue pressure on his business.[7]

During the wide-ranging deposition, which lasted several days, Tucker's attorney stated on the record that he believed the evidence was going to show a direct connection back to Homer Ferguson, through Harry McDonald. When asked to clarify, he said:

> I said there were certain persons on the Securities & Exchange Commission who were working on behalf of the Detroit auto interests. And I am thinking in particular of Mr. Harry McDonald, who now, I believe, is chairman of the commission but was not at that particular time. Anybody that says Mr. McDonald was not working against Mr. Tucker and his enterprise is just nuts, as far as I'm concerned: he had a direct financial interest in the Detroit auto enterprises through business interests of his own, he was the political

protégé of Senator Ferguson, whose family is up to their necks in the Chrysler Corporation, and I think we will get into that question at some later time.[8]

As for Ferguson, Tucker testified about a lavish anniversary party Ferguson had thrown at the Mayflower Hotel in Washington, DC. It was unclear how Tucker knew the details he gave, but he listed attendees of the party and explained how the check for the entire event was picked up by Chrysler's finance officer, B. E. Hutchinson. Rather than asking Tucker what evidence he had to back up the story, the attorney asked him about the Tucker Corporation expense account, and if Tucker had ever misused it.[9]

Tucker also gave another possible explanation for McDonald's actions, but the defense attorneys chose not to follow up on it. They asked Tucker why McDonald might have been coming after him unfairly, and Tucker said he had received a phone call in Chicago from McDonald's former business partner at McDonald, Moore & Hayes. Tucker told the attorney that Moore had called him and asked for the exclusive rights to sell Tucker stock in Michigan when the offering was finally made. Tucker declined to give Moore such a deal. But the attorney skipped over this topic and instead asked him what phone conversations he might have had with McDonald.[10] Tucker felt that McDonald's actions may have been spurred partially by his refusal to strike a deal with McDonald's former business partner.

Similarly, Tucker told his interrogator that although he could not prove it, he understood that James Goode had sought a job at the Washington, DC, law firm employed by the Tucker Corporation in its early days. Goode was turned down, and Tucker believed it resulted in a "sour grapes" attitude, which contributed to him attacking Tucker's enterprise. Tucker had been told that it was Goode who had initiated and written the opinion the SEC released after it had approved the stock offering, in which the SEC had warned investors to avoid the stock.[11]

————

Meanwhile, Tucker dealers filed claims against the Tucker Corporation to try to get their money back, arguing they had been defrauded. Boyd

Veenkant and Clyde Bates were typical claimants. Hundreds of dealers had joined the suit, and the court asked the attorneys to choose two representatives to bring forward as test cases.[12] These two had agreed to pay $4,000 each for dealerships, which committed them to buying two hundred cars apiece—cars that were never delivered. Now they wanted their money back. The court examined their claims and threw out their cases. They appealed.

An appeals court explained the legal standards for fraud, a description which the SEC had never properly applied to Tucker:

> Claimants contend that Tucker Corporation made fraudulent or false pretenses respecting its ability to manufacture and produce the Tucker automobile. The specific fraud relied upon is that the Tucker Corporation, through its publicity and advertisement in newspapers and magazines, represented that it was then in a position to bring forth the Tucker automobile, whereas, those in charge of Tucker's affairs knew, or should have known, that the funds available to Tucker were entirely insufficient to do so. In the alternative, claimants seek recovery on the ground that Tucker's finance failed, it was no longer in a position to manufacture Tucker automobiles; that claimants were thereby . . . entitled to a return of the price paid.[13]

The court noted that investors knew Tucker was a "newly organized manufacturing company" and still, they had invested their money less than a year after the company was launched. And allegations of fraud were tied to the dates the men had bought their dealerships—that is, had Tucker Corporation made fraudulent statements to them on or before the dates they had signed up?[14] Actions and statements made later could not have contributed to them being defrauded into signing their contracts. At the time, Tucker had indicated only that he would build automobiles in the future, and everyone knew it would be an expensive undertaking. What's more, the court wrote, "no automobiles available to the general public had been manufactured during the period of World War II. A terrific demand for new automobiles had been built up. Had Tucker been able to get into production while this demand continued, it is very likely each franchise would have become a valuable property right."[15]

Too late to save Tucker, the court concluded that "there is no indication in the claims filed that Tucker Corporation did not honestly intend to use its best efforts to produce automobiles."[16] And, perhaps to underscore its ruling, the court of appeals upheld the lower court's most contentious ruling. It ordered Bates to pay $500 he still owed under his franchise agreement. He had never fully paid off the note to the Tucker Corporation, and now he would have to pay the money to the trustee in charge of marshaling the corporation's remaining assets for distribution to creditors.[17]

27

Joseph Turnbull Testifies Again

As Preston Tucker gathered evidence and testimony for his day in court, the defendants planned to take the position at trial that Tucker had indeed defrauded his investors, making what they had written about him true. Truth is a defense to most defamation and libel actions, so if Tucker's operation were a fraud, there would have been nothing wrong with saying so. It was an improbable argument, however, considering that Tucker had been found not guilty of fraud by a federal court.

The defendants thought their best bet was to call on Joseph Turnbull, the SEC accountant who had been the prosecution's linchpin in Chicago, his testimony considered so important that the prosecutors had saved him to be their last witness. On July 19, 1955, the attorneys in the civil actions traveled to Boston—where Turnbull lived—to question him.

Once again, however, the accountant was not as helpful as Tucker's opponents hoped. They asked him to identify the summaries of "questionable transactions" Turnbull had made for the criminal trial. One summary was for corporate payments made to Preston Tucker, totaling $380,199.36. After a few questions confirming that Turnbull had created the summary and was familiar with it, the defense attorney turned him over to Tucker's attorney for cross-examination.

Turnbull had introduced the same summary at trial, and the defense had a field day with it then. This time was no different. Among the suspect items paid to Tucker was his salary for two years, totaling almost $100,000. Was it wrong for Tucker to have drawn a salary? Turnbull waffled: "That is a matter of opinion, I believe."[1] Did he know for a fact that Tucker was reimbursed by the corporation for expenses he hadn't incurred? He was unsure.[2] While Turnbull backpedaled, the defense attorney—the one who had called Turnbull as a witness—began objecting often—thirty-four times in just a few hours, not counting numerous other interruptions without specific objections. When Tucker's attorney started a question by asking, "But I think we can agree, can we not—?" the defense attorney replied, "I object to asking the witness for any agreements."[3] When Tucker's attorney pulled out the transcript from the criminal trial to show how Turnbull's testimony had changed over time, the attorney objected.[4] When Tucker's attorney agreed to give the defense attorney a "continuing objection" so it would be unnecessary for him to keep objecting, he continued objecting: "It is understood that I have a continuing objection that this isn't proper cross-examination."[5] He then objected eighteen more times, on the same grounds, despite having no need to do so.

Despite the waters being muddied by the defense attorney, Turnbull's testimony helped Tucker. Turnbull admitted he had not looked at any of the Tucker documents in six years, and even prior to that, he had not bothered to check the items he had listed as being questionable in the corporation's books. He had seen the two cars Tucker had sold to the company but did not bother to find out that Tucker had sold them for exactly what he paid for them. Other money for which Tucker had been reimbursed had likewise not been checked. Turnbull had no idea whether the expenses were legitimate or not.[6]

Tucker's attorney asked Turnbull point-blank if he had any knowledge that the expenditures claimed by Tucker and his associates were "not bona fide and proper." The defense attorney objected vigorously, of course, after which Turnbull said, "Well, I have no knowledge of those claims at all."

By this time, Turnbull had no strong opinion about the financial dealings of Preston Tucker or his corporation. All he had done was look at the books, write some summaries, and reach no conclusions about whether any of it was legitimate.[7] As far as he was concerned on the day of his deposition, Turnbull was not prepared to say that Tucker and his associates had actually done anything wrong.

When the deposition ended, the defense attorneys went to the judge and asked for Turnbull's deposition to be sealed. At the time, witnesses in civil cases routinely asked for testimony to be sealed, and courts thought little of granting the requests. The judge agreed in this case as well, and the transcript would remain sealed until 2014.

28

The Last Days of Preston Tucker

Preston Tucker wasn't relying solely on lawsuits to reclaim his good name. In the years following the publication of his *Cars* article, he also took steps toward reaching the goals laid out in that essay. Tucker hoped to design an all-new automobile that would at first be sold in the form of a kit, containing parts simple enough for buyers to assemble themselves.

As Tucker imagined it, the car would be fun to drive and cost under $1,000. Again, his goals were lofty, probably impossible, but he took steps toward reaching them. He invited an automotive designer named Alexis de Sakhnoffsky to Ypsilanti Machine and Tool. (Those who had wondered about why it had been held in his mother's name certainly now saw the wisdom in it: he had managed to hang on to this shop even though he had lost pretty much everything else related to the ill-fated Tucker Corporation.) Sakhnoffsky was a Russian-born designer who had worked on everything from boats to airplanes and often referred to himself as Count Sakhnoffsky.[1] He had worked on the design staff at the Auburn Automobile Company in 1931 and even designed a "beautiful" Kelvinator refrigerator in 1936.[2]

When Tucker brought the designer to his shop, he presented his new approach. Spread out across several workbenches were many parts necessary to assemble a car, which were readily available from automotive vendors and could be used in any model. Tucker asked Sakhnoffsky if he could design a sports car around these parts. If so, the manufacturing process would be drastically reduced and the tooling necessary to build the car would be minimized. Sakhnoffsky saw the "pitfalls" inherent in having to design around ready-made parts, but was "fascinated by the thought of becoming associated with such an incredibly imaginative man as Preston Tucker."[3] He said he would do it.

Sakhnoffsky listened spellbound to Tucker explain his ideas for the new car. Tucker told him that many cars' fenders accumulated dirt and mud, making them needlessly heavier. If a car's fenders could be removed, it would make it easier to clean, so he wanted removable fenders on the new car. He also wanted the headlights to steer with the direction of the car. And, of course, he wanted the cyclops center headlight. It was Tucker's automotive trademark.

Other ideas were imported from Tucker's previous automobile as well. The car would be rear-engine drive and the instrument panel easy to use. He and Sakhnoffsky examined ways to keep the cost down and knew that the cost of sheet metal dies would be their largest obstacle. Assembly would be expensive as well. Tucker wondered if some body panels could be made from composite materials and asked Sakhnoffsky to investigate other industries, like the recreational vehicle industry, where composite body panels were gaining popularity. For inspiration, Tucker gave Sakhnoffsky a Harry Miller sketch of a race car design. Sakhnoffsky went to work.[4]

Sakhnoffsky drew a car that fit Tucker's vision of a fun and sporty car, and Tucker began looking into ways to launch the new project. He knew he could not get financing on any scale, and he told Sakhnoffsky that they could arrange for the kit cars to be shipped to automotive garages once buyers had paid for them. The cars would be designed to be built in ten hours by a mechanic. If the mechanic was paid six dollars an hour, the assembly cost would only be sixty dollars. Tucker believed he could easily find mechanics willing to do the work. He also looked for banks willing to act as escrow agents, holding buyers' money until the cars were delivered.

———

In 1953 or 1954 Tucker developed a hacking cough. When it would not go away, he visited a local doctor. A chest X-ray revealed a spot on one of his lungs. It was lung cancer.[5] A lifetime of smoking had caught up with the Lucky Strike smoker. Tucker vowed that he was going to fight and asked around about treatment options. When everyone told him there was little to be done, someone told him about Dr. William F. Koch, a doctor from Michigan who claimed to have a cure for cancer. Koch's treatment, which he called Glyoxylide, had been sold in huge quantities before the FDA prosecuted him for fraud. During the trial, expert witnesses testified that the medicine was nothing more than distilled water, and the chemical Koch claimed to have been using was not known to cure anything. In his first trial the jury could not reach a verdict. In the second, a mistrial was granted when a juror became ill. Koch moved to Brazil and apparently continued treating patients there.[6] Tucker began traveling to South America for Glyoxylide therapy.

Toward the end of 1955, Tucker announced in an article he wrote for *Car Life* magazine titled "I Never Gave Up" that the "new Tucker" was very near ready to be sold to the public. The magazine's cover bore a beautiful artist's rendering of what would later be called the Carioca, captioned PRESTON TUCKER'S SECRET NEW CAR. Inside, Tucker retold some of his story and then described the Carioca. Like in the *Pic* article announcing the Tucker Torpedo, Tucker blurred the line between what he wanted to do and what he had already done: "I have this new car now!"[7]

He admitted he was starting from scratch because "when the trial was over I was broke." He had spent his time since the acquittal running Ypsilanti Machine and Tool and saving his money to launch the new car. He noted that his Tucker sedans were still on the road and were proving themselves to be quality cars. Even so, Tucker again emphasized that they were, in his mind, "obsolete."[8] He avoided specifics, probably because of how his optimistic figures had been used against him at trial, and simply noted that the Carioca would be "a utility car with sports car performance. It will sell for less than the lowest-priced stock car on the market today."[9]

He described the Carioca as a rear-engine car with rear-wheel drive. One difference from the Tucker '48 was that this time the engine would be air-cooled, making the system simpler and lighter.[10] The Carioca would be safe, containing many of the advanced features the Tucker '48 had, and even some it didn't. Along with the padded dash and the pop-out windshield, the Carioca would also have a collapsible steering column "that will give, instead of killing the unfortunate driver who happens to be behind it." But, again, Tucker was cautious about his descriptions: "Brakes will be the best we can get, probably disk brakes which we didn't have the time or money to develop to our satisfaction the first time around."[11]

After describing the car, Tucker indicated that he was hoping to raise $2 million to launch the company. He didn't explain how he was going to do so on such a shoestring budget but said he could do it. And he said he would love to build the cars in America if he could. But, he granted, "it may even be that I will have to start in another country. There have been offers but I have been reluctant to accept them. I love my country and I believe I have had a part in building it. I will leave it only as a last resort."[12] He did not seem optimistic on his chances of staying in the United States, at least while the political climate stayed the same. "When government agencies become the tools of private monopoly, individual initiative and enterprise are doomed."[13]

———

Tucker worked on his Carioca out of the office of his two-story facility not far from his house. A portion of the plant had been rented by Joe Butcko, the tool and die maker who had gone with Tucker to New Orleans. Butcko had not gone to Chicago to work for the Tucker Corporation, instead starting his own successful business. Tucker now made most of his income renting out space in his buildings. Butcko often stopped in to visit Tucker, who "in that great big building was all by himself."[14] He presented a different figure from the high-flying dealmaker of just a few years earlier. Tucker quietly confided that he had been diagnosed with lung cancer and had traveled to

South America seeking a cure. He was optimistic he could beat it, though, and told Butcko not to worry about him.[15]

Tucker gave Butcko advice on business. Butcko had told Tucker about how someone was threatening to sue him after a business deal had gone sour. Butcko thought it was unfair, since the other party hadn't lived up to its end of the bargain. Tucker told Butcko to simply call the attorney for the other side and tell them to file suit, so Butcko could file a counterclaim. By Tucker's reckoning, the other side would back down when they realized they faced a claim twice the size of their own. And they did. The advice saved Butcko $4,000.[16]

When no domestic backers materialized for his Carioca, Tucker entertained offers from elsewhere. Traveling back and forth to Brazil seeking a cure for his cancer, he had made connections there; he met Juscelino Kubitschek, a state governor in Brazil who would become the country's president in 1956. Kubitschek indicated to Tucker that tax breaks might be available for his venture if he was willing to build the cars in Rio de Janeiro. Brazil could not offer any financial assistance beyond tax breaks, but Tucker liked the idea and had apparently been thinking of Brazil when he named the new car the Carioca—the name of a popular Brazilian ballroom dance and a nickname given to residents of Rio de Janeiro.[17]

Around Christmas 1955, Butcko stopped by Tucker's house with a present—two bottles of White Horse Scotch, Tucker's favorite drink—to thank him for the advice he had given him on the threatened lawsuit. Tucker greeted him wearing a bathrobe. It was the only time Butcko had seen Tucker not wearing a suit and tie. The two sat at Tucker's dining room table and Tucker confided in him. "You know, Joe, I had a lot of friends and I did them a lot of favors and I paid a lot of people way the hell more than they were worth. You bring me two bottles of scotch and I don't even get a Christmas card from those bastards." Tucker was depressed. He told Butcko his cancer was progressing.[18]

In August 1956 the family held a huge picnic in the yard behind the Tucker home in Ypsilanti. "He wanted everybody to come home and be there. Everybody was dressed up but apparently everybody knew that he was sick and that he was going to die," recalls Cynthia Tucker Fordon, his granddaughter, who was six years old at the time.[19] She remembers that he still looked pretty healthy and did his best to enjoy the time with his family, especially the children who were there that day. He still had his sense of humor. When he had walked out wearing all white—suit, shirt, tie, shoes— one relative said, "Look, it's Jesus Christ!" Everyone laughed, even Preston, albeit a bit sheepishly.[20]

———

Tucker traveled to Brazil several times in 1956.[21] On his last trip he became seriously ill and returned to Ypsilanti. On the flight home the plane made an emergency landing, because Tucker could not breathe.[22] He was placed on a ventilator, and when he arrived in Michigan he was admitted to Beyer Memorial Hospital on September 1. The diagnosis was not good. When family members visited, he was in an oxygen tent.[23] In early December 1956 the *New York Times* reported he was in serious condition.[24] Shortly before Christmas he developed pneumonia and his condition rapidly deteriorated.[25] He died the day after Christmas.[26] His son Noble later told the press that his father had been exhausted from his travels, having flown to Brazil and back three times just that year.[27]

Tucker's funeral was a low-key affair considering the headlines he had made a decade earlier. Joe Butcko did not even hear that he had passed away until long after the funeral. The service was attended mostly by close friends, family, and Tucker's coworkers from his time with the Lincoln Park Police Department. Pallbearers included the current Lincoln Park police chief and two former chiefs, along with some officers on the force with whom he worked.[28] He was buried in Flat Rock, Michigan.[29] He was survived by his mother, his wife, three sons, and two daughters.[30]

After Tucker died, his lawsuits, still dragging through the courts, were dismissed. The parties were still not done with the discovery phase, so we will never know what Tucker and his attorneys might have proven if the suits had made it to trial. Most of the news stories reporting his death focused on his criminal trial and the failure of his corporation. Some of the notices reminded readers that his car had been dubbed an "engineering monstrosity."[31] No one spoke of the cars that survived, and no one defended his memory—at least, not then.

In 1960 Charles Pearson wrote *The Indomitable Tin Goose*, a biography of Tucker, which primarily focused on the time the two men had spent together. Some readers sensed Pearson was pro-Tucker, defending him because it was Pearson's article that had started the Tucker juggernaut in the first place. It would be several decades before someone with a bigger platform would come to the defense of Preston Tucker's legacy.

29

The Movie

In 1988 Francis Ford Coppola released *Tucker: The Man and His Dream*, starring Jeff Bridges as Preston Tucker. The director told an interviewer it was a labor of love: Tucker had always fascinated him. As a child, Coppola said, he saw his father spend $5,000 on Tucker Corporation stock—all of which he lost—and he had seen a Tucker '48 sedan in the flesh. His father had even placed an order for one.[1] Even after the car never arrived—and it was clear that the down payment would never be returned—the elder Coppola never said a bad word about Tucker. The filmmaker took it as a lesson: one had to admire Tucker for trying to do something original.[2] To Coppola, the Tucker '48 became "a mythical thing."[3]

In 1974 he bought the maroon Tucker sedan #1037[4] and tracked down Alex Tremulis for expert advice on restoring it. Interacting with one of Tucker's lead designers gave Coppola the idea to make a movie about Tucker, but Tremulis didn't seem all that impressed with the notion. He said, "Coppola doesn't really understand automobiles, I think. He's a difficult man. He's got 5,000 bottles of wine or whatever—la-di-da. He plays music at night—la-di-da."[5] Nothing came of the idea at the time, but Coppola loved his Tucker and bought another in 1980, the blue #1014.[6]

Over the next few years, Coppola would often return to the idea of adapting Preston Tucker's story into a film. At one point he took serious steps toward making it as a musical. Someone talked some sense into him and suggested he make it as a regular drama.[7] He mentioned Tucker's story to George Lucas, who liked the story of Tucker's battles: "The thing that fascinates me is that Tucker is about how you bring dreams into reality, which is something filmmakers do all the time. It is interesting to me to hear a story about how that happens—and how you have to go against the system."[8] George Lucas agreed to produce the film, while Coppola would direct.

Despite Alex Tremulis's opinion of the director's knowledge of cars, he agreed to join the project as a consultant. He visited the set and met the actor who would play him, Elias Koteas. Koteas was clean-shaven, while Tremulis always wore a mustache. Tremulis shook the actor's hand and reached up to stick a piece of black tape under the actor's nose.[9] Viewers of the movie will note that the producers agreed with Tremulis's suggestion: Koteas wore a mustache in the film.

Coppola sought advice from Preston Tucker's relatives and acquaintances. Vera, Tucker's widow, and four of his children consulted on the film set and signed off on the script. John Tucker even lent a pair of his father's cufflinks to Jeff Bridges, who wore them in the movie's climactic courtroom scene. "Having those Tucker cufflinks gave me a terrific energy and inspiration," Bridges recalled. "Having Preston's family around, so willing to talk and share their lives with us, was just like a gold mine for an actor."[10] Preston's granddaughter Cynthia Tucker Fordon spent time on the set and answered questions for the actors and filmmakers, ensuring such an attention to detail that Bridges handled his cigarettes the same way Preston did.[11]

Coppola reproduced many other aspects of the story quite realistically. He located a Ford assembly plant in Richmond, California, that had furnished Jeeps and other items during World War II, to replicate the Chicago Dodge plant.[12] Today, the plant is part of the Rosie the Riveter WWII Home Front National Historical Park. Keen-eyed movie viewers might notice mountains in the backgrounds of scenes set in Michigan, but such infidelities are minor. The attention to detail extended even to the design of the Tuckers' Chicago apartment building; Rick Fizdale, who has written a history of the building, notes that the apartment scenes in the movie—although not shot at the original location—were quite reminiscent of the actual interior of the apartment.[13]

To Tucker aficionados, the film is remarkable for another reason. Coppola wanted as many authentic Tucker sedans as possible in the movie and asked the Tucker community for help. Coppola's two Tuckers were featured in the film—his maroon #1037 played the role of the Tin Goose—and twenty-two more were volunteered by members of the Tucker Automobile Club of America. Many owners drove their cars during filming, putting both the cars and their owners into the movie.[14]

The movie cost $23 million to make—quite close to what Tucker himself had raised to launch his car company.[15] George Lucas saw further parallels between Tucker and Coppola, who had fought his own battles with an intransigent industry. "The character of Tucker has certain resemblances to Francis. They are both half creative genius and half enthusiastic promoter. They both have that ability to continue dreaming even after a dream has been deferred or delayed or somehow impeded."[16] Coppola saw the similarity too. While discussing *Tucker*, he told an interviewer, "All movies parallel your life."[17]

Tucker was not a financial success, but it was well received by critics, and it renewed the debate about whether Tucker had suffered at the hands of malevolent government bureaucrats or from his own incompetence or ill intent. The movie simplified some of the plotlines, choosing to pin all the blame for Tucker's failure on Homer Ferguson, working at the behest of the Detroit automakers. In the film, Tucker and Ferguson even meet in Washington, where Ferguson all but tells him he will be put out of business to protect Ferguson's constituents.

Many people compared Tucker to John DeLorean, another renegade carmaker who launched his own revolutionary car company to much fanfare in the 1970s, only to see the enterprise crash amid allegations of fraud and malfeasance. In 1982 DeLorean was also tried by the federal government, though he was charged not with securities violations but with drug trafficking. He was acquitted—the jury agreed with the defense that DeLorean was the victim of entrapment—after his attorney took a page from the Tucker trial and called no witnesses. Did he compare himself to Tucker? "Oh, sure, I see similarities," DeLorean told a reporter in 1988. But he had no regrets. "You give it a shot. You know it's better to have loved and lost than never to have loved at all." Tucker's daughter Marilyn also was reminded of her father when she watched DeLorean's trial unfold. "I've thought about the similarities between my father and DeLorean quite a bit," she told an interviewer.[18]

At least one Tucker expert involved in the movie thought it presented Tucker in a little bit too much of a glorified light. A Milwaukee Tucker collector named Al Reinert was consulted by the filmmakers because of his extensive knowledge of Tucker, gained as he traveled the country buying Tuckers and Tucker parts, and speaking with people who had built the cars. At the time of the movie, Reinert owned two Tuckers and was often asked about details to make the script and the sets more accurate. He told an interviewer in 1988 that there were two sides to Tucker, at least from what he had gathered over the years.

"Preston Tucker was a very advance-minded person. The man did have brains. The man was bucking the system." The downside? "In the end, he used these people. His methods were very, very shabby. The man was working way beyond his means. He just promised too much, too fast, and he couldn't deliver."[19]

30

After

After the criminal trial, Cliff Knoble went home and could not find work in advertising. The suspicion that he must have done something illegal hung over him despite his acquittal. He was in his fifties. His wife took jobs baby-sitting while he sold used cars and worked as a retail clerk. Eventually, he turned to writing. He didn't turn the corner financially until he received his first advance—one hundred dollars.[1]

Alex Tremulis had better luck. Brilliant automotive designers are not as common as admen. As a result, Tremulis had no trouble lining up job interviews. But at Nash Motors, his interviewer did not believe him when he said that he'd designed the Tucker '48. Tremulis later said, "The chief engineer greeted me with the statement, 'You are the eighth designer who claims to have designed the Tucker automobile.' I excused myself and went to my car and brought back my portfolio of my cars, aircraft and Duesenbergs. When he looked at my designs, he laughed and apologized . . . 'The other seven,' he said, 'were bums.'"[2]

Nash had no room on its payroll, so Tremulis ended up working for Kaiser-Frazer in Michigan, the company that could borrow any amount of money it wanted from the Reconstruction Finance Corporation. Later he

went to Ford Motor Company, where he led the Advanced Design department until 1963.[3] He then opened his own design consulting firm in Ann
Arbor, Michigan. One of his projects was the Gyronaut, a motorcycle specifically designed to break the land speed record, which it did at the Bonneville
Salt Flats. The motorcycle, using an engine that only put out 120 horsepower, managed a top speed of 245 mph.[4] Tremulis called it "the fastest
hunk of ballistic missilery you're ever going to see."[5]

In 1968 Tremulis moved to Ventura, California. He worked briefly with
people attempting to revive the Duesenberg nameplate and again on a land
speed record. This one was for a motor home, Ramona Motor Coach's
Travoy, which reached speeds in excess of 97 mph on a dry lake bed in the
California desert. Tremulis even piloted the coach during a high-speed run.
He also did design work for Honda and Subaru.[6]

Tremulis was recognized for his work during his lifetime, vindication for
a man whose most noted design was a car disgraced by legal problems. He
was inducted into the Automotive Hall of Fame in 1982. "It took me years to
get out of the Hall of Shame, but I finally made it. I kept going. I was a little
wilder than everybody else."[7] In 1987 the Society of Automotive Engineers
recognized several cars as "significant automobiles of the past half century,"
and included the Tucker '48. It was in good company: others in the group
were the Cord 810, the first Lincoln Continental, the Studebaker Starliner,
and the 1956 Corvette.

When the Coppola movie about Tucker came out, the wave of surrounding publicity led many reporters to track down Tremulis and ask him about
Tucker. In 1988 he told a journalist, "Preston was a terrific guy. Hell, we
loved him and worked our hearts out for him. He was one of the finest
people I've ever met."[8] Alex Tremulis died December 29, 1991.

Vera Tucker, Preston's wife, lived until 1995, long enough to see her
husband's legacy preserved in the Coppola movie. Shortly after its release, a
reporter asked her daughter, Marilyn McAndrew, what Vera thought of the
film. "She thought it caught the spirit of the family very well, and my father's
magnetic spirit." McAndrew had helped Coppola during filming and had
told the director, "My father is looking down on this and smiling."[9] Although

Vera had been living in Arizona when she passed away, she was buried in Flat Rock, Michigan, near Preston.

Philip Egan, who helped Tremulis bring his drawings to life and did most of the design work on the dashboard and interior of the Tucker, also had a successful career as a designer after the Tucker Corporation. He designed household appliances for Sears and then worked for a company designing hearing aids. Eventually, like Tremulis, he opened his own design firm. In 1989 he wrote *Design and Destiny*, his account of working at the Tucker Corporation four decades earlier. In 2008 Egan passed away. Like Tucker, he died on December 26.[10]

Otto Kerner Jr., the prosecutor of Preston Tucker and his associates, had an illustrious career after the trial—and then a spectacular crash. First he became a Cook County judge. Then, in 1960 and 1964, he was elected governor of Illinois. He said he planned to step down from the governorship in 1968 because of his wife's health but was almost immediately nominated to the US Court of Appeals by Lyndon Johnson. He took the bench in May 1968.[11] Many people believed he had stepped down as governor specifically so he could accept the judgeship.

In December 1971 Kerner was indicted, along with four other people, for fraud. The attorney general charged him with receiving discounted stock in two racetracks in return for political favors. The charges included bribery, conspiracy, tax evasion, and perjury before a grand jury. He was tried along with several other defendants in 1973, and convicted.[12] He became "the first sitting U.S. appellate judge to be convicted in the nation's history."[13] He was also the first in a series of Illinois governors to be incarcerated. Sentenced to three years in prison, he was released early, the parole board agreeing with his argument that his health required it and that his reputation had been so damaged that further prison time was unnecessary. He was right about his health; upon his release, he checked into a hospital to be treated for lung cancer. He died in 1976.[14] Kerner had spent the last few years of his life unsuccessfully appealing his convictions.

Drew Pearson, the muckraking radio man and newspaper columnist who virtually destroyed the Tucker Corporation with his June 6, 1948, radio broadcast, died in 1969. When he passed away, his bank account was overdrawn. His estate paid to settle two outstanding libel suits against him. Two publishers demanded the return of advances paid for books he failed to write. A farm he owned had lost $70,000 the year before he died. Pearson left behind seven different wills, assuring that his heirs would spend much time—and money—fighting over what little he had left behind.[15] One United Press International article summarized his career: "Government officials assailed many of his stories as inaccurate . . . or even blatant lies. Among those in high places who called him a liar were two presidents—Franklin D. Roosevelt and Harry S. Truman."[16]

The Tucker family home in Ypsilanti still stands. Shortly after the movie's release in 1988, a Michigan investor approached the owner about purchasing it and turning it into a Tucker museum. He hoped to set up a shop across the street from the home and to manufacture Cariocas as well. By the end of 1992, the plans for the museum and auto plant had fallen through and the owners placed the home back on the market.[17] At the time of this book's writing, the house is unoccupied.

31

The Tucker Legacy

Preston Tucker set out to launch a car company and build a revolutionary car that incorporated features he was convinced would become commonplace: aerodynamic styling, disc brakes, fuel injection, a safer passenger compartment. Not all these features made it into the initial run of Tucker '48s, but it seems clear that if the company had survived, more of them would have.

Preston Tucker is remembered today as a visionary. The curator of the National Museum of American History, Roger White, said, "Tucker thought of the automobile as a malleable object. He was kind of like Frank Lloyd Wright in that respect, unafraid to start from scratch."[1]

Still, Preston Tucker's legacy will always contain the element of the unknown. How might the future of the American automobile industry have been different if Tucker had succeeded? Roger White suggested that it does not matter. "If someone has a beautiful dream, but doesn't know how to achieve it, is he a great man or not? Whether Tucker was a great man or not, he was a quintessential American."[2]

There were two reasons Tucker did not succeed. The first was simply the problem of money. Tucker raised somewhere in the neighborhood of $25 or $28 million. Although he hoped to raise more as his company developed,

he underestimated the overall cost of competing with the major auto manufacturers of the time. Henry Kaiser, another carmaker who failed in his
efforts to conquer the car market in the post-WWII era, had managed to
raise more than $50 million to finance his operation. Later he said he would
have needed closer to $200 million to fortify his company for longer-term
success.[3]

Tucker was unrealistic about the difficulty of mass-producing automobiles, particularly at the price point he had promised consumers. He was a
salesman, and his true skill was salesmanship. He was not an engineer or an
astute businessman. Perhaps he could have succeeded if he had surrounded
himself with the right people and given them the authority to do their jobs,
but that never happened. Tucker was not a criminal; he was naive.

But even if Tucker could have raised enough money and hired the right
people, he would still have had to contend with the obstacles thrown up by
the government. Who was behind the push to shut Tucker down? Some
suspicion will always fall on Homer Ferguson. Tucker was convinced that
Senator Ferguson was his primary antagonist, but he had little more than
hearsay to back up this belief. Certainly, Harry A. McDonald, who was also
from Detroit, had a major hand in the attack on Tucker.[4] There is ample
evidence that the SEC, at the direction of McDonald, went out of its way to
harm the Tucker Corporation by telling Drew Pearson of the investigation
and then leaking its confidential report to the press. But what motivated the
SEC? Were they told to do it by someone else?

Another possibility is that employees of the SEC were simply frustrated
by their inability to do what they believed their jobs to be. The SEC was
tasked with protecting investors from unscrupulous promoters. In Tucker's
case, the SEC had overseen the doom-and-gloom warnings of the prospectus
and taken the extra step of issuing a statement warning investors to steer
clear of the offering. And yet investors still flocked to invest. What else could
the SEC do? Perhaps the effort to take down Tucker was simply viewed
as another step to protect investors from what the SEC perceived as a bad
investment. This is not to say they were right. However, it may explain their
motivation.

Not everyone believed Tucker was brought down by outside forces at all. In later years, Alex Tremulis said he did not think anyone in particular caused the downfall of Tucker. He chalked it up to mismanagement and a shortage of money. Were other manufacturers worried about Tucker? "I really saw very little professional jealousy take place," he insisted.[5] Of course, Tremulis was the designer of the car. He did not have day-to-day interaction with the business side of the Tucker Corporation. If someone had gone out of his way to shut down the Tucker Corporation, would Tremulis have been in a position to see it?

The prosecution of Preston Tucker and his associates should have caused every businessman in America to shudder. Tucker launched a car company and promoted it in an attempt to raise money. His promotional zeal was treated as a crime, and those who assisted him were charged with crimes as well. What if the SEC had decided to target other US companies for how they promoted their businesses? Would public relations executives face prison time for sending out press releases as Cliff Knoble had?

Moreover, if the prosecutors honestly believed what they told the jury—that Preston Tucker and his associates ran a scheme to steal money—then why weren't they also prosecuted for tax evasion? If the individuals had profited from the scheme, those proceeds would have been taxable. But it came out at the trial that the men had not misappropriated any of the funds from the company for their personal use. Neither the grand jury nor the prosecutors ever suggested that the tax returns of Tucker and his codefendants were improper. The returns must have been scrutinized; after all, Tucker was prosecuted in the same building where Al Capone had been found guilty of not paying federal taxes on income he had derived through an illegal enterprise.

Despite the prosecution and attacks, Preston Tucker will get the last word. The cars he built—the fleet of Tucker '48 sedans and the Tin Goose—have become a lasting reminder of Tucker's dream. And those cars have, for the most part, outlived Tucker's critics.

32

The Fleet of Tucker '48 Sedans

Of the fifty-one Tucker '48s built, including the Tin Goose, forty-seven survive. The fate of three of the missing sedans is also known. One was #1027, the vehicle that had crashed during road tests at Indianapolis, with Eddie Offutt hanging onto the steering wheel for dear life. Later, it was stripped for parts. Tucker #1018 was severely damaged when it bounced off a bridge abutment and wrapped around a tree near South Wales, New York. It split in half when it was yanked from the tree by an overzealous tow truck driver. And Tucker #1023 burned in a warehouse fire.[1] The owner retrieved the remains from the ashes and buried them.

It is a small enough number for Tucker fans to track and a remarkable testament to the quality of the cars that so many have survived.

At the auction of the Tucker Corporation assets in October 1950, many of the cars sold for just a little over a thousand dollars if they were missing an engine or a transmission. Complete cars were sold for $2,000 to $3,000—of the dozens of sedans sold, $3,000 was the maximum price. Some buyers bought more than one car, and many also picked up spare parts to complete their cars or just to have spares handy. The Tin Goose was among the cars sold. Tucker employees had replaced the 589-cubic-inch engine and had also installed the more conventional Cord transmission, replacing the fluid drive torque converter system, which had never worked properly. Employees had also replaced the car's bumpers. When it had been unveiled to the public, the Tin Goose's front bumper had been created out of wood and made to look like steel.[2] Stories surfaced that the car was sold at the auction for $2,500.[3]

The Tin Goose changed hands a few times and ended up in a field behind a barn in Pennsylvania. Les Schaeffer owned it, along with the front half of the crashed #1018. Its other half was missing and was probably scrapped, but the Tin Goose was mostly intact. Photos taken of the car around 1971 show it sitting on blocks, missing both bumpers, surrounded by weeds and dirt.

Then John Lemmo, former director of operations for the Cleveland Browns, bought the Tin Goose from Schaeffer. Lemmo already had a Tucker but was more interested in the prototype.[4] He rescued it from the field and restored it, painting it bright red, although the car had originally been maroon. He installed a production steel bumper on the front and an aluminum rear bumper that had been cast using a production bumper as a model. As a result, the car today looks only a little different than when it was unveiled in 1947.[5]

Lemmo brought the car to a gathering of Tucker fans in Ann Arbor, Michigan, in 1984. Alex Tremulis was there to see his creation after all those years. He commented to Lemmo about how much lead had been used to sculpt the car and asked him if he had ever weighed the car; Lemmo hadn't.[6] Tremulis used the occasion to comment on the sorry state of automotive design, remarking on the ugliness of cars in 1984. He said the Big Three were "torturing innocent sheet metal."[7]

Lemmo took the Tin Goose to the Kruse International automobile auction in Auburn, Indiana, for their twenty-fifth annual Labor Day auction of collector cars in 1995.[8] There, it was bought by the Swigart Museum, America's oldest car museum. Its antique automobile collection in Huntingdon, Pennsylvania, started as the private collection of W. Emmert Swigart, an insurance salesman fascinated by cars when they were still a new invention. He began collecting and preserving early cars and passed the collection to his son. Over time, the cars numbered in the hundreds and included many one-of-a-kind automobiles. But the collection did not contain a Tucker, so

Swigart bought two at the Kruse auction that day: the Tin Goose and #1013.[9] Although the Swigart Museum occasionally takes #1013 to car shows, it is almost always displayed next to the Tin Goose, which is always on display. The museum has an unwritten rule that while some cars rotate in and out of displays, the Tuckers don't.[10]

––––––

Many other Tucker sedans reside in museums, living the good life indoors, protected by velvet ropes and regularly polished. Tucker #1039, for example, currently resides in the Smithsonian Institution, safe and sound. Surprisingly, it has a criminal record. The silver sedan changed hands a few times after leaving the factory. In the early 1990s it was owned by an entrepreneur in Southern California. That man's business generated a lot of cash, and he invested some in the rare car. The cash flow was—according to federal agents—the product of a meth lab operation. Drug Enforcement Administration officers swooped in and shut down the business and seized the operator's assets, including Tucker #1039. It was 1992 and Tucker prices were climbing. The seizure of the unusual car made the news, and soon members of the Tucker Automobile Club of America were on high alert.

As part of a plea agreement, the defendant surrendered the Tucker to the government. Most nonliquid assets of criminal enterprises subject to seizure are slated for public auction, and Tucker #1039 was no exception. TACA members worried. What if the vehicle was sold to someone outside the United States? One Tucker had recently been sold to a car company in Japan, where it today sits in a museum, thousands of miles and an ocean away from its home. Might there be a way to keep Tucker #1039 in the country?

TACA asked its members to petition the White House, asking the DEA to donate the car to a museum. TACA offered to assume liability for the car's maintenance. Or, they suggested, the car could be given to the Smithsonian Institution, which did not yet own a Tucker. The DEA agreed to donate the car to the institution, which took possession of Tucker #1039 in 1993. The car is not always shown; the holdings of the Smithsonian are too large for everything to be on display. But from time to time, #1039 is available for visitors to see at the National Museum of American History in Washington, DC.

———

Most Tuckers, once they are acquired by museums, stay put. Such was not the case with Tucker #1036, which made a brief, well-publicized escape attempt from a Louisiana museum.

Detroit real estate mogul Bernard Glieberman bought and sold football teams as well as property. He and his son Lonie had bought the Ottawa Rough Riders of the Canadian Football League in 1991, but had since fallen out with the league—and much of Canada—when the team didn't live up to expectations. The Gliebermans' purchase price had been a dollar, which wasn't as good a deal as one might think. Along with a team that hadn't seen a winning season in over a decade, Glieberman acquired about a million dollars of debt. The elder Glieberman let his son run the team, and various personnel decisions soon caused them and the team to lose favor with what few fans the Rough Riders had left in Ottawa. So they sought to move the team to the United States, but the CFL blocked the move.

A compromise was struck: The CFL had decided to set up franchises in the United States, much as Major League Baseball has teams in both countries. Might the Gliebermans be interested in a CFL franchise in Shreveport, Louisiana? The Gliebermans sold their share of the Ottawa team and began setting up shop for the CFL's new Shreveport Pirates. While in Shreveport, Glieberman, who had bought #1036, loaned the car to the Ark-La-Tex Antique & Classic Vehicle Museum. When the car had left the Tucker plant in Chicago, it had been painted "Andante" green. By the time it got to the museum, it had been repainted copper. Although it had only been driven a few thousand miles since it had been built, it was badly in need of a professional restoration. At this point, Tucker #1036 was already too valuable to be driven all that often.

The Shreveport Pirates did not play well. In their first season at Shreveport's Independence Stadium, they won only three games to offset fifteen losses. They went 5–13 the next year. Grumbling in town led the

Gliebermans to look for a more hospitable place to play. They investigated moving the team to Norfolk, Virginia. But Shreveport officials were worried about some unfinished business. Unresolved issues over rent and use of the stadium led to a lawsuit. As the two sides squabbled, Bernard Glieberman suddenly realized he had a vulnerability: his Tucker was in Shreveport, and it was worth a lot of money. Would it get dragged into the litigation? Just to be safe—although details of this event are sketchy—Glieberman's attorney went to the museum and asked for the keys. The car was, after all, owned by Glieberman. The attorney got in the car and headed out of town, hoping to get the car away from Shreveport's legal clutches.

Tuckers are known for their speed, but one thing they need, not surprisingly, is gasoline. The attorney, in his haste to get out of town, didn't notice that the Tucker's gas gauge was on empty. Right outside of town, the car sputtered to a stop. The attorney coasted to the side of the road and wondered what to do next. A minute later, a friendly police officer stopped to see what was the matter with the stalled car. It's not every day a police officer gets to see a Tucker on the side of the road.

The Tucker was brought back to the museum. Shreveport officials ran to court and asked the judge to impound the vehicle in case it was needed later to satisfy a judgment against the Gliebermans. The judge agreed that the Tucker was a flight risk and placed the car under house arrest at the museum. A large sticker on the windshield warned: UNITED STATES MARSHAL. NO TRESPASSING.

The Gliebermans resolved their legal issues with Shreveport, and shortly after, the CFL decided that Americans weren't interested enough in their version of football to maintain teams south of the border. The sticker on Tucker #1036's window was removed and the car was released.

The car turned up again in 2014 when it was auctioned during the Pebble Beach car show, the Concours d'Elegance. The winning bid was $1.425 million, which, with the buyer's premium, means the new owner paid $1,567,500 to acquire it.[11] Other Tucker '48s have sold for much more. In 2012 a well-restored Tucker '48 was auctioned for $2.7 million by Barrett-Jackson. With the buyer's premium, the total purchase price was $2.9 million. That sedan was blue, #1043.[12]

———

Nick Jenin, a hotel operator in Florida, began collecting Tuckers in 1952, and by 1960 he owned ten. Jenin had gotten to know Tucker and simply loved the cars. He often took them to auto shows and charged admission to see "the Fabulous Tuckers." He told a reporter he paid between $3,500 and $6,500 for each of the cars. He drove one to New York City from Florida specifically to show it to reporters attending the International Auto Show at the New York Coliseum. On the drive north, a Florida state trooper pulled him over on the turnpike and asked if he could examine the car. When he realized he wasn't getting a ticket, Jenin obliged. Jenin said he stopped driving the cars because they caused a ruckus everywhere he went. More than a decade after the demise of the Tucker Corporation, people still knew the cars and what they stood for.[13]

Jenin decided to give one of the Tuckers to his daughter for daily driving. Knowing the idiosyncrasies of the car, he decided it would be best if the car—#1046—had a conventional drivetrain. He removed the Tucker engine and transmission and placed the car on an Oldsmobile chassis with an Oldsmobile drivetrain. His daughter drove the car once and told her father that the car drew too much attention for her to use it. So Jenin sold the car to a Mercury dealer. The new owner could not have his Tucker powered by Oldsmobile; he moved the car onto a Mercury chassis and drove it that way for a while. The car changed hands a couple times and eventually ended up with another collector, who painstakingly restored it to its original configuration with all Tucker parts and a Tucker drivetrain.[14]

———

Perhaps the most important person in the field of maintaining the Tucker legacy was a Virginia real estate investor named David Cammack. Cammack had seen the Tin Goose display at the Mayflower Hotel when Tucker toured the country. He was just a teenager, but he remembered in later years that the place was packed. He had hoped to see the infamous 589-cubic-inch engine, but the trunk wasn't open when he was there. Shortly after, the SEC investigation hit the news and Cammack, like many other Americans, lost interest in the car.[15]

In 1972 Cammack heard that a museum in New York was selling two Tuckers. By the time he called, one had already been sold. He bought the other, #1022. Cammack embarked on a fourteen-year restoration of the car. In the meantime, #1001 became available. He added that to his collection in 1973. In 1974 another Tucker called to him, and #1026 soon joined the others. Each car needed restoration, including new engines. Luckily, while Tucker had only ordered body panels for about fifty cars, he had obtained more than a hundred engines for his endeavor. Cammack had no problem locating new ones for his cars, although he spent quite a bit of time wheeling and dealing for them.[16]

When Cammack bought #1026, its previous owner also owned a Tucker test chassis and asked Cammack if he would like to add it to his collection. Soon Cammack was buying everything Tucker-related he could find. He eventually had an almost complete collection of the various engine configurations the Tucker Corporation had experimented with before settling on the Aircooled.[17] He displayed the nine engines on stands in his warehouse turned private museum in Virginia. Word got out that he was buying Tucker materials, and soon someone called with the ultimate find: fifty thousand blueprints and engineering drawings for the Tucker sedan and all of its components. They had been sold at the factory liquidation auction for $2,000, and the owner said he wanted the outrageous sum of $10 million for them. Cammack declined the offer.[18]

A few years later, the man with the blueprints passed away without selling them. His family, cleaning out his belongings, loaded up the blueprints and other papers and took them to the dump. The dump refused them, presumably because paper needed to be processed elsewhere. Someone in the family then wondered if the Tucker Automobile Club might be willing to help them dispose of the paper. Word soon got back to Cammack and he worked out "a much more reasonable price" for the drawings.[19]

Cammack's collection eventually included three beautifully restored Tucker sedans; #1026 is the only surviving Tucker with an automatic transmission—the Tuckermatic. Amazingly, Cammack never drove his cars, even though each was perfectly drivable. "I would have liked to have driven them, but after 14 years of restoration, I've lost my enthusiasm for driving them. I don't care to work on them. I'm getting too old to crawl up and down, cleaning them up." Cammack was notoriously generous with his collection, however. He kept a listed phone number and showed off his collection to anyone who asked. Tucker fans from around the globe appeared at his doorstep and were given personal tours by Cammack himself.[20]

People who spoke with Cammack were also intrigued to see that his own views on Tucker had changed over time. After hearing about the Tucker fraud allegations and losing interest in the automaker and his cars, he had bought his first Tucker simply as an investment. There were only so many around that they had to increase in value. But after he acquired his collection, he realized something: the remains of the Tucker Corporation were more than what would have been created by a fraudster, particularly the fifty thousand blueprints and engineering drawings. "I don't think there was any doubt that he was serious about building a car. I think all these drawings prove that. I think Tucker was absolutely honest. He was trying to do too much at one time. Everything was new," Cammack told a writer for *Hemmings Classic Car*.[21]

David Cammack passed away in April 2013 at the age of eighty-five. His will stipulated that his entire Tucker collection would go to the Antique Automobile Club of America, to be housed in their museum in Hershey, Pennsylvania.[22] There, a room had already been built to display the collection, paid for by a donation from Bill Cammack, Dave's brother.[23]

———

As mentioned, a few Tuckers have left the country. In August 2010 an Australian businessman bought #1045 in the United States for $1,140,000. He took the car to Australia, where he reportedly had to install emergency flashers on it to make it street legal.[24]

Tucker #1004 went to Japan, but not before it had an exciting life in the United States. First, it was one of the cars sold to dealers before the company went bankrupt. Pittsburgh Tucker Sales bought it in June 1948, and it was then purchased by a car dealer named Red Harris. It wound up in the possession of a man named Joe Merola, a twenty-four-year-old who wanted to try stock car racing. Merola found a local sponsor, painted the number 12 on the side, and entered a few races. The Tucker did not fare well, breaking down mechanically each time Merola raced. The culprit was a rear axle that kept breaking, traceable to the Aircooled motor developing too much torque. Merola retired from racing, never having won any races, and sold the car. Its next owner, Wayne Weaver, was a dealer in Clarion, Pennsylvania; he sold #1004 for $2,250 in 1963. The new owner kept the car for more than twelve years, mostly in a barn. While it was there, someone stole the battery and the radiator. In 1976 the owner decided to have the car restored. It was finished in 1978, and in 1988 #1004 appeared in the film *Tucker: The Man and His Dream*. The owner of the car died and his son sold the car a few years later to a business in Las Vegas. They, in turn, sold it to the Toyota Automobile Museum in Japan.[25]

Tucker #1035 spent a couple decades forgotten in a barn in Sao Paolo, Brazil. No one really knows how, but #1035 found its way to Brazil very early. While some thought it must have ended up there as part of Preston Tucker's efforts to promote his Carioca auto design in the mid-1950s, all sources indicate the car was already there before Tucker first visited the country. A man named Roberto Eduardo Lee had bought it for a collection of cars he had on display. In 1975 he died, and his personal museum was closed while his heirs fought over the one hundred cars Lee had left behind. During that time, thieves and vandals broke in. The Tucker was not stolen, but it was damaged. In 2011 the local government reached a deal with the heirs to retrieve the cars and put them back on display. This Tucker needs more than just a little work to get it back into proper form. Not only did it sit neglected for decades, but someone swapped out much of the car's drivetrain and chassis with that of a 1947 Cadillac. Members of TACA have offered their assistance and assure Tucker fans that the car can be restored to its original glory.[26]

Tucker #1007 is a typical museum Tucker. Sold first to Aircooled Motors for testing purposes, its engine was replaced, suggesting that the original engine may have been pushed to its mechanical limits. During the bankruptcy, the court declared the car an asset of the Tucker Corporation—which owned Aircooled—and the car was part of the liquidation auction on October 20, 1950. In 1953 Nick Jenin bought it and added it to his collection of Fabulous Tuckers. Jenin sold it in 1964 to a man in Texas who spent fifteen years restoring it. A few years later, he placed it in an auction, where it sold for a then-record price of $255,000. In 2001 the Petersen Automotive Museum bought a collection of cars that included this Tucker, but since they already had one, they turned around and sold it shortly after. The LeMay family bought it and placed it in the collection they keep in Tacoma, Washington.[27]

Tucker #1010 made headlines in late 2010 when it reemerged from years of obscurity. Aficionados had heard it was hidden away in the Northwest, but rumors and facts were so intermingled that no one knew for sure. It had been sold to Philadelphia Tucker Sales in July 1948. A few owners later, it was in California, where it was purchased by Don and Mignonette Wright in 1956. Don Wright was president of the Tucker Automobile Club for a couple years but did not like to talk about his own Tucker sedan. In fact, #1010 sat parked in his garage for decades. It was "dragged out of a ramshackle garage in Auburn, Wash., where it was parked for 54 years," and then sold at auction for $797,500.[28] It was "complete but not running." Someone had painted it an outlandish turquoise and the interior upholstery had been redone. The odometer displayed 9,819 miles, but most experts believe the car has been driven 109,819 miles, or possibly even 209,819. Rumors circulated that the car may even have spent time at the Bonneville Salt Flats doing high-speed runs in the late 1940s or early 1950s, but no documentation has surfaced to confirm that. It matters little: the auction winner was at least the eleventh owner of the vehicle and will probably restore it.[29] The high mileage will not detract from what will most likely end up being a million-dollar car.

One more Tucker '48 could still exist: Tucker #1042. Rumors abound that the car was smashed intentionally, or involved in some kind of shady transaction. Pieces of it have turned up, but the rest of it might be out there somewhere. With the prices of survivors heading skyward, it wouldn't matter what condition it was found in for it to have value.

———

If people today have heard anything at all about Preston Tucker, they likely know little more than that he tried to start a car company. If they've seen the Jeff Bridges movie, they think of him merely as a man who fought a valiant battle against government corruption and lost. But Tucker's legacy is more nuanced than that, and he deserves much more credit than most people give him. In a time when big corporations ruled the auto industry, his upstart company made waves. His stock offering was remarkably successful for such a speculative venture, and the car he imagined was ahead of its time. Many of the features he touted—like aerodynamic styling and new safety features inside and out—would later become standard on American roadways.

It is true that Preston Tucker had flaws. He underestimated the cost of setting up a car company, as well as the resistance he would encounter. And his detractors are quick to point out that he had little chance of success with or without government interference. But the cars Tucker built are still out there—forty-seven of the original fifty-one—a lasting memorial to his bold adventure.

His legacy is more than just the car, however. Tucker dared to compete in the highest levels of American business, and he came tantalizingly close to succeeding.

Acknowledgments

Thanks to Josh Bertocki, Laura Bieniewicz, Joe Butcko, Andrew Campbell, the Detroit Public Library, Martyn Donaldson, Rick Fizdale, Cynthia Tucker Fordon, the Gilmore Museum, Steve Harris, Harry S. Truman Library & Museum, Brad Hunt, Mary Jane Kamrowski, Leslie Kendall, Ken Lehto, Paul Lehto, Rick Lehto, Mark Lieberman, Glenn Longacre, Joe Lupinacci, Ian Lyngklip, Ryan Moran, National Archives Chicago, Gwynyth Oswin, the Petersen Automotive Museum, Yibin Ren, Simone Samano-McDaniel, Pat Swigart, Yuval Taylor, Steve Tremulis, John Tucker, and Leslie Lynch Wilson.

Notes

I. AN EARLY MORNING CAR CRASH

1. This story is told in many places. One is by Tucker himself: Tucker, "My Car Was Too Good," 4.

2. The crash is described several places, including Tucker, "Inter-Office Memorandum," n.d., but accompanied by a cover letter of October 18, 1948, courtesy of the Tucker Automobile Club of America archives; and the Tucker Corporation film *Tucker: The Man and the Car*, where it is said that Offutt was doing over 95 mph. The film was "Produced for the Public Relations Dept. of Tucker Corporation," but bears no copyright date. It can be dated based on the cars that it shows, and some of the scenes can be likewise placed. It was released after November 1, 1948. The film is available several places and can be seen on YouTube.

3. Some sources say it was a bruised knee, but Tucker, "Inter-Office Memorandum," described the accident in detail at the time and said it was his elbow. Tucker also wrote later that it was a bruised elbow. The confusion lends itself to the notion that the injury must have been slight, otherwise people would be more inclined to get the body part right when telling the story. Tucker, "My Car Was Too Good," 4.

4. Tucker, "Inter-Office Memorandum."

2. PRESTON THOMAS TUCKER

1. Pearson, *Indomitable Tin Goose*, 23–24.

2. Knoble, *Call to Market*, 193–194.

3. Cynthia Tucker Fordon, interview by the author, September 11, 2014.

4. Certificate of death for Shirley H. Tucker, State of Michigan, filed February 5, 1907. Sources often vary on his age when his father died. See "Preston Tucker of 'Auto Fame,' Dies," *Star-News* (Wilmington, NC), December 27, 1956. There, he was said to have been four when his father died.

5. David L. Barber, "Unique Car Builder Is Remembered Here," *Herald-News* (Reed City, MI), September 21, 1988, courtesy of John Tucker.

6. Data regarding Lucille and Shirley Preston as well as the living arrangements and so on are all from census records and other government documents. Thanks are in order to Tom Spademan, who unearthed all of this information for the author, particularly because the family history is rather complex and had been described inaccurately elsewhere. That the family often took in lodgers is also from Tucker Fordon, interview by the author.

7. White confirmed the employment details in his statement to the SEC. See SEC, *Tucker Corporation*, 511.

8. Pearson, *Indomitable Tin Goose*, 23, 27–29.

9. Ibid., 32.

10. According to the Tucker Corporation stock offering prospectus, Tucker worked for Ford from 1920 to 1924, but it is not indicated whether this was continuous. Tucker Corp., *Prospectus*, 16.

11. Pearson, *Indomitable Tin Goose*, 32–37.

12. The date of 1925 as the beginning of his sales career is from Tucker Corp., *Prospectus*, 16.

13. Pearson, *Indomitable Tin Goose*, 38.

14. Dates of Tucker's employment with the Lincoln Park Police Department courtesy of the Lincoln Park Preservation Alliance.

15. Pearson, *Indomitable Tin Goose*, 37–38.

16. Dates of Tucker's employment courtesy of the Lincoln Park Preservation Alliance; title of "zone manager" is from Tucker Corp., *Prospectus*, 16.

17. John Shea, "Fenders and Headlights Will Turn on Preston Tucker's New Motor Car," *Ottawa Citizen*, August 27, 1946.

18. That Tucker met Miller in 1925 is from Tucker Corp., *Prospectus*, 16.

19. The Lincoln Park Preservation Alliance, *Lincoln Park*, Images of America (Arcadia, 2005), 57.

20. Flyer labeled "Please Read All of This," signed "Preston T. Tucker for Mayor," courtesy of the Lincoln Park Preservation Alliance.

21. Election details courtesy of the Lincoln Park Preservation Alliance.

22. Peter H. Blum, *Brewed in Detroit: Breweries and Beers Since 1830* (Detroit: Wayne State University Press, 1999), 163.

3. HARRY MILLER

1. Some sources say he dropped out at fifteen. See Jason Stein, "In a Lifetime Filled with Achievements, There Was Only One Thing That Would Finally Slow Him," *Lakeland (FL) Ledger*, December 25, 2005.

2. Timothy Gerber, "Built for Speed," *Wisconsin Magazine of History*, Spring 2002, 33.

3. Ibid., 34.

4. Ibid.

5. Ibid., 35.

6. Ibid., 36.

7. Ibid., 37.

8. Stein, "In a Lifetime."

9. Jeffrey Steele, "The Tucker Mystique," *Chicago Tribune*, July 3, 1994, says it was 1929.

10. E. Y. Watson, "Miller Builds for Speedway: Plans Four-Wheel Drive Racer to Appear at Indianapolis," *Milwaukee Journal*, November 1, 1931.

11. "New Company Will Make Marmon Autos," *Deseret News*, January 9, 1934.

12. Larry Edsall, *Ford Racing Century: A Photographic History of Ford Motorsports* (Minneapolis: Motorbooks, 2003), 38.

13. David Lanier Lewis, *The Public Image of Henry Ford: An American Folk Hero and His Company* (Detroit: Wayne State University Press, 1987), 332; also letter from N. W. Ayer & Son, January 28, 1935, courtesy of the Lincoln Park Preservation Alliance.

14. N. W. Ayer & Son, January 28, 1935.

15. Ibid.

16. Beverly Kimes, *The Cars That Henry Ford Built* (New Albany, IN: Automobile Heritage Publishing & Communications, LLC, 2004), 112.

17. N. W. Ayer & Son, January 28, 1935.

18. Kimes, *Cars That Ford Built*, 112.

19. "Henry Ford Has Entered Ten of These in Big Race," *Milwaukee Journal*, May 17, 1935.

20. Edsall, *Ford Racing Century*, 37.

21. Ibid., 39.

22. R. G. Lynch, "Harry Miller Does a Right About Face," *Milwaukee Journal*, May 22, 1935.

23. Kimes, *Cars That Ford Built*, 112.

24. Lewis, *Public Image*, 332. Some sources say nine cars tried qualifying with only four making the field. See Edsall, *Ford Racing Century*, 37.

25. Edsall, *Ford Racing Century*, 40.

26. Many sources say that *all* the cars suffered steering failure, while some list the front-drive leak on the one car and steering gear failure on the others. See Kimes, *Cars That Ford Built*, 112; and Lewis, *Public Image*, 332.

27. Edsall, *Ford Racing Century*, 37.

28. Lewis, *Public Image*, 332.

29. Ibid.

30. Edsall, *Ford Racing Century*, 48.

31. Ibid., 37.

32. "Shaw, Mays, Rose Favored In Indianapolis Classic," *Ottawa Citizen*, May 28, 1941.

33. Bob Considine, On the Line, *St. Petersburg Times*, May 8, 1943.

4. THE TUCKER COMBAT CAR

1. Joe Butcko, interview by the author, September 8, 2014.

2. Mary Jane Kamrowski, interview by the author, September 11, 2014.

3. Tucker Fordon, interview by the author.

4. R. P. Hunnicutt, *Armored Car: A History of American Wheeled Combat Vehicles* (New York: Presidio Press, 2002), 32.

5. "Armored Tank Attains Speed of 114 M.P.H.," *Mechanix Illustrated*, February 1939, 59.

6. Hunnicutt, *Armored Car*, 32.

7. P. T. Tucker et al., "Gun Control Mechanism," US patent 2,366,072, December 26, 1944.

8. *Development of Aircraft Gun Turrets in the AAF*, Army Air Forces Historical Studies 54 (AAF Historical Office, June 1947), 108–109.

9. Ibid., 110.

10. US Air Force, "Bell P-39 Airacobra" (fact sheet), National Museum of the US Air Force official website, accessed March 3, 2014, www.nationalmuseum.af.mil.

11. US Air Force, "Tucker XP-57" (fact sheet), National Museum of the US Air Force official website, accessed October 25, 2013, www.nationalmuseum.af.mil.

12. US Air Force, "Bell P-39 Airacobra" (fact sheet), National Museum of the US Air Force official website, accessed March 3, 2014, www.nationalmuseum.af.mil.

13. *Aircraft Gun Turrets*, 110.

14. Ibid., 108–111.

15. P. T. Tucker et al., "Gun Mounting and Control Mechanism," US patent, 2,408,707, October 1, 1946.

16. "114-M.P.H. Anti-Aircraft Combat Car in Production," *Mechanix Illustrated*, January 1942, 87.

17. Shea, "Fenders and Headlights Will Turn."

18. *Tucker: The Man and the Car* (film).

19. Ibid.

20. The story of Tucker's turret being widely used by the US military is ubiquitous on the Internet and can also be found in scholarly works. See John Heitmann, *The Automobile and American Life* (Jefferson, NC: McFarland, 2009), 131. It's even discussed as if it were a fact in Egan, *Design and Destiny*, 12.

21. *Aircraft Gun Turrets*, 98.

22. Ibid., 109.

5. ANDREW HIGGINS

1. "Higgins Industries Buys Tucker Aviation," *Milwaukee Sentinel*, March 24, 1942.

2. Ibid.

3. Ibid.

4. Jerry E. Strahan, *Andrew Jackson Higgins and the Boats That Won World War II* (Baton Rouge: LSU Press, 1998), 102.

5. Butcko, interview by the author.

6. Ibid.

7. Ibid.

8. Tucker Fordon, interview by the author.

9. Butcko, interview by the author; Chevrolet's role in the business is also covered in Strahan, *Andrew Jackson Higgins*, 172–173.

10. Butcko, interview by the author.

11. Strahan, *Andrew Jackson Higgins*, 198.

12. Stein, "In a Lifetime"; "Race Engine Designer Dies," *Pittsburgh Press*, May 4, 1943.

6. TUCKER'S AUTOMOBILE PLANS

1. Egan, *Design and Destiny*, 11.

2. Alan L. Gropman, *Mobilizing U.S. Industry in World War II: Myth and Reality* (Washington, DC: Institute for National Strategic Studies, 1996), 35.

3. Ibid., 59.

4. Heitmann, *Automobile and American Life*, 119.

5. Gropman, *Mobilizing U.S. Industry*, 59. The exact date varies depending on the source. See Heitmann, *Automobile and American Life*, 119.

6. Gropman, *Mobilizing U.S. Industry*, 59–60.

7. Ibid., 62.

8. Alan Milward, *War, Economy, and Society, 1939–1945* (Oakland: University of California Press, 1979), 122–123, quoted in Gropman, *Mobilizing U.S. Industry*, 63.

9. John A. Byrne, *The Whiz Kids: Ten Founding Fathers of American Business—and the Legacy They Left Us* (New York: Doubleday Business, 1993), 81.

10. Ibid.

7. THE *PIC* ARTICLE

1. Pearson, *Indomitable Tin Goose*, 17.

2. Ibid.

3. Egan, *Design and Destiny*, 23.

4. Ibid., 24.

5. "New Tucker Trial Looms," *Reading (PA) Eagle*, October 12, 1949.

6. SEC, *Tucker Corporation*, 44.

7. Tucker, deposition, 39.

8. SEC, *Tucker Corporation*, 45.

9. *Tucker Topics* 1, no. 7: 3.

10. Tremulis, "Epitaph," 58.

11. SEC, *Tucker Corporation*, 45.

12. Ibid.

13. Pearson, "Streamlining That Car."

14. Egan, *Design and Destiny*, 24.

15. Heitmann, *Automobile and American Life*, 111.

16. Pearson, "Streamlining That Car."

17. Pearson, *Indomitable Tin Goose*, 61–62.

18. "Tucker Visions New Auto to Cruise at High Speed," *Milwaukee Journal*, August 13, 1946.

19. Shea, "Fenders and Headlights Will Turn."

20. "Engine-in-Rear Auto to Buck Car Industry," *Pittsburgh Post-Gazette*, July 8, 1946.

21. Leo Donovan, "Forecast from Detroit," *Popular Mechanics*, November 1946, 91.

22. Pearson, *Indomitable Tin Goose*, 19.

23. Egan, *Design and Destiny*, 38.

24. Ibid., photo 3.

25. Pearson, *Indomitable Tin Goose*, 19–20.

8. THE TUCKER CORPORATION

1. Pearson, *Indomitable Tin Goose*, 55–56.

2. SEC, *Tucker Corporation*, 47.

3. Rockelman, "Behind the Gasoline Curtain," 15.

4. SEC, *Tucker Corporation*, 49.

5. Pearson, *Indomitable Tin Goose*, 60.

6. SEC, *Tucker Corporation*, 49.

7. "The Story of the Tucker '48" (brochure), n.d., courtesy of the Tucker Automobile Club of America archives.

9. TUCKER ACQUIRES A PLANT

1. Tucker Corp., *Prospectus*, 8.

2. Pearson, *Indomitable Tin Goose*, 65.

3. George Meader, counsel for US Senate Special Committee Investigating the National Defense Program, to Senator Homer Ferguson, December 15, 1947, Homer Ferguson Papers, Bentley Historical Library, University of Michigan. On the other hand, Pearson said that Beasley told him Tucker claimed to have $12,000 to his name and that he had called Tucker's bank to confirm. Pearson, *Indomitable Tin Goose*, 63. I am going with the former version because it comes from sworn testimony and because Pearson, who was a friend of Tucker, may have been biased.

4. SEC, *Tucker Corporation*, 48.

5. Ibid. That it was a money order and not a check is from Tucker's testimony at his deposition. The SEC report does not indicate the form of the payment—merely that the funds came from Ypsilanti Machine and Tool.

6. Pearson, *Indomitable Tin Goose*, 64.

7. Tucker Corp., *Prospectus*, 5.

8. Rockelman, "Behind the Gasoline Curtain," 16.

9. Kamrowski, interview by the author.

10. The co-op was organized such that the tenants bought into the organization and then leased their units from the co-op itself. Owners like Tucker were often said to "own" or have "bought" their apartments, a description that elides the nuance of the situation but is not altogether inaccurate. This and all other information regarding the 999 apartment is from Rick Fizdale, interview by the author, September 13, 2014.

11. SEC, *Tucker Corporation*, 50.

12. Ibid., 51.

13. Ibid., 50.

14. Ibid., 52.

15. Tucker, deposition, 44.

16. Meader to Ferguson, December 15, 1947.

17. Pearson, *Indomitable Tin Goose*, 64.

18. SEC, *Tucker Corporation*, 52.

19. Ibid.

20. Ibid., 54.

21. Ibid.

22. Pearson, *Indomitable Tin Goose*, 74.

23. Ibid., 73.

24. Thomas T. Fetters, *The Lustron Home: The History of a Postwar Prefabricated Housing Experiment* (Jefferson, NC: McFarland, 2001), 31–37.

25. Tucker, "My Car Was Too Good," 5.

26. Douglas Knerr, *Suburban Steel: The Magnificent Failure of the Lustron Corporation, 1945–1951* (Columbus: Ohio State University Press, 2004), 76–77.

27. "Testimony to Be Heard on Plant Lease," *Sarasota Herald-Tribune*, November 22, 1946.

28. US Senate letter from Meader, December 15, 1947.

29. "Plans for Tucker's Car Plant Started in Night Club, Story," *Milwaukee Journal*, November 22, 1946.

30. "Testimony to Be Heard on Plant Lease," *Sarasota Herald-Tribune*.

31. "Plans for Tucker's Car Plant," *Milwaukee Journal*.

32. "Housing Inquiry Witness Missing," *Spokesman-Review* (Spokane, WA), November 25, 1946.

33. "Senate Committee Seeks Lost Witness in Housing Inquiry," *News and Courier* (Charleston, SC), November 24, 1946.

34. "Senate Committee Seeks Lost Witness," *News and Courier*.

35. Knerr, *Suburban Steel*, 84–88; "#259. Letter Accepting Resignation of Wilson Wyatt as Housing Expediter," Harry S. Truman Library and Museum official

website, accessed October 21, 2015, www.trumanlibrary.org/publicpapers /index.php?pid=1829.

36. Tucker, "My Car Was Too Good," 5.

37. SEC, *Tucker Corporation*, 55.

IO. BEFORE THE STOCK OFFERING

1. Pearson, *Indomitable Tin Goose*, 76.

2. Jeff Gordinier, "A Lot of Drive," *Los Angeles Times*, August 11, 1988.

3. "Tremulis: The Genius Behind the Tucker," *Automobile Quarterly* 26, no. 3 (1988): 248.

4. Ibid., 246.

5. Ibid.

6. Ibid., 248.

7. Pearson, *Indomitable Tin Goose*, 87.

8. Gordinier, "A Lot of Drive."

9. "Tremulis: The Genius," *Automobile Quarterly*, 248.

10. Ibid.

11. Ibid., 246.

12. Peter Gareffa, "1967 Gyro-X Self-Balancing Car to Be Restored," Edmunds.com, March 4, 2013, www.edmunds.com/car-news/1967-gyro-x-self-balancing -car-to-be-restored.html.

13. "Tremulis: The Genius," *Automobile Quarterly*, 248.

14. Ibid.

15. Ibid.

16. Ibid.

17. Ibid., 252.

18. Gordinier, "A Lot of Drive." There are slightly different versions of the story regarding how Tucker and Tremulis first met. One is that Tucker contracted with the design firm where Tremulis worked and then later offered Tremulis the job working at the Tucker Corporation. It seems a minor difference. See Egan, *Design and Destiny*, 28–29.

19. Tremulis, "Epitaph," 62.

20. "Tremulis: The Genius," 252.

21. Tremulis, "Epitaph," 62.

22. Gordinier, "A Lot of Drive."

23. "No Room for Dreams: Preston Tucker's Fate," *Toledo Blade*, September 18, 1988.

24. Tremulis, "The 1946–48 Tucker," 1.

25. Tremulis, "Epitaph," 58.

26. Tremulis, "The 1946–48 Tucker," 1.

27. Tremulis, "Epitaph," 58.

28. "Tremulis: The Genius," *Automobile Quarterly*, 252.

29. Tremulis, "The 1946–48 Tucker," 1.

30. Tremulis, "Epitaph," 58.

31. Pearson, *Indomitable Tin Goose*, 88.

32. Tremulis, "The 1946–48 Tucker," 1.

I I. THE TIN GOOSE

1. Tremulis, "The 1946–48 Tucker," 2. Egan wrote it was indeed Tremulis who gave the car the nickname the Tin Goose. See Egan, *Design and Destiny*, 75.

2. There is some debate regarding the year of the Oldsmobile. Egan suggests it was 1942; see Egan, *Design and Destiny*, 38. Pearson does not mention a year; see Pearson, *Indomitable Tin Goose*, 89. Alex Tremulis does not mention the donor Oldsmobile at all in his SAE paper, but in "Epitaph," 57, he calls it a 1942; Steve Tremulis, nephew of Alex, believes it was a 1941, based on a trim tag found among Alex Tremulis's tools, thought to be from the donor car to the Tin Goose.

3. Pearson, *Indomitable Tin Goose*, 89.

4. Egan, *Design and Destiny*, 35.

5. Ibid., 37.

6. Ibid., 38.

7. Ibid., 39.

8. Pearson, *Indomitable Tin Goose*, 95–96.

9. Egan, *Design and Destiny*, 39.

10. Ibid., 96.

11. Mark Lieberman and Ken Lehto, interview by the author, 2015. Ken Lehto is an automotive engineer with decades of experience in the automobile industry.

12. Tremulis, "The 1946–48 Tucker," 2.

13. Ibid.

14. Ad from the *New York Tribune*, reprinted in Egan, *Design and Destiny*, photo 4.

15. "Step into a New Automotive Age in the Rear Engine Tucker," advertising circular, courtesy of the Tucker Historical Collection and Library, Gilmore Car Museum.

16. "Torpedo Devotees Just Don't Tucker Out," *Argus-Press* (Owosso, MI), June 28, 1984.

17. "The Story of the Tucker '48" (brochure).

12. GETTING READY

1. Tucker Corp., *Prospectus*, 17; SEC, *Tucker Corporation*, 58.

2. Tucker Corp., *Prospectus*, 18–19.

3. Tucker, "My Car Was Too Good," 5.

4. "SEC Stop Order Issued on Tucker," *Toledo Blade*, June 11, 1947.

5. Biographical information of SEC chairmen from "SEC Historical Summary of Chairmen and Commissioners," US Securities and Exchange Commission official website, accessed August 27, 2013, www.sec.gov/about/sechistoricalsummary .htm.

6. "Harry M'Donald Ex-U.S. Aide, Dies," *New York Times*, July 4, 1964.

7. "Ten Names Put in Nomination for President; Hoover Remains Non-Committal," *Gettysburg Times*, June 27, 1940.

8. Harry A. McDonald, "1949 and the Securities Business," talk given at the Chicago Stock Exchange, March 3, 1949, transcript available at the US Securities and Exchange Commission official website, www.sec.gov/news/speech /1949/030349mcdonald.pdf, p. 1.

9. Harry A. McDonald, "The Structure and Works of the S.E.C.," remarks given in Detroit, MI, September 26, 1947, transcript available at the US Securities and Exchange Commission official website, www.sec.gov/news/speech /1947/092647mcdonald.pdf.

10. Tucker, deposition, 869–870.

11. "Drivers End Race Boycott," *San Jose News*, May 22, 1947.

12. "Qualifiers for 500," *Milwaukee Journal*, May 29, 1947.

13. Bob Gilka, "Veteran Mauri Rose Wheels to Second Triumph in '500'," *Milwaukee Journal*, May 31, 1947.

14. Bob Gilka, "Unique Rear Engine Car Will Run in Race Here," *Milwaukee Journal*, June 3, 1947.

15. Bob Gilka, "27 Cars to Qualify for 14 Places Here," *Milwaukee Journal*, June 6, 1947.

16. *Tucker Topics* 1, no. 1, courtesy of Mark Lieberman.

17. Ibid.

13. THE TIN GOOSE UNVEILED

1. Pearson, *Indomitable Tin Goose*, 109.

2. Ibid.

3. Ibid., 109–111.

4. Egan, *Design and Destiny*, illustrations 13 and 22.

5. Egan, *Design and Destiny*, 77.

6. Pearson, *Indomitable Tin Goose*, 109–111.

7. Egan, *Design and Destiny*, 78.

8. Pearson, *Indomitable Tin Goose*, 109–111.

9. Egan, *Design and Destiny*, 78.

10. Pearson, *Indomitable Tin Goose*, 109–111.

11. Ibid., 112.

12. Ibid.

13. Ibid., 113.

14. Egan, *Design and Destiny*, 78.

14. THE STOCK OFFERING

1. "Tucker Corp. to Sell Stock," *Pittsburgh Post-Gazette*, June 27, 1947.

2. Tucker Corp., *Prospectus*, 1.

3. Ibid.

4. Pearson, *Indomitable Tin Goose*, 107.

5. SEC, *Tucker Corporation*, 2.

6. Ibid.

7. Tucker, deposition, 858.

8. SEC, *Tucker Corporation*, 56.

9. Tucker Corp., *Prospectus*, 3.

10. Pearson, *Indomitable Tin Goose*, 107.

11. Tucker Corp., *Prospectus*, 3.

12. Ibid., 6.

13. Ibid., 4.

14. Ibid., 5.

15. Ibid., 5.

16. Ibid.

17. Ibid., 11.

18. Ibid., 12.

19. Ibid., 5.

20. Ibid., 6.

21. Ibid.

22. Ibid., 17.

23. Ibid., 18.

24. Ibid., 18–20.

25. Ibid., 27.

26. Pearson, *Indomitable Tin Goose*, 120.

27. "California Bans Tucker Stock Sale," *Pittsburgh Press*, August 1, 1947.

28. SEC, *Tucker Corporation*, 66.

29. Pearson, *Indomitable Tin Goose*, 115–116.

30. Ibid., 116.

31. Ibid., 118.

32. Cowan, "Tucker: The Man, the Myth," 230.

33. Pearson, *Indomitable Tin Goose*, 118.

34. Ibid., 122–123.

35. W. L. Bussell, "Pittsburghers Lose $500,000 in Tucker Bust," *Pittsburgh Press*, June 12, 1949.

36. Knoble, *Call to Market*, 197.

37. Tucker Corp., *Annual Report*, 3.

38. "Tucker Was Here," *Newsweek*, March 14, 1949.

39. Ibid.

40. Tucker Corp., *Annual Report*, 2.

I5. POST-TIN GOOSE

1. *Tucker Topics* 1, no. 2, courtesy of Mark Lieberman.

2. Ibid.

3. Pearson, *Indomitable Tin Goose*, 124.

4. Ibid.

5. Ibid., 125.

6. Ibid., 126.

7. Knoble, *Call to Market*, 190.

8. Ibid., 191.

9. Ibid.

10. Ibid., 196; date of hire is from the lawsuit Knoble later filed. See also "Tucker Is Sued on Salary Deal," *Spokane Daily Chronicle*, August 31, 1948.

11. Tucker Corp., *Annual Report*, 1.

12. Ibid., 4.

13. Ibid., 2.

14. Tucker Corp., *Prospectus*, 6.

15. Tucker Corp., *Annual Report*, 2–3.

16. Ibid., 9.

17. Ibid., 20.

18. Ibid., 21.

16. GEARING UP FOR PRODUCTION

1. Egan, *Design and Destiny*, 83.

2. Tremulis, "Epitaph," 60.

3. Robin Miller, "Indy's Unluckiest Legends: Part 1," *Racer*, May 20, 2013, www .racer.com/indycar/item/55512-indys-unluckiest-legends-part-1.

4. Tremulis, "Epitaph," 60.

5. Egan, *Design and Destiny*, 83.

6. Edward Miller, "Tucker Torpedo Is Gone, but It's Not Forgotten," *Free Lance-Star* (Fredericksburg, VA), October 18, 1984.

7. Tremulis, "Epitaph," 59.

8. Mark Lieberman, interview by the author, 2015.

9. Some sources say it was fourteen states. See Gordinier, "A Lot of Drive."

10. Egan, *Design and Destiny*, 88; Tremulis mentioned the Tucker logo in Gordinier, "A Lot of Drive."

11. Tremulis, "Epitaph," 58.

12. Gordinier, "A Lot of Drive."

13. Margalit Fox, "Philip Egan, a Designer of a Fabled Sedan, Dies at 88," *New York Times*, January 12, 2009.

14. *Tucker Topics* 1, no. 3.

15. Ibid.

16. Ibid.

17. SEC, *Tucker Corporation*, 511.

18. Ibid., 512.

19. Ibid., 514.

20. Ibid.

21. Ibid., 514–515.

22. *Tucker Topics* 1, no. 4: 1.

23. Ibid., 11.

24. Egan, *Design and Destiny*, 93.

25. Pearson, *Indomitable Tin Goose*, 132.

26. Egan, *Design and Destiny*, 95.

27. Pearson, *Indomitable Tin Goose*, 132.

28. Lieberman, interview by the author.

29. William S. Bergstrom, "Memories Revived in Tucker Hometown," *Evening News* (Newburgh, NY) August 22, 1988.

30. Pearson, *Indomitable Tin Goose*, 132–133.

31. Ibid., 138.

32. Ibid.

33. Ibid.

17. THE FIRST CAR OFF THE ASSEMBLY LINE—#1001

1. Egan, *Design and Destiny*, 98–99.

2. *Tucker Topics* 1, no. 5: 14.

3. Ibid.

4. Pearson, *Indomitable Tin Goose*, 139.

5. *Tucker Topics* 1, no. 5: 15.

6. Egan, *Design and Destiny*, 102.

7. "Tucker 'Dream' Car Still Just That," *Dealer News*, March 10, 1948.

8. Tucker Corp., *Prospectus*, 6.

9. Egan, *Design and Destiny*, 111.

10. Veenkant v. Yorke, 256 F.2d 808 (1958).

11. "Tucker Lines Up Enough Steel for 240 Cars a Day," *Dealer News*, March 17, 1948.

12. "Tucker Torpedo Out in June," *New York Times*, February 12, 1948.

13. *Tucker Topics* 1, no. 5: 2.

14. Ibid., 3.

15. Ibid., 3–4.

16. Egan, *Design and Destiny*, 104.

17. "Tucker Buys Plant for Making Motors," *Dealer News*, March 31, 1948.

18. Ibid.

19. *Tucker Topics* 1, no. 5: 12.

20. Ibid. Some sources said the show was a half hour long, but the company's own publication would seem to be a more accurate source.

21. Ibid.

22. Pearson, *Indomitable Tin Goose*, 148–149.

23. Egan, *Design and Destiny*, 110.

18. THE ACCESSORIES PROGRAM

1. Knoble, *Call to Market*, 201.

2. *Tucker Topics* 1, no. 7: 3.

3. *Tucker Topics* 1, no. 6: 3.

4. Pearson, *Indomitable Tin Goose*, 146.

5. Knoble, *Call to Market*, 203.

6. Ibid., 201.

7. Pearson, *Indomitable Tin Goose*, 151.

8. Tremulis, "Epitaph," 5, 64.

9. *Tucker Topics* 1, no. 6: 6.

10. Ibid., 11. Campini's first name is sometimes spelled "Secundo."

11. Ibid.

12. Pearson, *Indomitable Tin Goose*, 130.

13. Tucker, "My Car Was Too Good," 6.

14. Pearson, *Indomitable Tin Goose*, 131.

15. Ibid.

16. Drew Pearson, "More on the Ferguson-Thomas Issue," *St. Petersburg Times*, September 28, 1948.

17. Tucker, "My Car Was Too Good," 6.

19. THE END OF THE DREAM

1. Some sources say he was fifty-two. *Tucker Topics* wrote that he was fifty-one. See *Tucker Topics* 1, no. 7: 3.

2. "Ralph Hepburn Killed at Indianapolis Speedway," *Pittsburgh Post-Gazette*, May 17, 1948.

3. "Last Rites for Racing Driver Ralph Hepburn," *Dealer News*, May 26, 1948.

4. *Tucker Topics* 1, no. 7: 16.

5. Ibid.

6. Tucker, deposition, 881–882.

7. Ibid., 885.

8. "Tucker Told to Let SEC Scan Books," *Detroit Free Press*, June 16, 1948.

9. Egan, *Design and Destiny*, 113; Pearson, *Indomitable Tin Goose*, 152.

10. "Tucker Shows New Automatic Transmission; 28 Basic Parts," *Dealer News*, June 30, 1948.

11. Securities and Exchange Act of 1934, sec. 24(b).

12. *Tucker Topics* 1, no. 7: cover.

13. Ibid., 1.

14. Ibid., 3.

15. Arthur Herman, *Joseph McCarthy: Reexamining the Life and Legacy of America's Most Hated Senator* (New York: Free Press, 2000), 232.

16. Ibid., 233.

17. Knoble, *Call to Market*, 207.

18. Tucker, "My Car Was Too Good," 6.

19. Pearson, *Indomitable Tin Goose*, 153, says $6 million.

20. Knoble, *Call to Market*, 207.

21. Tucker, "My Car Was Too Good," 6.

22. Knoble, *Call to Market*, 207.

23. Drew Pearson, "Tucker Auto in Mire," *St. Petersburg Times*, June 10, 1948.

24. Tucker, "My Car Was Too Good," 7.

25. "Let SEC Scan Books," *Detroit Free Press*.

26. Untitled story, *Dealer News*, June 16, 1948.

27. SEC, *Tucker Corporation*, 514.

28. Pearson, *Indomitable Tin Goose*, 140–141.

29. "Tucker Confident Firm to Receive 'Clean Bill,'" *Milwaukee Journal*, July 2, 1948.

30. Lieberman, interview by the author.

31. "Tucker Shows New Automatic Transmission," *Dealer News*.

32. Pearson, *Indomitable Tin Goose*, 142.

33. "TUCKER NEWS BUREAU Release Wednesday PM's," dated June, from context it is clearly from 1948, courtesy of the National Automotive History Collection, Detroit Public Library.

34. "TUCKER NEWS BUREAU," dated June 23, courtesy of the National Automotive History Collection, Detroit Public Library.

35. Tucker, "My Car Was Too Good," 7.

36. SEC, *Tucker Corporation*, table of contents (unnumbered page), under subheading IV, "Investor Witnesses."

37. "Tucker Confident," *Milwaukee Journal*.

38. SEC, *Tucker Corporation*, 3.

39. Ibid., 4.

40. Preston Tucker, "An Open Letter to the Automobile Industry in the Interests of the American Motorist," *Pittsburgh Post-Gazette*, June 14, 1948.

41. Egan, *Design and Destiny*, 112–113.

42. "Tucker Confident," *Milwaukee Journal*.

43. Ibid.

44. Ibid.

45. Ibid.

46. Gordinier, "A Lot of Drive."

47. Egan, *Design and Destiny*, 112.

48. Pearson, *Indomitable Tin Goose*, 153, 156.

49. "Tucker Auto Receivership Is Demanded," *Pittsburgh Post-Gazette*, July 15, 1948.

50. "Tucker Receiver Requested in Suit," *Milwaukee Journal*, July 15, 1948.

51. Ibid.

52. "Grand Jury to Probe Tucker Auto Company," *St. Petersburg Times*, February 17, 1949.

53. SEC, *Tucker Corporation*, 516.

54. Pearson, *Indomitable Tin Goose*, 156.

55. Egan, *Design and Destiny*, 113; "Tucker Auto Plant Resumes," *Dealer News*, July 28, 1948.

56. "Tuckers Being Built," *New York Times*, August 18, 1948.

57. Tom McCahill, "We Drive and Test the New TUCKER Car," *Mechanix Illustrated*, August 1948, 81.

58. Ibid.

59. Ibid., 82, italics in original.

60. Ibid.

61. Egan, *Design and Destiny*, 159.

62. Ibid., 159–160.

63. "Tucker Is Sued," *Spokane Daily Chronicle*.

64. Knoble, *Call to Market*, 211.

65. "Hughes to Buy into Tucker Auto Firm?" *Milwaukee Sentinel*, August 12, 1948.

66. "Hughes Purchase of Tucker Interest Denied," *Dealer News*, August 18, 1948.

67. Byrne, *Whiz Kids*, 163.

68. Tremulis, "Epitaph," 65.

69. Tucker "Inter-Office Memorandum." The higher-octane fuel could have resulted in a stalling condition simply because the compression and the ignition timing on the vehicle were set up for a lower-octane fuel. It does seem less likely that aviation fuel would result in vapor lock when the fuel is usually optimized for use at high altitude.

70. Ibid.

71. Tremulis, "Epitaph," 65.

72. Dan Leabu, "Tucker Corporation Departmental Correspondence," November 11, 1948, courtesy of Mark Lieberman.

73. "Tucker Takes Long Holiday," *Milwaukee Journal*, November 24, 1948.

74. Ibid.

75. "Tucker Plea for Loan Rejected, Capital Hint," *Milwaukee Journal*, November 30, 1948.

20. BANKRUPTCY

1. Veenkant v. Yorke, 256 F.2d 808 (1958).

2. "Suit Charges Tucker Auto Was '42 Olds," *Chicago Daily Tribune*, October 15, 1948.

3. "Suit Asks Tucker Receiver," *Chicago Daily News*, October 14, 1948.

4. "Tucker Faces More Charges," *Eugene Register-Guard*, October 21, 1948.

5. "Suit Charges Tucker," *Chicago Daily Tribune*. As noted elsewhere, the donor car for the Tin Goose was most likely a 1941 Oldsmobile.

6. "Tucker Faces More Charges," *Eugene Register-Guard*.

7. "Court Orders Tucker Action," *Milwaukee Journal*, December 16, 1948.

8. "Judge Rejects Inquiries Now in Tucker Suit," *Milwaukee Journal*, December 17, 1948.

9. "Backer Appears for Tucker Corp.," *New York Times*, January 3, 1949.

10. Ibid.

11. "Tucker Angel Identified," *New York Times*, January 26, 1949.

12. "Court Grants Tucker's Plea to Reorganize," *Milwaukee Journal*, March 3, 1949.

13. Tucker, "I Never Gave Up," 12.

14. Turnbull, deposition, 10.

15. Cliff Knoble, "As It Looks to Me" (newsletter) 1, courtesy of the National Automotive History Collection, Detroit Public Library.

21. THE SEC REPORT

1. SEC, *Tucker Corporation*, 1.

2. Ibid., table of contents (unnumbered page).

3. Ibid., 42.

4. Ibid.

5. Ibid., 63.

6. Ibid.

7. Ibid., 64.

8. Ibid.

9. Ibid., 72.

10. Ibid., 67.

11. Ibid., 73.

12. Securities Exchange Act of 1934, sec. 24(b).

13. Tucker, "My Car Was Too Good," 71; Thomas B. Hart to Preston Tucker, January 17, 1949, National Archives, Chicago, IL.

14. *Tucker: The Man and the Car* (film).

15. Ibid.

22. THE GRAND JURY

1. "U.S. to Investigate Tucker, Company," *New York Times*, February 14, 1949.

2. Ibid.

3. Details of Hayden's interactions with the federal government and his receipt of the SEC report are all from his deposition in the matter of Tucker v. Evening News, October 3, 1950, National Archives, Chicago, IL.

4. Some sources said he brought twelve Tucker '48s. See "Tucker Was Here," *Newsweek*.

5. "Tucker Puts on Show for Jury," *Spokesman Review* (Spokane, WA), February 22, 1949.

6. "Federal Jury Begins Inquiry on Tucker Auto," *New York Herald Tribune*, February 22, 1949.

7. "Torpedo's Wake," *Time*, June 20, 1949, 77.

8. Pearson, *Indomitable Tin Goose*, 178.

9. Ibid.

10. McDonald, "1949 and the Securities Business," www.sec.gov/news/speech/1949/030349mcdonald.pdf, p. 8.

11. Details of Hayden's interactions with McDonald and the report are all from his deposition.

12. Ibid. Pearson and Tucker also talk about the headlines with slight variations in wording: Pearson, *Indomitable Tin Goose*, 176; Tucker, "My Car Was Too Good," 72.

13. Hayden, deposition, 21, among many.

14. One such article was Clarence R. Dore, "Federal Probe Torpedoes Dreams of Investors, Public," *Pittsburgh Press*, June 12, 1949. Dore wrote for the Chicago Daily News Service, which distributed his stories to other news outlets. His article contained much of the information found only in the SEC report, but he may have simply pulled the information from the articles written by others.

15. "Preston Tucker Pleads Innocent," *St. Petersburg Times*, June 24, 1949.

16. Scott, "Ordeal by Trial," 4.

17. Knoble, *Call to Market*, 212.

18. "Jury Indicts Preston Tucker, Seven Auto Firm Associates," *Milwaukee Journal*, June 10, 1949.

19. Dore, "Federal Probe Torpedoes Dreams."

20. "Tucker Was Here," *Newsweek*.

21. Dore, "Federal Probe Torpedoes Dreams."

22. "Torpedo's Wake," *Time*, 77.

23. Ibid.

24. Other sources reported varying potential penalties, but most contemporaneous news accounts use the same figures as *Time*. See "Tucker, Auto Promoter, Seven Associates, Are Indicted on 31 Counts," *Argus-Press* (Owosso, MI), June 10, 1949.

25. "Torpedo's Wake," *Time*, 77–78.

26. Ibid., 78.

23. *COLLIER'S* AND *READER'S DIGEST*

1. "Defendant's Answer to Plaintiff's Interrogatories #1," Regina Hay file, National Archives, Chicago, IL.

2. Lester Velie, "The Fantastic Story of the Tucker Car," *Collier's*, June 25, 1949, 13.

3. "Defendant's Answer to Plaintiff's Interrogatories #24," Regina Hay file, National Archives, Chicago, IL.

4. "Defendant's Answer to Plaintiff's Interrogatories #30," Regina Hay file, National Archives, Chicago, IL.

5. Lester Velie, "The Fantastic Story of the Tucker Car," *Reader's Digest*, September 1949, 1–2.

6. "Defendant's Answer to Plaintiff's Interrogatories #33," Regina Hay file, National Archives, Chicago, IL.

7. Velie, "Fantastic Story," *Collier's*, 71.

8. Ibid., 69.

9. Ibid., 15.

10. Ibid., 72.

11. Ibid., 6.

12. "Defendant's Answer to Plaintiff's Interrogatories #38," Regina Hay file, National Archives, Chicago, IL.

13. Alfred Prowitt, "Good-bye to Tucker's Dream Car," *Coronet*, November 1949.

24. THE TRIAL

1. Scott, "Ordeal by Trial," 1.

2. "Tucker Pleads Innocent," *St. Petersburg Times*.

3. Scott, "Ordeal by Trial," 4.

4. Knoble, *Call to Market*, 216.

5. John C. Tucker, *Trial and Error: The Education of a Courtroom Lawyer* (New York: Basic Books, 2004), 4.

6. Scott, "Ordeal by Trial," 4.

7. "Indict Reader's Digest, Colliers, Tucker Firm Attorney Asks Court," *Southeast Missourian*, October 3, 1949.

8. Tremulis, "Epitaph," 57.

9. Ibid.

10. SEC, *Tucker Corporation*, table of contents (unnumbered page), under subheading V, "Supporting Witnesses."

11. "Group Hopes to Salvage Tucker Auto Corporation," *Reading Eagle*, September 18, 1949.

12. "Tucker Surrenders Chicago Car Plant," *Spokane Daily Chronicle*, October 4, 1949.

13. "Preston Tucker Wouldn't Know His Own Auto," *St. Petersburg Times*, August 5, 1949.

14. "Eight Tucker Jurors Chosen," *Pittsburgh Post-Gazette*, October 5, 1949; "Tucker Trial Starts; "Lease Is Canceled on Auto Plant," *St. Petersburg Times*, October 5, 1949.

15. "Lease Is Canceled," *St. Petersburg Times*.

16. Pearson, *Indomitable Tin Goose*, 182.

17. "Lease Is Canceled," *St. Petersburg Times*.

18. "SEC Act Killed Tucker Credit, Defense Claims," *Schenectady Gazette*, October 5, 1949.

19. Ibid.

20. Kamrowski, interview by the author.

21. Fizdale, interview by the author.

22. "Tucker Trial Likely to Last into Next Year," *Pittsburgh Press*, October 7, 1949.

23. Pearson, *Indomitable Tin Goose*, 185.

24. "Mistrial Ends Tucker Trial," *Milwaukee Sentinel*, October 11, 1949.

25. "New Tucker Trial Looms," *Reading (PA) Eagle*.

26. "New Trial Ordered in Tucker Case," *Ottawa Citizen*, October 11, 1949.

27. Scott, "Ordeal by Trial," 446; "Mail Fraud Case Mistrial Demanded," *Pittsburgh Post-Gazette*, October 11, 1949.

28. "Mail Fraud Case," *Pittsburgh Post-Gazette*; "Tucker Trial Off, New One Is Set," *Pittsburgh Post-Gazette*, October 12, 1949.

29. "Mistrial Declared in Tucker Case; to Start Again," *Daytona Beach Morning Journal*, October 12, 1949.

30. Scott, "Ordeal by Trial," 446.

31. "Designer Testifies in Tucker Case," *Reading Eagle*, October 20, 1949.

32. "Government Opens New Tucker Trial," *Deseret News*, October 24, 1949.

33. "Conditions of Kaiser-Frazer Loan Outlined," *Argus-Press* (Owosso, MI), October 25, 1949.

34. "Kaiser-Frazer Asks New Loan," *Pittsburgh Post-Gazette*, October 20, 1949.

35. "Kaiser-Frazer Obtains New Loan," *Lodi (CA) News-Sentinel*, October 25, 1949.

36. Tremulis, "Epitaph," 57.

37. Scott, "Ordeal by Trial," 447.

38. Tremulis, "Epitaph," 57.

39. Scott, "Ordeal by Trial," 447.

40. Ibid.

41. "Tucker Ads Protested, Official Says," *Pittsburgh Post-Gazette*, November 3, 1949.

42. SEC, *Tucker Corporation*, 488.

43. Ibid., 490–491.

44. Scott, "Ordeal by Trial," 447.

45. Ibid.

46. SEC, *Tucker Corporation*, 495.

47. Ibid., 497.

48. "Tucker Stock Plan Stopped," *Milwaukee Journal*, November 5, 1949.

49. SEC, *Tucker Corporation*, 498.

50. Ibid., 499.

51. Pearson, *Indomitable Tin Goose*, 187.

52. Scott, "Ordeal by Trial," 447.

53. "Tucker Stock Plan Stopped," *Milwaukee Journal*.

54. Kamrowski, interview by the author.

55. Ibid.

56. "Kaiser-Frazer Loan Is Upheld," *Spokesman-Review* (Spokane, WA), November 18, 1949.

57. Scott, "Ordeal by Trial," 447.

58. Ibid.

59. "'Threatened,' Tucker Trial Witness Says," *Pittsburgh Press*, November 21, 1949.

60. Scott, "Ordeal by Trial," 448.

61. SEC, *Tucker Corporation*, title page. Goode is listed as a contributing attorney, Corbin as a contributing accountant.

62. "'Threatened,'" *Pittsburgh Press*.

63. Scott, "Ordeal by Trial," 448.

64. "'Threatened,'" *Pittsburgh Press*.

65. Knoble, *Call to Market*, 217–218.

66. "Gulf Official Heard at Tucker Trial," *Pittsburgh Press*, December 12, 1949.

67. Ibid.

68. Ibid.

69. Harry A. McDonald, address to the thirty-eighth annual convention of the Investment Bankers Association of America, Hollywood, FL, December 4–9, 1949, transcript available at the US Securities and Exchange Commission official website, www.sec.gov/news/speech/1949/1204-0949mcdonald.pdf, p. 2.

70. Tucker, "My Car Was Too Good," 72.

71. Scott, "Ordeal by Trial,"448.

72. SEC, *Tucker Corporation*, 392.

73. Ibid.

74. Ibid., 393.

75. Ibid., 399.

76. Ibid., 401.

77. Scott, "Ordeal by Trial,"448.

78. Pearson, *Indomitable Tin Goose*, 191.

79. Scott, "Ordeal by Trial,"448.

80. Ibid., 449.

81. Ibid.

82. Pearson, *Indomitable Tin Goose*, 193–194.

83. Turnbull, deposition, 78–79.

84. Ibid., 84–85.

85. The number of witnesses is given variously as either seventy-two or seventy-three. Tremulis said seventy-two; see Tremulis, "Epitaph," 58. One newspaper reported the figure as sixty-three: "Tucker, Aides Acquitted in Suit over Dream Car," *Pittsburgh Post-Gazette*, January 23, 1950.

86. "Trial of Tucker Nears Jury Stage," *Wilmington (NC) Morning Star*, January 17, 1950.

87. Scott, "Ordeal by Trial,"449.

88. "Question of Faith," *Time*, January 30, 1950, 77.

89. Pearson, *Indomitable Tin Goose*, 195.

90. Scott, "Ordeal by Trial,"450.

91. "Tucker Cleared of Fraud Charges," *Pittsburgh Press*, January 23, 1950.

92. "Tucker, Aides Acquitted," *Pittsburgh Post-Gazette*.

93. Egan, *Design and Destiny*, 113.

94. Knoble, *Call to Market*, 219.

95. "Question of Faith," *Time*, 77.

96. "Tucker, Aides Acquitted," *Pittsburgh Post-Gazette*.

97. Scott, "Ordeal by Trial,"450.

98. Harry A. McDonald, "Today at the S.E.C.," address given at the forty-third annual dinner of the Detroit Stock Exchange, February 21, 1950, transcript available at the US Securities and Exchange Commission official website, www.sec.gov/news/speech/1950/022150mcdonald.pdf, p. 1.

99. Ibid., 9.

100. Tremulis, "Epitaph," 58.

101. "Preston Tucker in Court Again," *St. Petersburg Times,* January 27, 1950.

102. Tucker v. Kerner, 186 F.2d 79 (7th Cir. 1950).

103. The prospectus outlined the process by which shareholders could dissolve the company or merge it, etc. Any major action of that sort required 60 percent of the Class A stock to be voted in favor of the action. That would only require 2,400,000 shares of the Class A. Clearly, someone could have taken over the Tucker Corporation and done anything they wanted with it for a relatively small investment in 1949 or 1950.

104. Fizdale, interview by the author.

105. Kamrowski, interview by the author.

106. Tucker Fordon, interview by the author.

107. Ibid.

25. THE CIVIL SUITS

1. "Tucker Sues Gov't Employes for Damages," *Schenectady Gazette,* March 22, 1950.

2. Tucker, "My Car Was Too Good," 72.

3. Turnbull, deposition, 17. This statement was made by Tucker's attorney on the record.

4. Tucker, deposition, 41.

5. Hayden, deposition; Tucker, "My Car Was Too Good," 71–72.

6. Tucker, "My Car Was Too Good," 72.

7. Ibid.

8. Hayden, deposition.

9. Turnbull, deposition, 19.

10. Scott, "Ordeal by Trial," 451.

11. "Defendant's Answer to Plaintiff's Interrogatories #12," Regina Hay file, National Archives, Chicago, IL.

12. Scott, "Ordeal by Trial,"451.

13. Tucker v. Kerner, 186 F.2d 79 (7th Cir. 1950). It would appear that the statements of the judge were not made on the record. Otherwise, they would not have been considered hearsay.

14. "Public Auction" notice, flyer, courtesy of the Tucker Automobile Club of America archives.

15. "Report of Sale, in the Matter of Tucker Corporation," courtesy of Mark Lieberman and John Tucker.

16. Preston Tucker to Earl T. Simoneau, May 1, 1950, courtesy of Sean Tucker.

17. Tucker experts often group the Tucker sedans into three categories: Category 1: finished and built by Tucker at factory. Category 2: cars that were started on the assembly line but finished outside of the factory. Category 3: assembled from parts entirely outside of the factory.

18. Schmidt v. US, 198 F.2d 32 (1952). Strangely, the opinion does not give the appellant's first name.

19. Ibid.

20. "Kaiser-Frazer Granted Loan by Government," *Prescott (AZ) Evening Courier*, December 6, 1950.

21. "Kaiser-Frazer Loan Scored by Senate Unit," *Deseret News*, July 19, 1951.

22. Pearson, *Indomitable Tin Goose*, 220.

23. "SEC Probers Find No Blot on Integrity of McDonald," *Spokane Daily Chronicle*, February 15, 1952.

24. "Kaiser-Frazer to Pay on Loan," *Spokesman-Review* (Spokane, WA), June 25, 1952.

25. "Kaiser-Frazer to Buy Willys in 62 Million Dollar Deal," *Milwaukee Sentinel*, March 22, 1953.

26. Tucker, "My Car Was Too Good," 5.

27. "Answer of Defendant, The Evening News Association, to Plaintiff's Interrogatories," in Tucker v. The Evening News, National Archives, Chicago, IL.

28. Affidavit of Harry A. McDonald, April 7, 1952. The document is a single page and is not titled or captioned in any meaningful way. It can be found in the Tucker files at the National Archives, Chicago, IL.

26. PRESTON TUCKER SPEAKS OUT

1. Tucker, "My Car Was Too Good," 3.

2. Ibid.

3. Ibid., 7.

4. Ibid., 74.

5. "Report of Nathan Yorke, Trustee of Tucker Corporation," January 10, 1956, in the matter of Tucker Corporation, N.D. Ill. case no. 48 B 530.

6. Tucker, "My Car Was Too Good," 74.

7. Tucker, deposition, 858.

8. Ibid., 835–836.

9. Ibid., 876–877.

10. Ibid., 866–867.

11. Ibid, 858.

12. Veenkant v. Yorke, 256 F.2d 808 (1958).

13. Ibid.

14. Ibid.

15. Ibid.

16. Ibid.

17. Ibid.

27. JOSEPH TURNBULL TESTIFIES AGAIN

1. Turnbull, deposition, 39.

2. Ibid., 26.

3. Ibid., 41.

4. Ibid., 60–61.

5. Ibid., 51.

6. Ibid., 54.

7. Ibid., 58–59.

28. THE LAST DAYS OF PRESTON TUCKER

1. "Count in Suit," *Milwaukee Journal*, April 9, 1941.

2. Auto Row Notes, *Milwaukee Journal*, August 2, 1931; see also "New 1936 Kelvinator" (ad for the Kelvinator), *Ottawa Citizen*, April 15, 1936.

3. Sakhnoffsky, "Tucker Number Two," 69.

4. Ibid.

5. Kamrowski, interview by the author.

6. Wallace F. Janssen, "Cancer Quackery: Past and Present," *FDA Consumer*, July–August 1977.

7. Tucker, "I Never Gave Up," 10.

8. Ibid.

9. Ibid., 12.

10. Ibid., 14–15.

11. Ibid., 58.

12. Ibid.

13. Ibid.

14. Joe Butcko, interview by the author.

15. Ibid.

16. Ibid.

17. Sakhnoffsky, "Tucker Number Two," 69.

18. Butcko, interview by the author.

19. Tucker Fordon, interview by the author.

20. Kamrowski, interview by the author.

21. "Inventor of Tucker Car Dies," *Daytona Beach Morning Journal*, December 27, 1956.

22. Kamrowski, interview by the author.

23. Ibid.

24. "Preston T. Tucker in Hospital," *New York Times*, December 7, 1956.

25. "Preston Tucker, Auto Builder, Dies," *Southeast Missourian*, December 27, 1956.

26. Certificate of death for Preston Thomas Tucker, National Archives, Chicago, IL.

27. "Auto Manufacturer Preston Tucker Dies," *Lewiston Daily Sun*, December 27, 1956.

28. Lincoln Park Preservation Alliance, *Lincoln Park*, 58.

29. Scott, "Ordeal by Trial,"9.

30. "Preston Tucker, Car Maker, Dies," *New York Times*, December 27, 1956.

31. "Preston Tucker Dies," *Lewiston Daily Sun*.

29. THE MOVIE

1. Cowan, "Tucker: The Man, the Myth," 230.

2. Jill Kearney, "Francis Ford Coppola: His Latest Hero Dreamed of Producing a New Automobile," *Mother Jones*, September 1988.

3. Abigail Tucker, "The Tucker Was the 1940s Car of the Future," *Smithsonian*, December 2012.

4. Cowan, "Tucker: The Man, the Myth," 232.

5. Gordinier, "A Lot of Drive."

6. Cowan, "Tucker: The Man, the Myth," 232.

7. Kearney, "Francis Ford Coppola."

8. Cowan, "Tucker: The Man, the Myth," 231.

9. Gordinier, "A Lot of Drive."

10. Cowan, "Tucker: The Man, the Myth," 233.

11. Tucker Fordon, interview by the author.

12. Cowan, "Tucker: The Man, the Myth," 233.

13. Fizdale, interview by the author.

14. Cowan, "Tucker: The Man, the Myth." It appears that this would make the total number of authentic Tuckers in the movie to be twenty-four, counting the two belonging to Coppola, but it is unclear; the twenty-two figure may have included his as well.

15. IMDb.com, accessed October 29, 2015, gives the movie's budget as $23 million, while other sources sometimes say $24 million. See, for instance, Gordinier, "A Lot of Drive."

16. Cowan, "Tucker: The Man, the Myth," 231.

17. Kearney, "Francis Ford Coppola."

18. James Risen, "Uncanny Parallels Noted for DeLorean, Tucker," *Victoria (TX) Advocate*, August 14, 1988.

19. Patrick Jasperse, "A Car Collector's Moment of Glory," *Milwaukee Journal*, August 19, 1988.

30. AFTER

1. Knoble, *Call to Market*, 221–222.

2. "Tremulis: The Genius," *Automobile Quarterly*, 256.

3. Ibid., 258.

4. Ibid.

5. Gordinier, "A Lot of Drive."

6. "Tremulis: The Genius," *Automobile Quarterly*, 258.

7. Gordinier, "A Lot of Drive."

8. "No Room for Dreams," *Toledo Blade*.

9. Bergstrom, "Memories Revived."

10. Fox, "Philip Egan."

11. The federal appeals court wrote in an opinion that Kerner stepped down as governor specifically to take the judgeship with the Court of Appeals. US v. Isaacs and Kerner et al., 493 F.2d 1124 (7th Cir. 1974).

12. US v. Isaacs and Kerner et al., 493 F.2d 1124 (7th Cir. 1974). Some writers argued later that Kerner's conviction was inappropriate, because the legal theory upon which part of it was based—"honest services" being the basis for a mail fraud conviction—was overturned later by the Supreme Court. It seems unlikely that all his convictions would have been overturned, however. One count for which Kerner was convicted was his perjury before the grand jury. The striking down or rewriting of the mail fraud statute would have had no effect on Kerner's culpability for lying under oath.

13. Stephan Benzkofer, "First Illinois Governor to Do Time was Known as 'Mr. Clean,'" *Chicago Tribune*, December 11, 2011.

14. Ibid.

15. "Seven Drew Pearson Wills Form Legal Knot in Settling Estate," *Lakeland (FL) Ledger*, January 28, 1975.

16. "Death Claims Drew Pearson," *Bulletin* (Bend, OR), September 1, 1969.

17. Jim Irwin, "Tucker Museum Idea Seems Stalled," *Toledo Blade*, December 29, 1992.

31. THE TUCKER LEGACY

1. Abigail Tucker, "1940s Car of the Future."

2. Ibid.

3. Philip S. Egan, "The Real Life Tucker; A Dream as Bright as Its Chrome," *New York Times*, September 18, 1988.

4. Pearson, *Indomitable Tin Goose*, 177.

5. Gordinier, "A Lot of Drive."

32. THE FLEET OF TUCKER '48 SEDANS

1. Mike Schutta, "Racing Rarity: Identity of the Tucker 48 That Competed in NASCAR Is Finally Revealed," *Hemmings Classic Car*, March 2012, www .hemmings.com/hcc/stories/2012/03/01/hmn_feature1.html.

2. Stan Gilliland, e-mail to Mark Lieberman, December 4, 2013, provided to the author by Lieberman.

3. Miller, "Tucker Torpedo Is Gone."

4. "No Room for Dreams," *Toledo Blade*.

5. Lieberman, interview by the author.

6. Miller, "Tucker Torpedo Is Gone."

7. Ibid.

8. "The Tucker Prototype Will Be Auctioned for the First Time During Kruse International's 25th Auburn Auction!," PR Newswire, July 5, 1995.

9. Lieberman, interview by the author; Pat Swigart, interview by the author, 2015.

10. Swigart, interview by the author.

11. "Lot 140: 1948 Tucker 48," RM Sotheby's official website, accessed October 29, 2015, www.rmauctions.com/lots/lot.cfm?lot_id=1067570.

12. "1948 Tucker Torpedo," Barrett-Jackson Salon Collection official website, accessed October 24, 2013, www.saloncollection.com/2012/1948-tucker-torpedo/ (site discontinued); Jeremy Korzeniewski, "Barrett-Jackson 2012," *Autoblog*, January 21, 2012, www.autoblog.com/2012/01/21/barrett-jackson-2012-1948-tucker-torpedo-bid-up -to-over-2-6-mi/.

13. Agnes Nash, "The Car Arrived Before Its Time," *Miami News*, May 8, 1960.

14. Lieberman, interview by the author.

15. David LaChance, "David Cammack: Decades of Collecting Have Produced a Tucker Collection That Has No Equal," *Hemmings Classic Car*, June 2007, www.hemmings.com/hcc/stories/2007/06/01/hmn_feature20.html.

16. Ibid. This article indicates that 150 Tucker engines had been produced, but the number was probably 125. Lieberman, interview by the author.

17. Missing from his collection was a Jacobs engine, which had been considered, as well as a high-performance Franklin, which had also been experimented with at the Tucker factory.

18. LaChance, "David Cammack."

19. Ibid.

20. Ibid.

21. Ibid.

22. Daniel Strohl, "Tucker Collector David Cammack Dies," *Hemmings Daily*, April 10, 2013, http://blog.hemmings.com/index.php/2013/04/10/tucker-collector-david-cammack-dies/.

23. LaChance, "David Cammack."

24. "Tucker Torpedo for Motorclassica," *Next Car*, October 20, 2010, www.nextcar.com.au/n.2010.au.101020.motorclassica.html.

25. Schutta, "Racing Rarity."

26. Daniel Strohl, "Long-Neglected Tucker Exhumed, Headed for Restoration," *Hemmings Daily*, February 15, 2011, http://blog.hemmings.com/index.php/2011/02/15/long-neglected-tucker-exhumed-headed-for-restoration/.

27. "1948 Tucker Model 48," LeMay Family Collection Foundation official website, accessed October 21, 2015, www.lemaymarymount.org/vehicle.php?vID=729.

28. Paul Duchene, "Unearthed Tucker," *Chicago Tribune*, January 27, 2011, http://articles.chicagotribune.com/2011-01-27/classified/sc-cons-0127-autocover-20110127_1_tucker-automobile-club-alex-tremulis-pilot-cars.

29. Ibid.

Bibliography

Cowan, Lisa E. "Tucker: The Man, the Myth, the Movie." *Automobile Quarterly* 26, no. 3 (Third Quarter 1988).

Egan, Philip S. *Design and Destiny: The Making of the Tucker Automobile*. Orange, CA: On the Mark, 1989.

———. "Tremulis: The Genius Behind the Tucker," *Automobile Quarterly* 26, no. 3 (Third Quarter 1988).

Knoble, Cliff. *Call to Market*. New York: Frederick Fell, 1963.

Pearson, Charles T. *The Indomitable Tin Goose*. New York: Abelard-Schuman, 1960.

———. "Streamlining That Car." *Pic*, January 1946.

Rockelman, Fred. "Behind the Gasoline Curtain." *Bulb Horn*, July–August 1966.

Sakhnoffsky, Alexis de. "Tucker Number Two: The Carioca." *American Quarterly* 4, no. 1 (Spring/Summer 1965).

Scott, Robert F. "Ordeal by Trial: The Decline and Fall of Preston Tucker." *American Quarterly* 2 (Winter 1963–1964).

SEC. *Tucker Corporation: Report of Investigation by Securities and Exchange Commission*. SEC, December 20, 1948. National Archives, Chicago, IL.

Tremulis, Alex. "Epitaph for the Tin Goose," *American Quarterly* 4, no. 1 (Spring/Summer 1965).

———. "The 1946–48 Tucker: A Great Promise Unfulfilled." SAE Technical Paper Series #872001. Society of Automotive Engineers, 1987.

Tucker, Preston. Deposition in the matter of Hay v. Crowell-Collier. Beginning July 13, 1954. Civil action 9507. National Archives, Chicago, IL.

———. "I Never Gave Up." *Car Life*, December 1955.

———. "My Car Was Too Good." *Cars*, March 1952.

Tucker Corp., *Annual Report*. Tucker Corp., January 1948. Courtesy of the Tucker Automobile Club of America archives.

———. *Prospectus*. Tucker Corp., July 7, 1947. Courtesy of the Tucker Automobile Club of America archives.

Turnbull, Joseph A. Deposition in the matter of Tucker v. Evening News. Beginning July 19, 1955. Civil Action 9078. National Archives, Chicago, IL.

Index